Introduction to Microsoft Works®

(Macintosh Version 3.0)

A Problem Solving Approach

Al Schroeder
Emilio Ramos

Richland College

Macmillan Publishing Company
New York

Maxwell Macmillan Canada
Toronto

Maxwell Macmillan International
New York   Oxford   Singapore   Sydney

Cover art: Marjory Dressler

Editor: Charles E. Stewart

Cover Designer: Thomas Mack

Production Buyer: Pamela D. Bennett

This book was set in Times Roman and was printed and bound by Von Hoffman Press, Inc. The cover was printed by Von Hoffman Press, Inc.

Microsoft Works is a registered trademark of Microsoft Corporation.

The Publisher offers discounts on this book when ordered in bulk quantities. For more information, write to: Special Sales Department, Macmillan Publishing Company, 445 Hutchinson Ave., Columbus, OH 43235, or call 1-800-228-7854.

Macmillan Publishing Company
866 Third Avenue
New York, New York 10022

Macmillan Publishing Company is part of the
Maxwell Communication Group of Companies.

Maxwell Macmillan Canada, Inc.
1200 Eglinton Avenue East, Suite 200
Don Mills, Ontario M3C 3NI

Library of Congress Cataloging-in-Publication Data

Schroeder, Al.
  Introduction to Microsoft Works (Macintosh version 3.0) : a problem solving approach / Al Schroeder, Emilio Ramos.
            p. cm.
  Includes index.
  ISBN 0-02-407796-8
  1. Macintosh (Computer)--Programming. 2. Microsoft Works.
  I. Ramos, Emilio. II. Title
  QA76.8.M3S37   1994
  005.369--dc20   94-18944
                                                                             CIP

Printing: 1 2 3 4 5 6 7 8 9   Year: 4 5 6 7 8

Preface

Introduction

Many educational institutions are searching for a practical and economical alternative to teaching application software concepts. Students are looking for a practical and economical way of using application software. Because of these factors, there is a shift from using products such as WordPerfect, Lotus 1-2-3, and dBASE to the use of integrated software packages.

Stand-alone programs, such as WordPerfect, Lotus, and dBASE have gained prominence in both industry and education. They provide more capabilities in one area, and that is their greatest strength. But for the person who uses several applications (e.g., word processing and spreadsheets) an integrated program like Microsoft Works may have the features needed. Fully integrated programs, such as Microsoft Works, are intended to provide an alternative that includes word processing, spreadsheet, graphics, database and communications capabilities in a single program. Moreover, the purchasing costs and upgrade costs are reduced to a single program rather than several, and the learning and use of the applications are simplified by having to know only one set of commands.

Microsoft Works is considered one of the best integrated application programs currently available. It has combined ease of use, low cost, and a high level of capability to gain prominence in the educational and personal use markets. This text teaches the fundamentals of using Works in a Macintosh environment.

Objectives of This Text

Upon completing this book, students will

1. Understand the differences between integrated software and stand-alone software, and know the process for installing application software onto a system and interfacing with it.

2. Understand word processing concepts and be able to efficiently use the word processing tool in Microsoft Works.

3. Understand spreadsheet concepts and be able to efficiently use the spreadsheet tool in Microsoft Works.

4. Understand business graphics concepts and be able to efficiently use the business charting tool in Microsoft Works.

5. Understand database concepts and be able to efficiently use the database tool in Microsoft Works.

iii

6. Have a practical knowledge of integrated applications and be able to integrate all application tools in Microsoft Works.

Organization of the Text

The text provides a general introduction to microcomputers in Chapter 1, followed by an introduction to application software and Microsoft Works in Chapter 2. Subsequent topics include word processing, spreadsheets, graphics, database, and integrated applications. It is intended that Chapters 1 and 2 be covered prior to any other chapters, but application areas can be covered in the order of preference.

Within each application area, chapters are divided into three sections. Each chapter begins with a generic introduction to the topic, followed by a section that applies Works commands to the topic and then a tutorial dealing with a sample problem. The generic section explains what types of problems the tool is solving and the benefits of automating the solutions. The command section (always stressing menu choices and mouse control, in this environment) explains specific commands in Works which relate to the type of problem defined. The tutorial section provides a sample problem related to the generic section of the chapter and uses the commands and features of Works explained in the chapter to guide the student step by step through the problem solution.

The chapter organization provides the instructor the flexibility of lecturing on the uses of the application in solving problems and the specific Works commands that correlate to the area. Alternatively, the instructor can have the students read the sections independently as background reading. The tutorial can be completed by the students as a guided walkthrough by the instructor, or as an independent activity for each student. The organization provides the ability to use lecture time to cover the material or have the book used only in the laboratory portion of the course.

For students who have no background in the application area (e.g., spreadsheets) and no computer experience, the generic section should be read to provide an understanding of the purpose of the tool. The second section of each chapter can then correlate Works commands to the application. The beginner should then complete the tutorial to reinforce the commands and features. The tutorial also provides an illustration of how Works can be used to solve problems in the area. A student with background in the area may skip the generic section. A student who is computer literate may use the second section of the chapter as a reference and skip the tutorial. The organization allows the student to use any or all of the sections as needed to become familiar with the topic and with Works.

Conventions

Each chapter has three sections: a generic section, a command section, and a tutorial section. In all sections, keys used in combination with each other are represented two ways. If one key is held down while the other is pressed (e.g., CTRL/PAGEUP), the slash (/) is used to separate the two keys. If one key can be pressed and released, then the second key pressed (e.g., HOME + RETURN), then the keys are separated by a plus (+). In the tutorial section of each chapter, a key symbol is used to represent the key, and a picture of a mouse is used to represent the mouse button. In the command section, capital letters are used when referencing a key. In the command and tutorial sections, references to menu items will appear as they do on the menu, which typically means that the first character of each word will be uppercase.

The tutorial section of each chapter includes descriptions of the process and specific step by step instructions to complete the exercise. The numbered statements will be indented and must be followed in sequence to complete the tutorial. Characters and words to be typed are in boldface and appear slightly larger than other text. Keys to be pressed are represented in picture form, indicating the key to be pressed.

Appendices

Appendix A is a discussion of the tool palette that is available to all of the Works applications.

Appendix B explains the draw feature of Works.

Appendix C includes an explanation of the communications application in Works. If you want to include a study of communications using Works, this section can be used as a teaching module.

Appendix D lists the keys used to move the insertion point around in the Works applications.

Appendix E contains a list of keyboard shortcuts to enter commands that are used often. This provides an alternate way to communicate with the program.

Acknowledgments

The authors would like to thank the Macmillan staff who participated in this project. We would also like to thank the reviewers of this material. They included Patricia M. Thomas, Karen Guessford, and Diane Buckey. Each of them provided quality feedback regarding the manuscript. Special thanks to Karen Guessford, who was instrumental in designing the layout of the book.

Teaching Outline

The following charts show several scenarios for fitting the materials in our text to your particular course structure.

Quarter			Short Course	
Week	One quarter literacy course without programming	One quarter literacy course with programming	Hours	Short course in Microsoft Works (16 lecture/lab hours)
1	Ch. 1	Ch. 1, 2	1, 2	Ch. 1, 2
2	Ch. 2	Ch. 3	3, 4	Ch. 3
3	Ch. 3	Ch. 4	5, 6	Ch. 4
4	Ch. 4	Ch. 5	7, 8	Ch. 5
5	Ch. 5	Ch. 6	9, 10	Ch. 6, 7
6	Ch. 6	Ch. 7	11, 12	Ch. 8
7	Ch. 7	Ch. 8	13, 14	Ch. 9
8	Ch. 8	Programming	15, 16	Ch. 10
9	Ch. 9	Programming		
10	Ch. 10	Programming		

	Semester		
Week	One semester application software course without programming	One semester literacy course without programming	One semester literacy course with programming
1	Ch. 1	Ch. 1	Ch. 1
2	Ch. 2	Ch. 2	Ch. 2
3	Ch. 3	Ch. 3	Ch. 3
4	Ch. 4	Ch. 4	Ch. 4
5	Additional word processing exercises	Ch. 4	Ch. 5
6	Ch. 5	Ch. 5	Ch. 6
7	Ch. 6	Ch. 6	Ch. 7
8	Additional spreadsheet exercises	Ch. 6	Ch. 8
9	Ch. 7	Ch. 7	Ch. 9
10	Additional graphics exercises	Ch. 7	Ch. 10
11	Ch. 8	Ch. 8	Programming
12	Ch. 9	Ch. 9	Programming
13	Additional database exercises	Ch. 9	Programming
14	Ch. 10	Ch. 10	Programming
15	Appendix C - Communications	Ch. 10	Programming

Dedication

To Sarah

Your warm and beautiful smile is an inspiration to all who know you.

Dad

Contents

Chapter 1. The Microcomputer System

Objectives 1
Introduction to the Microcomputer 2
    The Central Processing Unit 4
    Main Memory 4
    Input Devices 5
        The Keyboard 5
        The Mouse 6
        Other Input Devices 6
    Output Devices 6
        Monitors 6
        Printers 7
        Other Output Devices 9
    Storage Devices 9
        Floppy Disks 9
        Hard Disks 10
        Other Storage Devices 10
    The Operating System 10
        Booting the System 10
        System Commands 11
        Preparing Data Disks 11
        File Names 12
Hands-on System Operation 13
    Booting a Computer System with a Hard Drive 13
Summary 13
Questions 14
Exercises 15

Chapter 2. Integrated Application Software

Objectives 17
Solving Problems with a Computer 18
    Stand-Alone Programs 19
    Integrated Programs 20
    Why Microsoft Works? 20
The Macintosh Environment 21
    The Macintosh Desktop 21
    The Background 22
    The Mouse 22
        Point 23
        Click 23

Press 23
Drag 23
Double Click 24
Shift-Click 24
The Icons 24
Types of Icons 24
How Icons Are Used 25
Windows 28
Title Bar 28
Vertical Scroll Bar 28
Horizontal Scroll Bar 29
Size Box 30
Dialog Boxes 30
Managing Folders and Files 30
Creating Folders and Files 31
Moving and Copying Folders and Files 32
Deleting Folders and Files 32
Renaming Folders and Files 32
Getting Started with Works 32
Introduction to Microsoft Works 32
The Works Interface 33
The Works Opening Dialog Box 33
Creating and Saving a Document 34
Exiting Works 34
Hands-on with Works 35
Booting the System 35
Formatting a Disk 36
Creating the Document 38
Saving the Document 39
Closing the File 40
Exiting Works 40
Copying Files 41
Renaming a Document 42
Creating a Folder 43
Moving a Document 44
Removing the Backup Disk 44
Deleting a Document 44
Removing Disk1 46
Shutting Down the System 46
Summary 46
Questions 47
Exercises 47

Chapter 3. The Word Processing Tool
Objectives 49

What Is Word Processing? 50
    Word Processing in Industry 50
    Word Processing in the Home 51
    Automating Word Processing 51
Creating a Document 52
    The Word Processing Window 52
    Entering a Document 54
    Saving and Continuing 55
    Spell Checking 57
    Editing a Document 58
        Moving the Insertion Point 58
        Inserting Text 59
        Deleting Text 59
        Selecting Text 60
        Block Operations 60
    Printing 61
    Saving and Exiting 62
Hands-on Word Processing 63
    PART I 63
        Typing a Letter 63
        Checking the Spelling 66
        Saving the Letter 69
        Printing the Letter 71
        Closing the File 72
        Exiting Works 72
    PART II 73
        Retrieving the Document 73
        Making Changes 75
        Block Changes 77
        Saving the Letter 81
        Printing the Letter 81
        Closing the File 82
        Exiting Works 83
Summary 83
Questions 84
Exercises 85
Problems 87

Chapter 4. Document Formatting with the Word Processor
Objectives 89
Layout and Presentation Features 90
    Planning a Document 90
    Formatting a Document 90
    Enhancing a Document 92
Page Layout and Formatting with Works 93

Margin Settings 93
Headers and Footers 95
Numbering Pages 96
Viewing the Layout 96
Formatting Text 97
Justification and Centering 98
Line Spacing 99
Boldfacing and Underlining 100
Indenting Text 100
Hands-on Layout and Formatting with Works 102
Retrieving the Letter 102
Indenting Text 103
Changing the Margins 106
Adding a Footer and Page Number 107
Viewing the Layout 109
Adjusting the Line Spacing 111
Justifying the Text 112
Centering Text 114
Adding Formatted Text 114
Using Boldfacing and Underlining 115
Saving the Letter 117
Printing the Letter 117
Closing the File 118
Exiting Works 118
Summary 119
Questions 119
Exercises 120
Problems 123

Chapter 5. Spreadsheets
Objectives 125
What Is a Spreadsheet? 126
Numbers and Tables 126
Financial Applications 127
Automating the Spreadsheet 128
Creating a Spreadsheet with Works 129
The Spreadsheet Window 129
The Cell Pointer and Cell Reference 131
Range 132
Data Labels 132
Data Values 133
Formulas 134
The SUM Function 135
Saving a Spreadsheet 135
Editing Data 137

Printing a Spreadsheet 137
Displaying Formulas 139
Saving and Exiting 139
Hands-on with Spreadsheets 140
    PART I 140
        Creating the Spreadsheet 140
        Entering Labels 143
        Entering Values 143
        Entering Formulas 144
        Saving the Spreadsheet 144
        Printing the Spreadsheet 146
        Displaying and Printing the Formulas 147
        Closing the File 148
        Exiting Works 149
    PART II 151
        Retrieving the Spreadsheet 151
        Editing the Spreadsheet 152
        Saving the Spreadsheet 155
        Printing the Spreadsheet 155
        Closing the File 156
        Exiting Works 156
Summary 157
Questions 157
Exercises 158
Problems 160

Chapter 6. Managing the Spreadsheet
Objectives 163
Managing the Spreadsheet 164
    Applying the Spreadsheet 164
    Manipulating the Worksheet 164
    Manipulating the Data 166
Modifying Worksheets and Manipulating Data with Works 167
    Worksheet Modification 167
        Adding Rows and Columns 167
        Deleting Rows and Columns 167
        Adjusting Column Width 168
        Formatting Cells 169
    Data Manipulation 172
        Deleting Cell Contents 172
        Moving Cell Contents 172
        Copying Cell Contents 173
        Functions 174
    Display and Print Options 174
Hands-on Spreadsheet Manipulation 175

Retrieving the Spreadsheet 175
Moving the Data 177
Adding New Columns 178
Copying Data 179
Changing Column Width 182
Formatting the Cells 184
Adding Data 186
Saving the Changes 187
Printing the Spreadsheet 188
Deleting Cells 189
Saving the Template 190
Closing the File 190
Exiting Works 190
Summary 191
Questions 192
Exercises 192
Problems 194

Chapter 7. Charting
Objectives 197
What Are Business Graphics? 198
Bar Chart 198
Pie Chart 200
Line Chart 201
Features of Charting 201
Chart Development with Works 202
Creating a Chart 202
Viewing a Chart 204
Saving a Chart 205
Printing a Chart 205
Enhancing a Chart 205
Titles 205
Labels and Grids 206
Chart Range 206
Chart Location 206
Chart Size 206
Using the Tool Palette 207
Managing Charts 207
Hands-on Charting 208
PART I 208
Creating a Series Chart 208
Sizing and Moving the Chart 211
Saving the Chart 211
Printing the Chart 212
Closing the File 212

Exiting Works 213
PART II 213
    Creating a Pie Chart 213
    Saving the Chart 216
    Printing the Chart 216
    Closing the File 217
    Exiting Works 217
PART III 218
    Duplicating the Chart 218
    Modifying the Chart Definition 220
    Saving and Printing the Chart 220
    Closing the File and Exiting Works 221
Summary 222
Questions 223
Exercises 223
Problems 224

Chapter 8. Database Management
Objectives 227
The Database Tool 228
    What Is a Database? 228
    Planning a Database 228
    Creating and Maintaining a Database 229
    Automating the Database 229
Creating a Database File withWorks 230
    The Database Window 230
    Data View 233
        Characteristics of Data View 233
        Formatting Fields 234
        Entering Records 236
    Saving a Database 236
    Printing Records in Data View 237
    Updating a Database 237
        Retrieving a Database 237
        Updating a Field 237
        Adding or Deleting a Record 238
        Restructuring the Database in Design View 238
        Multiple Data Views 240
    List View 241
        Entering List View Mode 241
        Cell Pointer Control 242
        Changing Field Width 242
        Naming Fields 242
        Formatting a Field 242
        Adding a Field 243

Deleting a Field 243
Moving a Field 243
Updating a Record 244
Deleting a Record 244
Adding a Record 245
Moving a Record 245
Printing in List View 245
Hands-on with Database 245
    PART I. Managing a Database in Data View 245
        Creating the Database 245
        Creating the Fields 247
        Entering Records 251
        Saving the Database 251
        Browsing the Records 252
        Adding a Record 253
        Modifying a Record 253
        Adding a Field 254
        Moving a Field 256
        Deleting a Field 257
        Formatting a Field 257
        Adding Data 259
        Printing the Records 260
        Printing the Form 260
        Closing the File 261
        Exiting Works 262
    PART II . Managing a Database in List View 262
        Creating the Database 262
        Creating the Fields 263
        Entering Records 265
        Saving the Database 265
        Changing to List View 266
        Changing the Field Width 267
        Adding a Record 268
        Modifying a Record 269
        Deleting a Record 269
        Adding a Field 270
        Formatting a Field 272
        Deleting a Field 272
        Moving a Field 273
        Printing the Records 274
        Closing the File 275
        Exiting Works 275
Summary 276
Questions 276
Exercises 277

Problems 278

Chapter 9. Applying the Database
Objectives 281
Using the Database Tool 282
    How the Data Is Used 282
    Selecting Data 282
    Sorting Data 283
    Summarizing Data 284
    Reporting the Results 285
Using the Database in Works 285
    Sorting Records 285
    Searching the Database 285
        Finding a Field Entry 285
        Matching Multiple Field Entries 287
        Selecting a Group of Records 287
    Using the Report Writer 289
        Creating a Report 289
        Printing a Report 291
        Modifying a Report 291
        Managing Report Formats 291
        Summarizing Data 292
Hands-on with Database 294
    PART I. Creating the Database 294
    Creating the Fields 295
    Sorting Records 298
    Multiple Level Sorts 300
    Searching the Database 302
        Finding a Field 302
        Finding Multiple Records 303
        Selecting a Group of Records 304
        Using Multiple Rules 305
    Saving the Database and Exiting 308
    PART II. Retrieving the Database 308
    Reports 308
        Creating a Report Format 308
        Summarizing Data 310
        Creating a Report with Rules 312
        Printing a Report 315
    Saving the Database and Exiting 316
Summary 316
Questions 317
Exercises 318
Problems 319

Chapter 10. Integrating Works

Objectives 321
Integrated Applications 322
    Multiple Tools 322
    Windows 322
Integrating the Microsoft Works Tools 322
    Using Multiple Tools 323
    Using Windows 323
    The Clipboard 326
        Using the Clipboard to Integrate Documents 326
    Form Letters 328
    Printing the Merged Document 331
Hands-on Integrating Documents with Works 332
    PART I 332
        Including a Spreadsheet in a Text Document 332
        Including a Chart 335
        Saving and Exiting 337
    PART II 338
        Creating Form Letters 338
        Printing the Form Letter 341
        Saving and Exiting 342
Summary 342
Questions 343
Exercises 343
Problems 344

Appendix A. Tool Palette 346

Appendix B. Draw 347

Appendix C. Communications 350
The Communications Process 350
    The Modem 351
    Software Communications Terminology 351
    The Communications Tool 352
    Making the Connection 353

Appendix D. Keyboard Control 355
    Word Processing 355
    Spreadsheet 355
    Database 356

Appendix E. Keyboard Shortcuts 357
   Word Processing 357
   Spreadsheet 358
   Database 358
   Communications 359
   Draw 360

Index 361

Chapter 1

The Microcomputer System

Objectives

After completing this chapter you will

1. Be familiar with the basic microcomputer system.

2. Understand the function of the central processing unit.

3. Understand the uses of and differences between RAM and ROM.

4. Be able to distinguish among the different input/output devices.

5. Understand the differences between a floppy disk and a hard disk.

6. Understand how to boot a microcomputer system.

7. Know how to prepare a disk to accept information.

Introduction to the Microcomputer

Computer technology was one of the major topics of discussion during the 1980s and will continue to be throughout the 1990s. The computer revolution during the past decade has been compared in importance to such other great events as the invention of the automobile and the telephone. Few human creations have been able to touch every facet of our lives as extensively as the computer. It is still fashionable to talk about hardware, software, word processors, spreadsheets, and related topics.

The technological advances in the microelectronics industry have revolutionized our personal lives and the manner in which we operate in society. Computers surround us in every shape and form: at the grocery store checkout counter, the teller machine at the bank, and in the microcomputers on our desks at home.

It is the microcomputer, or personal computer as it is sometimes called, that has captured the attention of millions of people. The capability to take power away from the large and expensive mainframe computers and put it on our desks has made the personal computer an instant success. The microcomputer area is the fastest growing sector of the computer industry. With prices of entire systems well within reach of the average person, the personal computer has now moved into the home, creating a link between it and the professional office.

A microcomputer system is a collection of microcomputer components that work concurrently to achieve a goal. It can be thought of as a desktop computer system with the capability to acccpt data as input, manipulate the input, perform mathematical and logical operations, and print and store the results of these operations. Fig. 1.1 shows a typical microcomputer system.

Fig. 1.1 A typical microcomputer system

The term *microcomputer system* usually denotes a set of computer hardware and software that is used as a single unit. Whenever this book refers to the microcomputer or personal computer (PC), it is actually addressing the system as a whole.

We can divide the microcomputer into its hardware and software subsystems. The hardware consists of the physical parts that make up the microcomputer. Some of these parts are the keyboard, the metal box that protects the electronic circuits, the monitor, and other electronic devices. In more general terms, the hardware can be categorized by the function that each component performs:

1. Central processing unit

2. Main memory

3. Input devices

4. Secondary storage devices

5. Output devices

Later in this chapter a more detailed explanation of each of the subcomponents of the personal computer hardware is offered.

The software consists of the instructions that tell the computer what to do. Software can be categorized according to the purpose for which it was created and is used. The major categories are the following:

1. System software

2. Application software

System software programs contain instructions that control the functioning of the computer and the communication between the computer components and the user. Within the system software are the operating system, utility programs, and some languages used to create application software.

Application software programs were developed to solve specific problems. Some examples of application software are word processors, spreadsheets, databases, and telecommunication programs. A special type of application software is the integrated software package, which incorporates several applications into one system. This book concentrates on teaching the use of a specific integrated software package in order to solve problems. The rest of the chapters explain in detail the different software programs included in the integrated package and how the user can take advantage of the power of the microcomputer to solve everyday problems.

The Central Processing Unit

The central processing unit, also referred to as the CPU, is responsible for performing the calculations and logical operations that a program requires of the microcomputer. It also decides which instructions are executed first and controls communications among the hardware devices. It consists of the arithmetic/logic unit (ALU) and the control unit.

It is the ALU that actually performs all arithmetic calculations such as addition, subtraction, multiplication, and division. In addition, it performs all logical operations (comparisons). The control unit determines which one of the instructions in a program is executed next and directs the flow of instructions from input devices to and from main memory and secondary storage and to output devices.

Main Memory

Main memory, also called primary storage, is composed of storage addresses, or locations. Each of these locations has a unique address number, and they all hold the same amount of information, a byte. A byte can be thought of as the amount of memory required to store one character. Each byte is composed of eight bits. A bit is the smallest amount of information that can be stored inside the microcomputer. The amount of memory that a microcomputer has is normally measured in bytes. A personal computer typically has at least 640 kilobytes (K). A kilobyte is 1,024 bytes. Today's Apple Macintosh microcomputers are being sold with two to four megabytes (MB) or more of memory. A megabyte is 1,024,000 bytes and is referred to as a million bytes.

Memory is usually divided into RAM (random access memory) and ROM (read only memory). RAM is where programs are stored during execution (at run time). These instructions tell the microcomputer what to do whenever a specific application is running. Data, which is typed into the computer, is also stored in RAM for further processing by the CPU. Instructions stored in RAM can be accessed very quickly. However, when the power to the microcomputer is turned off, all the instructions stored in RAM are lost unless previously saved. The contents of RAM can be changed by the user and the application programs at any time.

ROM contains instructions that tell the computer what to do during the startup, or booting process. Booting is the process the microcomputer goes through when it is first turned on. During this time the hardware goes through a self-check and uses a minimum set of instructions to begin communicating with the user. The instructions to perform these operations are stored in ROM. The instructions in ROM are installed at the factory, and application and system software use the instructions stored in ROM. These instructions cannot be altered; hence the name "read only memory."

Input Devices

Input devices are used to accept data from external sources such as users. The input received is converted by the input device into signals that the CPU can understand. The most popular input devices are

1. The keyboard

2. The mouse

The Keyboard

The keyboard is the most common input device. Fig. 1.2 shows a Macintosh keyboard. Some of the important keys to recognize are

1. The RETURN key is used to indicate the end of an instruction or command to the microcomputer.

2. The ENTER key is used to indicate the end of an instruction or command to the microcomputer.

3. The ESC key is sometimes used to terminate a command or an instruction.

4. The DELETE key is used to erase or delete keystrokes entered from the keyboard.

5. The PAGE UP and PAGE DOWN keys are used to position the pointer at different places in the application in use.

6. The CTRL and COMMAND keys are used in conjunction with other keys to indicate actions the microcomputer must take.

Fig. 1.2 Macintosh keyboard

7. The SHIFT and CAPSLOCK keys are used to change from lower-case to uppercase letters.

8. The NUM LOCK key allows use of the numeric keypad.

9. The function keys F1 through F15 may be used by application software to assist users to perform certain tasks.

The Mouse

The mouse is a small input device that fits in the palm of the hand. It is moved across a flat surface to control the placement of a pointer on the screen. When the mouse is moved to the left on the surface of a desk, the pointer on the screen moves to the left. When the mouse is moved to the right, the pointer moves to the right on the screen, and so on.

On top of the mouse is one or more buttons. Many application software packages allow menu selections by the user moving the pointer across the screen and pressing the mouse button. The mouse can also be used in icon-driven systems, such as the Macintosh, to manage the processing and execute commands. For some applications, such as desktop publishing, a mouse is indispensable.

Other Input Devices

Other types of input devices can be used by microcomputers. Some of them are

1. Touch screen. Touch screens are used by touching areas of the screen to enter data.

2. Graphic tablet. These special tablets can be used to input graphic data such as pictures.

3. Light pen. Touching the screen with a pen indicates instructions to the microcomputer.

4. Voice input. Commands can be entered by the user with spoken words.

Output Devices

Output devices allow the display of data and information on some media for viewing by the user. If the output takes the form of print on paper, it is called hard copy. If the output is on the monitor, it is called soft copy. The most commonly used output devices are

1. Monitors

2. Printers

Monitors

Monitors are output devices that use cathode ray tube (CRT) technology, also employed in the commercial TV industry. The image produced on these screens is sent from the computer to the CRT electronically. Inside, the CRT has an electron beam that strikes the phosphorus-coated screen of the monitor. When the coating is struck by the beam, light is emitted by the electrons in the phosphorus. A higher beam intensity produces a brighter picture. It is the phosphorus-emitted light that produces images on the screen.

Computer monitor screens are normally divided into addressable dots that can be illuminated. Each addressable dot is called a pixel or picture element. As an electron beam inside the CRT scans each pixel, its intensity can be varied to turn the pixel on or off. The number of pixels that a screen can address (turn on or off) determines the resolution of the monitor. More pixels on the screen will produce a higher resolution.

The quality of the output depends on the type of monitor being used. In general, monitors are either monochrome or color. Other factors to consider are the size of the screen and density of pixels. Fig. 1.3 shows a color monitor.

Fig. 1.3 Monitor

The graphics component of the computer has the electronics necessary to understand the output requests of the CPU and translate them into a format that can be used by a monitor to display the output. With some Macintosh systems, the monitor is built into the system. Other models have an external monitor and provide the flexibility of using different monitors sold in the Macintosh series.

Printers

Printers can be grouped into two major categories:

1. Impact printers

2. Nonimpact printers

Impact printers produce an image on paper by driving a series of pins against a ribbon (dot matrix printers) or by hitting fully formed characters that are on a disk with a hammer against a ribbon (daisy wheel printers).

The pins on a dot matrix printer are normally arranged in the shape of a rectangle, typically from nine to twenty-four pins high and from one to five pins wide. A larger number of pins forming the rectangle will produce better quality letters on the paper. Dot matrix printers operate at a variety of speeds, from fifty characters per second to one thousand characters per second. This type of printer can produce text and graphics output. Most models work in a bi-directional mode; that is, they print from left to right and right to left as they move down the paper.

Daisy wheel printers produce sharp, solid characters of high quality. The output quality of a daisy wheel printer is superior to that of a dot matrix printer. The main reason is that characters are fully formed on the daisy wheel as opposed to being a series of dots. The drawbacks of the daisy wheel printer are its slow speed and inability to produce graphic output.

Nonimpact printers use technologies such as thermal printing, ink jet printing, and laser technology. Thermal printers, like dot matrix printers, have a print head consisting of wires that get hot and leave an imprint on heat-sensitive paper. Ink jet printers spray ink onto the page. They provide a higher quality and faster alternative to the impact dot matrix printers. Laser printers are top-of-the-line devices, having excellent print quality, speed, and quietness of operation. They use technology similar to that of a photocopier. The output produced by a laser printer is composed of characters and graphics suitable for business output and presentations. Fig. 1.4 shows a laser printer.

Fig. 1.4 Laser Printer

Printers sold with the Macintosh series of computers include a nine-pin dot matrix printer (ImageWriter), ink jet printers (StyleWriter and DeskWriter), and laser printers (LaserWriter).

Other Output Devices

There are many other types of output devices being used by microcomputers. Some of them are

1. Voice output. The telephone company commonly uses this type of output when a number is requested from a telephone operator.

2. Plotter. Plotters are used mainly to produce high quality graphical output that also requires color.

3. Photographic camera. Special adapters can be used to take a snapshot of the screen and produce either a slide from the graphic on the screen or just a normal picture on photographic paper.

Storage Devices

Since the information stored in RAM can be lost if the microcomputer is turned off or if a power failure takes place, computer systems require the use of secondary or permanent storage systems. By placing data and programs into secondary storage, they can be loaded back into RAM at a later time for more viewing or modification. The two major types of storage devices for microcomputers are

1. Floppy disk (diskette)

2. Hard disk

Floppy Disks

The floppy disk, also called a diskette, floppy, or simply a disk, is one of the typical storage devices for the microcomputer. It is normally available in two sizes: 5 1/4 inches and 3 1/2 inches in diameter. A floppy disk consists of a circular piece of plastic (Mylar plastic), coated with an oxide material. This material is similar to the coating used in cassette technology. The Mylar plastic is enclosed in a protective jacket that can consist of plastic or paper. The jacket has an opening to expose a portion of the disk surface so the disk drive can read and write information to and from the disk. Floppy disks typically store between 360,000 bytes and 2.8 million bytes of information. On most microcomputers, floppy disk drives are labeled A or B. On icon driven systems, such as the Macintosh, the drives available will be pictured on the screen and can be given any name the user desires. A drive is referenced by selecting the icon on the screen. Macintosh systems currently being sold store 1.4 megabytes on high density disks and .7 megabytes on low density disks.

Hard Disks

A hard disk, or fixed disk, as it is sometimes called, stores data on platters that are permanently mounted inside the computer and cannot be removed. On a hard disk, the read/write mechanism, all moving parts, and the metal disks that store the information are enclosed in a sealed metal case. This avoids contamination of the storage surface by dust or any other foreign particles. The hard disk is similar to the floppy disk. However, the hard disk can store 20 million bytes or more of data. Also, the time to transfer data is faster with the hard disk than with the floppy disk. Macintosh hard disks typically contain 40 megabytes, but may contain 80 megabytes or more. On the Macintosh systems, the icon for a hard disk will be different from the icon for a floppy drive.

Other Storage Devices

Some other storage devices are

1. Disk cartridge. Disk cartridges use technology similar to a cassette tape. They can store large amounts of data inexpensively, and they are portable.

2. Compact disk read only memory (CD-ROM). This technology is relatively new, but it holds great promise for the microcomputer user. A CD-ROM can hold large amounts of information, and it can also store audio and video data in digitized format. This enables microcomputers to display normal computer output mixed with sound and full motion video.

The Operating System

The operating system is a set of system programs that controls the hardware of the microcomputer. It allows the user to communicate with the hardware without the need to understand the inner workings of the machine. Without the operating system, the user would have to learn machine language, which consists of zeros and ones. Computing would never have reached the masses without the aid of the operating system. The Macintosh series of computers uses a proprietary system, which is icon driven. The system is disk based and is loaded into memory when the machine is turned on.

Booting the System

The process of turning the microcomputer on and loading (placing) the operating system from a disk into main memory is called booting the system. The process varies from computer to computer, but the basic steps can be generalized as follows:

1. A floppy disk that contains the operating system is placed into a disk drive. If the computer has a hard disk, then the floppy disk would not be used, and there should be no disk in the floppy disk drive.

2. The microcomputer is turned on. Instructions are loaded first from read only memory (ROM) into main memory (RAM), and then the memory-resident portion of the operating system is loaded into RAM.

3. The instructions loaded from ROM, also called the boot instructions, transfer control of the microcomputer to the operating system.

4. Finally, the operating system prompt is displayed. This prompt is an indication to the user that the operating system is ready to accept commands from the keyboard. At this point, application software can be loaded into RAM and executed.

After the operating system has been placed in memory, it usually resides there until the computer is turned off. In some instances, it may be necessary to boot the system after the computer is on. This is referred to as a "warm boot" and is typically conducted by a menu command or combination of keys on the keyboard. The Macintosh system provides a Restart command on the Special pull-down menu to conduct a warm boot.

System Commands

The three techniques of communicating with operating systems are by typing commands, selecting commands from menus, and selecting icons from the screen. The Macintosh operating system communicates to you through icons and menus, and assumes a working knowledge of the mouse. Commands are issued by selecting the appropriate icons from the screen or window. A command may then display a dialog box to use to communicate further details regarding the command issued. Storage areas are created and deleted by selecting these options from windows. Files are moved from one area to another by selecting the appropriate icon with the mouse and moving the icon to the new storage area. Files are copied from one disk to another using the same technique. Files are deleted by moving them to an icon signifying trash or disposal.

Preparing Data Disks

After a data disk is purchased, it must be formatted in order for the disk drive to use it as a secondary storage medium. Formatting is a function that the operating system performs on all new disks so it knows how the surface of the disk is subdivided and numbered. An analogy to this concept would be a post office that just received a large number of mail boxes. As the mail boxes are installed, each will receive a number. This process is performed only once when the mail boxes are new. Afterward, when mail is received, post office personnel know where to place the mail so it can be retrieved by its proper owner.

In the same manner, the operating system needs to know the different addresses on the disk so it can place data in its proper place. When a program requires data that is stored on the disk, it asks the operating system for the particular location of the data. The operating system gives the address to the program so it can find the data. Also, the operating system needs to know if both sides of the disk are being used or only one side, where and how many bad spots are on the disk, where to store the data, and how to free space when the user deletes data in the future.

All of the above functions are performed by the format command. At this point it is not important to understand how the format command performs its work or exactly what is taking place in the system. However, it is important to understand that most new disks will need to be formatted once before they are used to store files.

When a disk is placed in a drive, the system will attempt to read from it. If it has not been properly formatted, the system will display a message and give you the option of formatting the disk. Each disk can be given a volume name for later reference.

Once a disk has been formatted, a disk drive can write information on the disk and read the information from the disk. The format command can be a dangerous command. Any data residing on a disk will be destroyed by the formatting operation. Make sure that there is no valuable data on the disk before the formatting operation is invoked.

File Names

Every file saved on a disk must have a name, which is used by the operating system to locate the data stored in the file. The file name is provided by you before data is saved to the disk. Normally a program will prompt you for a file name when you choose the Save As option from within an application program.

System files are denoted by icons, typically with associated names. Microsoft Works files will be pictured as files, with each having a unique name. When the contents of a particular file is being modified, the name will be followed by a two letter code indicating the type of file it is. WP indicates word processing, SS indicates spreadsheet, and DB indicates database.

Hands-on System Operation

Booting a Computer System with a Hard Drive

1. Turn the machine on. (This is called a "cold boot.")

When you turn the machine on, it automatically conducts the booting process. After some checks, you should see a screen similar to Fig. 1.5. You are now ready to enter commands. Prior to turning the machine off, select the Shut Down option from the Special pull-down menu. The procedure is covered in detail in Chapter 2.

2. Select Shut Down from the Special pull-down menu.

3. Turn the machine off.

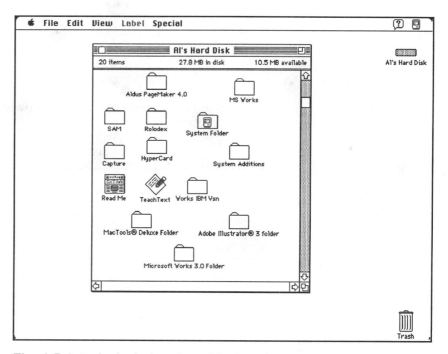

Fig. 1.5 A typical window for a Macintosh running under System 7

Summary

The microcomputer revolution has touched all our lives. A microcomputer system is a set of components that work together to achieve a computing goal.

The microcomputer system is composed of hardware and software. The basic components of the hardware are the input devices, output devices, central

13

processing unit, main memory, and secondary storage devices. Software can be categorized into system software and application software.

The system software that serves as the interface between the computer and the user is the operating system. In the Macintosh series of computers, the operating system is proprietary. Without it, the machine and user could not communicate with each other.

Before a disk can be used for the first time, it must be prepared so that it can accept data. The process by which a disk is prepared is called formatting. Formatting is accomplished with the use of the format command. Disks need to be formatted only once. After the disk is formatted, it can be placed in a disk drive and documents or files can be stored on it.

Questions

1. Why is the microcomputer an important step in the evolution of technology?

2. What are the components of a microcomputer system?

3. What are the components of the hardware?

4. What are the major types of software?

5. What are application programs?

6. What are system programs?

7. Describe the elements of the CPU and explain the function of each.

8. What is a byte?

9. What is the difference between main memory and secondary storage?

10. What are RAM and ROM?

11. What is meant by booting the machine?

12. Describe two input devices.

13. Describe how the CRT works.

14. What is a pixel?

15. Describe how impact printers work.

16. Describe two different types of nonimpact printers.

17. What is the difference between a floppy disk and a hard disk?

18. What is the purpose of the operating system?

19. How can a disk be prepared to accept data from the computer?

Exercises

Exercise 1

Review and report on the hardware components of the Macintosh systems in your lab. Identify and report on the process to boot the system in your lab.

Chapter 2

Integrated Application Software

Objectives

After completing this chapter you will

1. Understand the basic microcomputer system.

2. Understand the difference between stand-alone programs and integrated programs.

3. Understand how to manage files.

4. Know the initial screens of Microsoft Works.

5. Know how to create, save, delete, rename, copy, and back up files in Microsoft Works.

Solving Problems with a Computer

Three decades ago many real-life problems required some device that could perform thousands of calculations relatively quickly. Some of the early calculation machines were not fast enough to efficiently process data and could not handle large amounts of information. Their limitations created barriers to the advancement of science and the evolution of business practices.

One of the largest and most ambitious projects ever undertaken, putting people on the moon, was faced with such problems. If the United States was to be successful in sending people to the moon and bringing them back alive, technology had to progress rapidly. As a result of the efforts made by scientists and engineers, computers were developed and refined to handle more data at faster speeds. The end result was machines that could help people solve problems by taking the routine and tedious work away from their users, allowing them to concentrate on designing solutions to problems.

The computer is a workhorse capable of working 24 hours a day and 7 days a week. Computers can do thousands of tasks accurately without getting tired. They are fast, reliable, and have large storage capacities. If they are used properly and with the right software, computers help individuals and companies do the following tasks:

1. They increase productivity by performing dangerous, routine, or boring jobs, and jobs that require many calculations in a short amount of time.

2. They help managers make good decisions. Managers need to look at large amounts of data in order to make decisions that might affect thousands of people. A computer, instructed by a problem-solving program developed by humans, can help decision makers understand the data and gather information from it.

3. They also reduce the cost of doing business, because computers increase productivity and help in decision making.

4. They solve many tasks in scientific and engineering applications that otherwise could not be solved without the use of computers that can perform millions of calculations per second.

However, computers by themselves are useless. The hardware requires instructions that tell it what it is supposed to do. These instructions are stored in programs called software. Programs used for word processing, accounting, database, or telecommunications are called application software.

Stand-Alone Programs

The following are the five most commonly used application programs on a microcomputer:

1. Word Processing. It is used to type memos, letters, and other documents. The user enters words by typing on a keyboard and the computer stores them in memory. The user can then change any of the text, change margins, add boldfacing, and provide other enhancements to the documents. Finally, the letters or documents can be stored on a disk or printed on a printer.

2. Spreadsheet. It is used by people who work with numbers, such as accountants or statisticians. Numbers, formulas, and text can be entered into the spreadsheet, and questions such as "What if?" can then be asked of the program. The results are displayed on the computer monitor or printed on a printer.

3. Computer Graphics. Business graphics allow the user to see pictorial representations of a series of numeric values. The graphs can be produced by using data stored in a spreadsheet. The ability to see numerical values in a graphical representation allows managers to have a better understanding of the information required to make business decisions.

4. Database. It allows the user to enter, update, retrieve, and sort data in a manner that is organized efficiently. With this type of program a manager can produce quick reports from large amounts of data stored on the computer. Also, some database packages allow many types of inquiries to be performed, and the information can be accessed and displayed in many different formats.

5. Telecommunications. This type of software program allows one computer to talk or communicate with another. A person with a microcomputer, a modem, and the appropriate telecommunications program can access other personal computers and larger computers, called mainframes, which may reside locally or on the other side of the world.

All of the above software programs can be purchased and used individually; hence the name stand-alone programs. Each one can provide many sophisticated features to the user. Since the programs are used independently of each other, the data produced by one is not easily available to the others. For example, assume that a manager wants to send a month-end report to his or her supervisor, who resides in a different state. This problem requires three of the five types of programs mentioned. The manager will use a spreadsheet to produce a balance sheet for the entire month. A letter will be typed with a word processor that explains the numbers found in the balance sheet. The manager then needs to send both documents to the supervisor through the use of a telecommunications program. Since the word processor is independent of the spreadsheet, the manager will have to send two documents instead of just one.

This is one of the limitations of stand-alone programs. Data produced by one package sometimes needs to be included in another. Unless the data is retyped for each document, the process is difficult to perform and sometimes impossible. One solution to the problem is to use programs that work under an integrated interface that allows data transfer from one program to another.

Integrated Programs

Integrated programs combine the most commonly used application programs, including word processing, spreadsheet, database, graphics, and tele-communications, into a single software package that is easy to use. All the application programs included share a common interface, or command structure. This means that once the user learns how to save a word processing document, the same command is also used to save documents in the spreadsheet and other application programs included in the integrated package.

Since the application programs have a common interface, it is easier to learn the second, the third, and the fourth after learning the first. This will significantly reduce the time required to become productive with the software. In addition, moving among the different programs and transferring data between them is relatively easy. This also reduces the time required to complete a project and aids in providing a better final product.

Why Microsoft Works?

Microsoft Works is a collection of software applications designed for use at home, school, and the workplace. All of these applications come in a single package from Microsoft Corporation that is sold through most computer hardware and software dealers. The basic applications included in the Works package are word processing, spreadsheet with charting, database and reporting, and telecommunications.

All of the applications in Works are fully integrated. This feature helps users be more productive at work and at home. For instance, suppose that a person has a mail order system that he or she is running from home. The mailing addresses and personal data can be stored in the database application of Works. If a special promotion takes place, a "form" letter to be sent to all customers can be created with the word processor included in Works. Then data from the data-base can be merged with the form letter to create a mass mailing in an efficient and cost effective manner. Also, as payments are received from customers, the amounts can be posted in the database. Later the data can be incorporated into a spreadsheet for financial analysis, and charts can be created to map the progress of the company. This type of functionality and the power of each of the applications within the Microsoft Works program are the reasons for its success in both the Macintosh and the IBM PC environments.

To run Microsoft Works on the Macintosh, you must have the following hardware equipment:

1. A Macintosh, Quadra, or Centrix computer system with at least 4 MB of RAM

2. An 800K double-sided disk drive and a hard disk

3. Operating System 6.02 or higher. This is the Macintosh operating system. (For this book, System 7 was used.)

4. A printer, if documents are to be printed on paper

5. A modem, if communication with other computers is desired

6. Hypercard, if the Microsoft Works online tutorial is to be used

The Macintosh Environment

The Macintosh computer system uses a graphical oriented "desktop" that allows users to perform most functions by selecting items on the screen with a mouse. Regardless of which Macintosh computer Works is stored on, starting the Macintosh is about the same. If the computer has a hard disk, then it is automatically the startup disk. The startup disk is a special disk that contains the commands necessary for the computer to perform its functions. The startup disk contains the System Folder and the Finder. Both make up part of the Macintosh operating system; a discussion of them is beyond the scope of this book. If the computer does not have a hard disk (all new models of the Macintosh come with a hard disk) then the startup disk will be one of the floppy disks that came with the machine. Due to the low cost of hard disks on the market, and since all new Macintosh systems have a hard disk, the rest of this book will assume that Works is stored on the hard disk and that the hard disk is the startup disk.

The Macintosh Desktop

Depending on the type of Macintosh available, the procedure to turn on the machine will vary slightly. On some models, there is a switch on the back of the machine; on others, a special key on the upper part of the keyboard is the ON switch. In either case, when the computer is turned on, the first display that is available to the user is the Macintosh desktop. Fig. 2.1 shows a picture of the desktop. The content will be different from computer to computer depending on what is stored in the system, but generally the layout is the same.

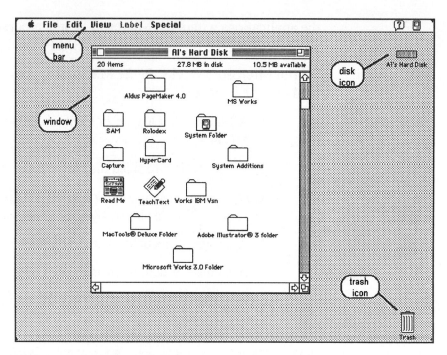

Fig. 2.1 Macintosh desktop

The desktop contains a background area, which is the shaded area in Fig. 2.1. It contains a menu bar across the top, an icon for each disk on the system, and a trash can icon. It also contains a window displaying the contents of the system disk. We will call this the Opening System Disk window.

The Background

The shaded surface within the border in Fig. 2.1 is the background for all of the objects on the desktop. All items are placed on the desktop in the same manner as a person places papers, books, and artwork on top of a desk. The objects available on the desktop are icons, menu bars, windows, and dialog boxes. Items are selected with the aid of a pointer that moves across the desktop. It is controlled from the keyboard and from a mouse.

The Mouse

The mouse is a major component of the Macintosh computer system. It is used to manage the windows and to select icons and menu items. The mouse is rolled on a flat surface. As the mouse moves, the mouse pointer moves on the desktop in a corresponding direction. The pointer symbol is an arrow symbol when the system is booted. In Microsoft Works, the pointer will appear as an arrow, but will also appear in other shapes, including a vertical bar, a cross, and a hand. Each symbol has a specific purpose that will be explained as it is introduced in the text. There are six different mouse actions required to perform most functions on the Macintosh. These are point, click, press, drag, double click, and shift-click.

Point

An icon is a pictorial representation of an application or a document. To point to an icon, roll the mouse on the flat surface until the pointer is on the icon desired. The direction of movement of the mouse on the flat surface is imitated on the desktop. The movement technique is used to point to windows, bars, menu items, and any symbol or identifier on the desktop.

Click

To click the pointer on an icon, the pointer must overlap the chosen icon. With the pointer over the chosen icon, press the mouse button and release it quickly. This selects the object. The object selected changes color to indicate that it is now active. To deselect an icon, point to another part of the desktop and click the mouse button. If you are pointing to something else, this will make it active. Pointing to a blank area in the active window and clicking the mouse button will deselect all icons.

Press

Pressing the mouse button means holding it down while an action takes place. Pressing is commonly done to select a menu item and then a submenu item. It can also be used to select an icon and move (drag) it to another area of the desktop.

Drag

Dragging means placing the mouse pointer over an object, then pressing the mouse button and holding the button down while the mouse is moved across a flat surface, thus moving the object across the desktop, and then releasing the mouse button. The effect of dragging depends on the application running when the dragging takes place. If an icon is selected in a window, and it is dragged, the effect is to move the icon across the desktop until the mouse button is released. Dragging the mouse pointer inside a text document highlights the characters that it is dragged over. A window can be dragged by placing the pointer on the title bar, pressing the mouse button, dragging the window to a new location, and then releasing the mouse button.

Double Click

Double clicking means pressing and releasing the mouse button twice in rapid succession. Double clicking on an icon selects the icon and performs an action on the selected option. In the Finder, double clicking on a folder opens the folder. Double clicking on a program icon launches (executes) the program. Double clicking on a file loads the program that the file belongs to and loads the file into memory.

Shift-Click

Shift-clicking allows the selection of multiple elements. For example, to select three folders, press the shift key and hold it down while moving the mouse pointer to each of the icons and clicking on them. Once all the icons are selected, dragging on one moves all of them at the same time.

The Icons

Types of Icons

An icon is a picture representing an option. Fig. 2.1 shows a disk icon, the trash can icon, and the Opening System Disk window with several folder icons.

All disk icons will typically be displayed on the upper right side of the desktop. Any disks currently in use by the system will be displayed. Even though you may have only one floppy drive, there may be several floppy disks in use by the system at the same time, and there is typically one hard disk in use. Each disk is named to identify it. The icon for a hard disk is a small rectangular box, and the icon for a floppy disk is in the shape of a floppy disk jacket. The active disk will be shaded or colored differently. When the system is booted, the system disk will be the active disk. Generally, the system hard disk will be the only disk on the system when it is turned on.

The trash can icon is on the lower right side of the desktop and is always present, even though it may be hidden from view by a window. It is used to delete unwanted files from the disks. Any files to be deleted are first placed in the trash can icon. Then the trash is emptied by selecting an Empty Trash command from a menu.

Other icons generally reside in the windows. There are three types. Folder icons, shown in Fig. 2.2, look the same and indicate a folder containing other folders and/or files. Folder icons typically don't have pictures in them, but there are exceptions (see System Folder in Fig. 2.1).

The second type of icon, shown in Fig. 2.2, is a program icon. Although many program icons are in the shape of a rectangle, each one contains a different picture. And some, such as the SAM Intercept icon in Fig. 2.2, are not in the form of a rectangle.

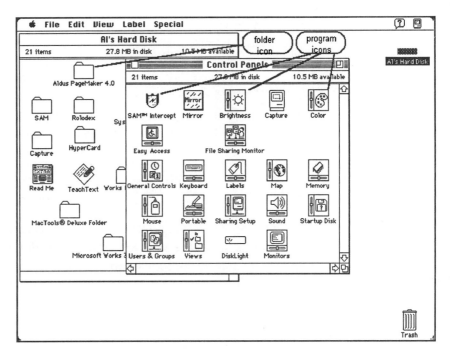

Fig. 2.2 Folder and file icons

The third type of icon represents a document. Document icons are typically characterized by a rectangular format with the upper right corner folded over, or dog-eared (see the document files in Fig. 2.5), but they may also take on a different shape (see the Apple File Exchange program in Fig. 2.4). They commonly contain pictures depicting the type of document file they are.

How Icons Are Used

Document icons identify documents containing data. In Microsoft Works, these can include text, database, spreadsheet, communications, and draw documents, each of which is characterized by a separate icon (see Fig. 2.3). These are used to store and process data.

Program icons represent programs that can be launched (executed) to run a specific application. For example, the Sound program pictured in Fig. 2.2 provides the sound messages to you in response to incorrect actions. The user can modify the volume and message in the program, and the program will be launched by the other programs to send the message. System programs are used to manage and control operations. Application programs are used to solve problems. Microsoft Works is an example of an application program. The Works Opening dialog box is shown in Fig. 2.3 and is characterized by the types of documents it produces.

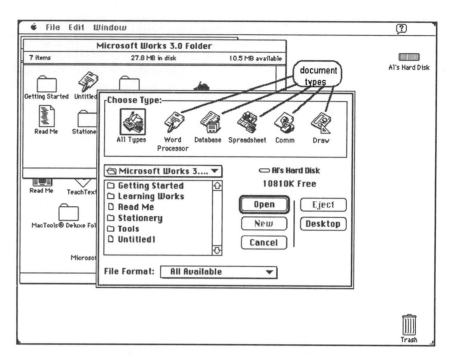

Fig. 2.3 Works Opening dialog box

Folder icons are containers, holding documents, programs, and other folders. The Apple File Exchange folder shown in Fig. 2.4 contains programs, documents, and folders. By creating a hierarchical structure of folders, the desktop can stay organized; programs and their corresponding files will be easier to manage. A folder within a folder is said to have a child/parent relationship, with the outer folder being the parent and the folder in it the child.

At the top of the desktop (see Fig. 2.3) is the menu bar. The menu bar contains options for pull-down menus with commands and selection items on them. The Apple menu on the left (picture of an apple) is always present; it includes items pertaining to system control and operation.

The other menu items will vary, depending on operation status and the program running at the time. The options available on them will also vary, depending on system and program status. The menus contain commands that are used to create folders, empty the trash can icon, and perform other functions to operate the Macintosh.

To access any of these menus, move the mouse pointer to the menu and press and hold the mouse button, causing a pull-down menu to appear (see Fig. 2.5). In this menu, one of the choices, Show Clipboard, is used to view the contents of the clipboard.

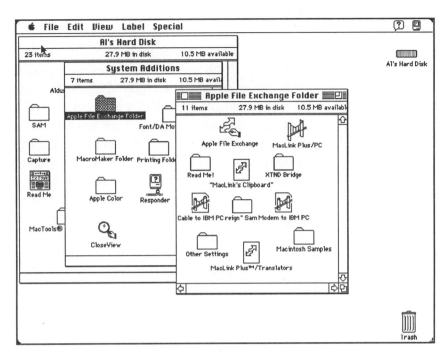

Fig. 2.4 Folders, documents, programs, and system program icons

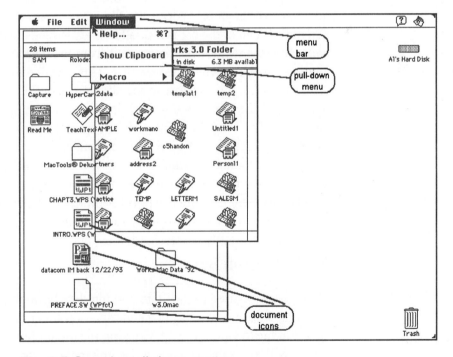

Fig. 2.5 Sample pull-down menu

Windows

A window is a rectangular portion of the screen that displays some type of information. Programs use windows to display the results of calculations, queries, or any other action required of them. A window contains a work area, a title bar, a vertical scroll bar, a horizontal scroll bar, a close box, and a size box. It may also contain other characteristics that are associated with a particular function. For example, the Control Panels window shown in Fig. 2.2 has a line under the title bar with specific information regarding the disk. Although many windows may be on the desktop, only one is active. It is characterized by shaded lines on the title bar. In Fig. 2.2 there are two different windows displayed on the desktop. The active window is the one with the title Control Panels. Clicking the mouse on any other window makes it active and the previously active window becomes inactive. The active window will always appear in the foreground (all of it showing), with other overlapping windows in the background (appearing to be behind it). The size and position of any window can be changed, and any one of them can be made the active window (the one that the user wants to work with) at any moment.

Title Bar

The title bar is the bar across the top of the window (see Fig. 2.6). It contains the name of the disk, folder, data file, or program that the window represents. On the left end of the bar is a small box, called the close box. Selecting this box will close the window and remove it from the desktop. On the right end of the bar is a small box within a small box. This is called the zoom box. Selecting the box will zoom the window to the size of the desktop. Selecting the box again will return the window to its original size. The close box and zoom box are selected by moving the pointer to the box and clicking the mouse button. If the window is not active, the bar will be clear. If the window is active, the bar will have lines running through it, giving it a shaded effect. When the window is active, the bar can be used to move the position of the window on the desktop. This is done by placing the pointer on the bar, pressing the mouse button, dragging the window to its new location, and then releasing the mouse button.

Vertical Scroll Bar

Scroll bars are used to facilitate moving data through the windows. The bar on the right side of a window is the vertical scroll bar (see Fig. 2.6). It contains an arrow at the top, pointing up. Clicking the mouse button with the pointer on the arrow will move the data down one line in the work area (move the window up one line). Pressing the mouse button with the pointer on the arrow will scroll the data down through the window (move the window up through the data). The bar contains an arrow on the lower end that points down. This arrow is used in the same way, causing the data to move up in the window (the window appears to move down). If there is only one page (window) of data, the bar will be clear. If there is more than one window, the bar will be shaded.

When the data is more than one page (window), a box will be displayed on the bar indicating the relative position of the data in the window to all the data. For example, if there were five pages (five windows) of data, and you were on the third page, the box would appear to be about three-fifths of the way down the scroll bar. You can use the box to scroll through the data by placing the pointer on the box, pressing the mouse button, and dragging the pointer in the desired direction. Releasing the mouse button terminates the scrolling process. You can also place the pointer ahead of the box, in either direction, and click the mouse button, causing the data to scroll a page (window) through the data in that direction. For data with multiple output pages (paper pages), such as a letter, the box will contain a number that indicates the actual output page number, given the current specifications.

Horizontal Scroll Bar

The horizontal scroll bar is the bar on the bottom of the window (see Fig. 2.6). It contains the same characteristics as the vertical scroll bar and works the same way. If the data is not wider than the window, it will be clear. If the data is wider, it will be shaded and will include the arrows and the box.

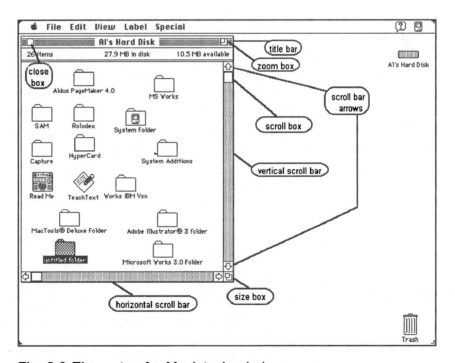

Fig. 2.6 Elements of a Macintosh window

Size Box

The small box in the lower right corner of the window, linked to another small box, is called the size box (refer to Fig. 2.6). It is selected by placing the pointer on it and pressing the mouse button. Dragging the pointer in any direction will resize the window, making it wider, narrower, taller, or shorter. This box is used to help manage the display of multiple windows on the desktop by resizing them as appropriate.

Dialog Boxes

Dialog boxes are distinguished from windows in that they have no title bar or scroll bars. They are used by programs to communicate information to and from the user. A dialog box may contain as little as a message and a button to acknowledge receiving it, or it may have many boxes and buttons, along with messages to the user.

There are three types of boxes that are used in a dialog box. A text entry box is used to enter data into the program. A text entry box is rectangular in shape, with the length of the rectangle defining the visible entry size. A check box (in the shape of a square) is used as a toggle switch to turn an option on or off. If it has an X in it, selecting it will erase the X and turn the option off. If it is empty, selecting it will place an X in it and turn the option on. A list box contains a list of names. The list is used as a reference list or a selection list from which to choose the desired item.

There are two types of buttons used in dialog boxes. A rectangular or oval type button is used to select a command option from the dialog box. The second type, called a radio button, is a round button used to select alternative options. The round button represents a toggle switch and is clear if it is off and shaded with a dot if it is on. Sometimes turning on one radio button in a dialog box will cause another one to be turned off (in mutually exclusive options).

You will also see messages and icons in dialog boxes. The messages are used to describe status, define options, and identify boxes and buttons. The icons are used to provide options in picture form rather than through boxes and buttons.

Managing Folders and Files

All documents created are called files, and the processes required to create, store, delete, and copy them are called file management. All documents created with application programs will have to be stored on a hard or floppy disk. Otherwise, when the power to the computer is turned off, all work will be lost. From time to time, old files will need to be deleted from the disk or copied to other disks in order to have multiple backup documents in case an accident destroys the originals.

Before you use the computer, make sure that a floppy disk has been prepared to accept files. Floppy disk preparation is outlined in Chapter 1. Review it as necessary. When the first letter of a document is typed or when you choose "Create New File" from a menu, the file is automatically created in main memory. As explained before, main memory is volatile (its contents are erased when the power to the computer is turned off). For this reason, the file stored in memory will need to be saved on a disk for more permanent storage. This process should be repeated often since power failures can take place at any time. It is frustrating to work on a document for two hours and see it disappear if, for some reason, the power is interrupted.

Eventually, all files should be copied onto a disk other than the original or working disk. This process is called backup. The reason for backing up files is that the original disk may get damaged and information stored on it can be lost. Even though there are programs on the market that help you recover files after an accident erases them, sometimes they can't be recovered. Therefore, all files stored on the working disk should be backed up at the end of each session, and the backup disk should be stored in a safe place. If any files are damaged, the backup disk can be used to restore the files to their recent state.

Creating Folders and Files

Files on a Macintosh disk are organized into folders. Folders are the counterparts of a file drawer in a file cabinet. In an office, file folders are organized by function or subject and stored in appropriate cabinet drawers. The same process applies to a computer disk.

Although files and programs do not have be placed into folders, doing so organizes the desktop and makes finding and accessing programs and data files easier.

Folders can be created by clicking on the File pull-down menu, dragging the mouse until New Folder is selected, and then releasing the mouse button. This creates an empty folder where files and programs can be placed. The default name of the new folder is "untitled folder" as in Fig. 2.6. As soon as the folder is created, typing a new name that represents the future contents of the folder will replace the default name.

Files, on the other hand, are created by application programs such as word processors, spreadsheets, databases, and others. Usually, to create any type of data file on the Macintosh, a program must first be launched, then a new file created, and then the file saved to disk before a file icon shows on the desktop. Program files are placed on the desktop by copying or moving them from another disk onto the desktop.

Moving and Copying Folders and Files

To move folders and files from one area of the desktop to another, the desired item is selected and then the icon is dragged to the destination on the desktop. When trying to drag the program icon, an outline of the figure moves with the mouse pointer. Placing this outline over the new folder and releasing the mouse button causes the program to be placed in the folder.

The process of copying what an icon represents is similar to moving, except that copying is performed from one disk to another. First the icon is selected. Then the icon outlined is dragged and positioned over the outline of the disk icon where the copy is to be placed. The mouse button is released and the copying takes place.

Deleting Folders and Files

The process of deleting a folder or a file is the same. The item to be deleted is dragged to the trash can icon. When the object is placed over the trash can, it changes color. When the mouse button is released, the item is placed in the trash can, and the trash can will change sizes, showing a bulge. Items placed in the trash can be retrieved by opening it. When the user is certain that the items in the trash can are to be erased, the Special pull-down menu is displayed and the Empty Trash option is selected. This action erases the files represented by the icons from the disk.

Renaming Folders and Files

To change the name of a folder, click on the name at the bottom of the icon. The icon will become active and the name will appear shaded or colored. You can type the new name to replace the old name, or you can create an insertion point in the existing name by clicking the mouse with the pointer next to any character, and then edit the name. Clicking on anything outside the name box or pressing the RETURN key completes the process. A file name is changed using the same procedure.

Getting Started with Works

Introduction to Microsoft Works

Microsoft Works is a collection of software applications designed for use at home, school, and the workplace. The applications come in a single package from Microsoft Corporation that is sold through most computer and software dealers. The basic applications included in the Works package and their functions are listed below.

1. Word Processing. It can be used to write letters, school term papers, memos, and business correspondence.

2. Spreadsheet with Charting. It can be used to prepare, analyze and present personal and professional business budgets, cost estimates, and mathematical calculations in both numerical and graphical form.

3. Database and Reporting. It can be used to organize and print mailing lists, inventories, receipts, and phone numbers.

4. Telecommunications. It can be used to connect to online information services, electronic bulletin boards, or other computers.

5. Draw. It can be used to create simple drawings to be used as separate output or in conjunction with other Works materials, such as a text document.

Before Microsoft Works can be used on a computer, it must be installed. The process of installation is clearly outlined in the Works manual and requires just a few steps. Please refer to the Works manual for installation.

The Works Interface

Works is more than just the application software outlined above. Information contained in one of the applications can easily be used in any of the other applications. For example, an office budget can be prepared with the spreadsheet, a graph of the projected costs can be created, and then the worksheet and the graph can be incorporated into a memo. The memo can then be sent electronically to other users for review, and it can be printed on a variety of printers.

All the applications work in a similar manner because they all share the same menu interface. This means that the windows in each of the application programs that make up Works are similar and sometimes identical. Therefore, a user can apply what he or she learns in one application to the use of another of the Works applications. This will reduce the time required to learn and use all of the tools included in the package.

The Works Opening Dialog Box

In order to start using Works, the Works program must first be retrieved, or loaded, from the disk and placed in main memory. This process is called executing, or launching, the program. The procedure for launching the program consists of locating the Microsoft Works icon and double clicking on it. A Works Opening dialog box will be displayed on the screen (see Fig. 2.7). The type of application to be used can be selected from the icons in the dialog box. A new file can be created or an existing file can be opened and placed in memory.

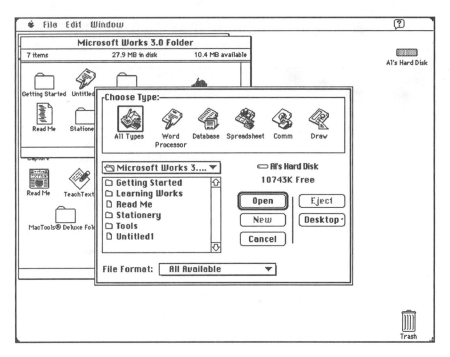

Fig. 2.7 Works Opening dialog box

Creating and Saving a Document

To create a document, such as a text document, the Word Processor icon is selected by double clicking on it. This displays an empty window on the desktop. The computer waits for input from the user.

Once the document is completed, it should be saved for future use. To save the document, the File pull-down menu is selected, and the mouse pointer is dragged to the Save or Save As option. The dialog box shown in Fig. 2.8 is displayed. The name of the file that will contain the data is typed in the box named "Save Document As:."

Exiting Works

To exit Works, close any open documents, select the File pull-down menu, drag the mouse pointer to Quit, and select it. Then close the Microsoft Works 3.0 Folder window by clicking on the close box on the left end of the title bar.

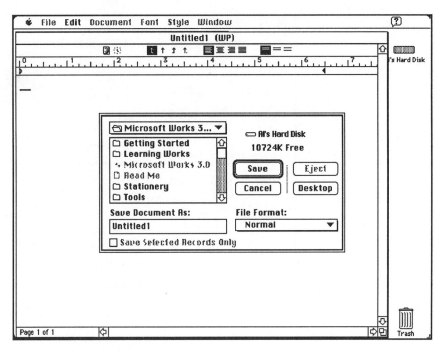

Fig. 2.8 File Save As dialog box

Hands-on with Works

Booting the System

    1. Turn the computer on.

The On switch may be on the back of the computer or on the upper part of the keyboard.

You should see a screen similar to the one shown in Fig. 2.9. It shows the Opening System Disk window.

NOTE: If the Opening System Disk window is not open, double click on the hard disk icon to open it.

To boot the system with the machine on, use the Restart command on the Special pull-down menu. To become familiar with it, perform the restart now.

    2. Move the pointer to the Special item on the main menu.

    3. Press and hold the ⌐⟍.

    4. Drag the pointer to the Restart option.

    5. Release the ⌐⟍.

You should have a time delay while the system boots. Then it will display the Opening System Disk window shown in Fig. 2.9.

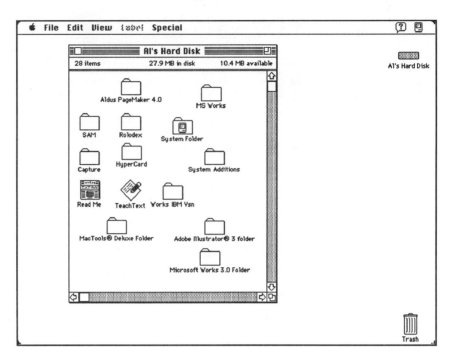

Fig. 2.9 Opening System Disk window

Formatting a Disk

You will now format two diskettes.

    1. Place a diskette into the floppy disk drive.

You should see a dialog box, shown in Fig. 2.10, indicating the disk is not readable (or not a Macintosh disk). Select the Initialize button to initialize it.

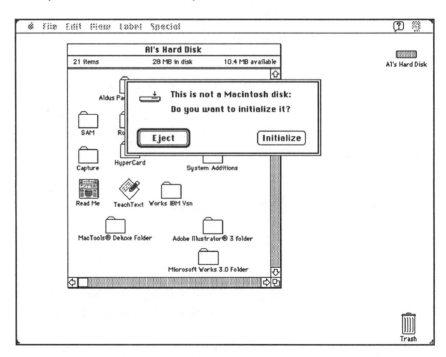

Fig. 2.10 Dialog box indicating disk is unreadable

2. Move the pointer to [Initialize].

3. Click the ⌱.

You should get a dialog box with a warning that the disk will be erased. Select the Erase option.

4. Move the pointer to [Erase].

5. Click the ⌱.

You should get a dialog box with a request to name the disk. Name it DISK1.

6. Type **DISK1.**

7. Press [return] (or select the OK button).

You will see the message "Formatting disk" in the dialog box, followed by other messages as the disk is being formatted. When the disk is formatted, it will be shaded dark, meaning it is now the active disk.

Now eject the formatted disk, but leave it pictured on the desktop.

8. Move the pointer to the Special item on the main menu.

9. Press and hold the ⌱.

10. Drag the pointer to the Eject Disk option.

11. Release the ⌱.

The disk should eject.

12. If you get the prompt "Please insert the disk:," insert it and repeat steps 8 through 11.

Now move the picture of the diskette to the trash can icon since the disk is no longer in the system.

13. Move the pointer to the DISK1 icon.

14. Press and hold the ⌱.

15. Drag the pointer to the trash icon.

16. Release the ⌱.

The picture should be gone from the window. It does not need to be emptied from the trash can because the disk has already been removed from the system. If the disk were in the drive, it would be ejected as a result of this process.

Now format the second disk and name it BACKUP.

17. Repeat steps 1 through 16, naming the disk "BACKUP."

You now have two floppy disks available for use, one named DISK1 and the other named BACKUP. You should place a paper label on each disk and identify it by name.

Creating the Document

From the Opening System Disk window, select the Works Application folder (named Microsoft Works 3.0 Folder in Fig. 2.9).

    1. Move the pointer to the Microsoft Works 3.0 Folder.

    2. Double click the 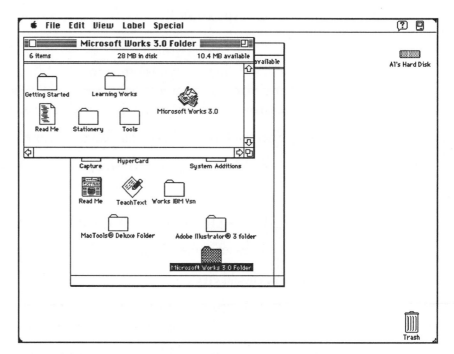.

From the Works Application window, select the Microsoft Works program (see Fig. 2.11).

Fig. 2.11 Microsoft Works 3.0 Folder window

    3. Move the pointer to the Works icon containing the small pictures.

    4. Double click the .

You should now see the Works Opening dialog box (see Fig. 2.12).

    5. Insert the disk named DISK1 into the floppy drive.

You should see the icon appear on the desktop, indicating that it is now the active disk.

You are now ready to use the disk to store data.

    6. Move the pointer to the Word Processor icon.

    7. Double click the to create a word processing file.

You should have a word processing window named Untitled1 (WP) or Untitled"n" (WP).

Click on Desktop

8. Type the following sentence: **This is the time for all good men and women to come to the aid of their country.**

This is your document. It is now stored in memory.

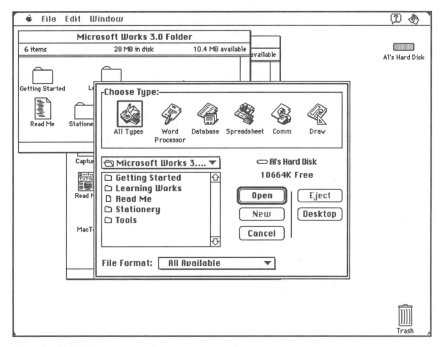

Fig. 2.12 Works Opening dialog box

Saving the Document

Now save it on your disk, using the File pull-down menu. Since you want to name the document, use the Save As option.

1. Move the pointer to the File item on the main menu.

2. Press and hold the ⌒.

3. Drag the pointer to the Save As option (see Fig. 2.13).

4. Release the ⌒.

You should see a dialog box with the name Untitled1 (or Untitled"n") highlighted.

5. Type the name **FIRST DOCUMENT**.

The name at the top of the dialog box should be DISK1. (If the name is not DISK1, select the Desktop button, then select DISK1 from the list of names.)

6. Move the pointer to ⌷ **Save** ⌷ and click the ⌒.

You are returned to the document in memory, but a copy is now saved on DISK1.

39

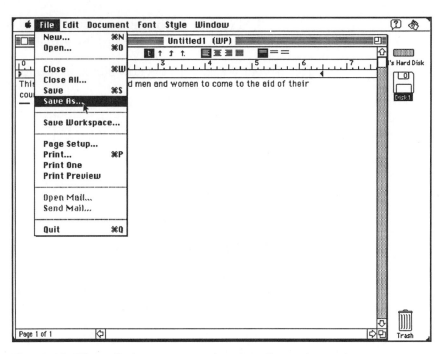

Fig. 2.13 File pull-down menu showing Save As option

Closing the File

1. Move the pointer to the close box on the left end of the title bar.

2. Click the .

The file is closed from memory, and you are returned to the Works Opening dialog box.

Exiting Works

Select Quit from the File pull-down menu.

1. Move the pointer to the File item on the main menu.

2. Press and hold the ⌖.

3. Drag the pointer to the Quit option.

4. Release the ⌖.

You should see the Microsoft Works 3.0 Folder window.

5. Move the pointer to the close box on the left end of the title bar.

6. Click the ⌖.

You should see the Opening System Disk window.

Since you no longer need the hard disk, you will close the window.

7. Move the pointer to the close box on the title bar.

8. Click the 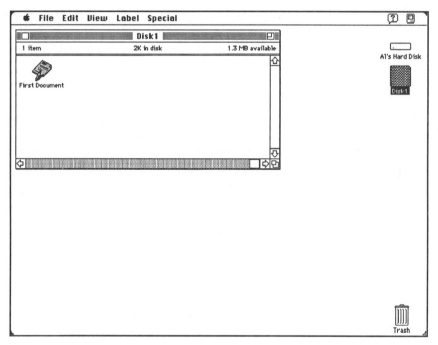.

The desktop should be clear of all open windows.

Copying Files

To protect the file, you will make a copy onto the disk named BACKUP.

First, open the DISK1 window.

1. Move the pointer to the DISK1 icon.

2. Double click the 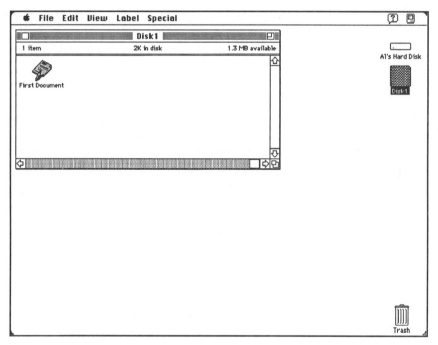.

You should have a screen similar to Fig. 2.14, with the FIRST DOCUMENT file displayed in the DISK1 window.

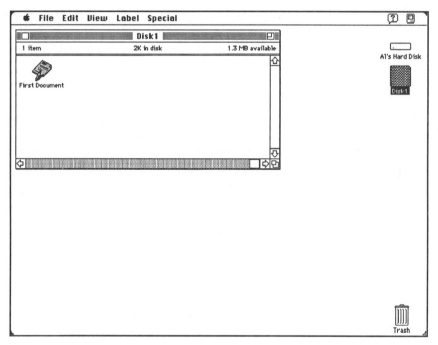

Fig. 2.14 DISK1 window containing FIRST DOCUMENT

Now remove DISK1.

3. Move the pointer to the Special item on the main menu.

4. Press and hold the 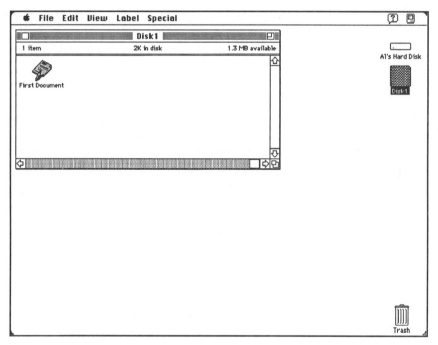.

5. Drag the pointer to the Eject Disk option.

6. Release the 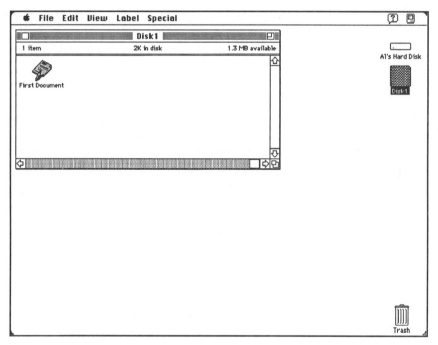.

7. Remove the disk.

8. If you get the prompt "Please insert the disk:," insert it and repeat steps 3 through 7.

9. Insert the disk named BACKUP into the drive.

You should now see icons for both floppy disks.

Open the disk named BACKUP.

10. Move the pointer to the BACKUP icon.

11. Double click the ⬤.

You should now have an open window for the BACKUP disk, containing no files.

12. If the two windows overlap too much, position them on the desktop by using the title bar to drag them and the size box to resize them.

Both windows should be accessible.

13. Move the pointer to the FIRST DOCUMENT icon.

14. Press and hold the ⬤.

15. Drag the pointer inside the BACKUP disk window.

16. Release the ⬤.

The system will eject the BACKUP disk and tell you to first insert DISK1 in order to read the file, and then the BACKUP disk to store it. When this task is completed, you should see the FIRST DOCUMENT icon in both windows, indicating it is on both disks.

17. Follow the directions, inserting the proper disk as necessary, until the file is copied to the BACKUP disk.

The file is now copied.

Renaming a Document

To further define the document as a backup copy, change the name of the file to FIRST BACK.

1. Move the pointer to the name FIRST DOCUMENT on the file in the BACKUP window.

2. Click the ⬤.

The name should now be highlighted.

3. Type **FIRST BACK**.

4. Press ⎍ **return** ⎍.

Your desktop should look similar to Fig. 2.15.

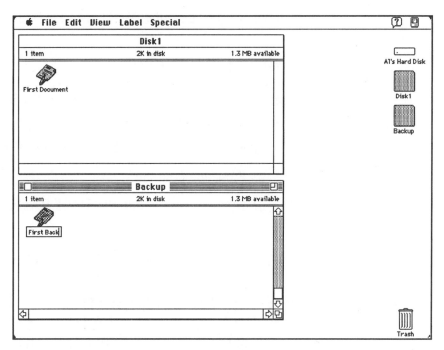

Fig. 2.15 Backup copy of FIRST DOCUMENT on BACKUP disk

Creating a Folder

As you put more files on the BACKUP disk, you may want to organize them into folders. Create a folder on the BACKUP disk and put the FIRST BACK file in it.

1. If the BACKUP disk is not active, place the pointer in the BACKUP disk window and click the ⌒.

2. Move the pointer to the File option on the main menu.

3. Press and hold the ⌒.

4. Drag the pointer to the New Folder option.

5. Release the ⌒.

You should now see a folder icon in the BACKUP disk window.

6. With the name "untitled folder" highlighted, type **TEXT BACKUP** to name the folder, and press ‖ **return** ‖.

7. To open the folder, place the pointer on it, and double click the ⌒.

8. Position the window, as necessary, using the title bar and size box, so that you can work with all three windows. (If a window disappears, you can select the file name from the Window pull-down menu.)

You now have a folder called TEXT BACKUP inside the BACKUP window.

Moving a Document

You can move a document from a window to a folder inside the window. Move the document called FIRST BACK into the folder just created.

1. Move the pointer to the FIRST BACK document.

2. Press and hold the ⬚.

3. Drag the pointer into the TEXT BACKUP folder.

4. Release the ⬚.

FIRST BACK is now in the TEXT BACKUP folder.

Removing the Backup Disk

1. If the TEXT BACKUP folder is not active, make it active by moving the pointer in it and clicking the ⬚.

2. Move the pointer to the close box, and click the ⬚ to close the window.

You should now have an active BACKUP disk window with a TEXT BACKUP folder in it.

3. Move the pointer to the close box, and click the ⬚ to close the window.

Since you no longer need the BACKUP disk for reference, you can drag it to the trash can to remove it.

4. Move the pointer to the BACKUP disk icon.

5. Press and hold the ⬚.

6. Drag the pointer to the Trash icon.

7. Release the ⬚.

8. If you get the prompt "Please insert the disk:," insert it and repeat steps 4 through 7.

The disk should be ejected, and the icon should be gone from the desktop.

Deleting a Document

Insert DISK1 into the drive, so that you can reference it.

You may no longer need a working copy of FIRST DOCUMENT. You have a backup copy for historical reference. You can now delete the working copy.

1. Move the pointer to the document named FIRST DOCUMENT.

2. Press and hold the ⌒.

3. Drag the pointer to the Trash icon.

4. Release the ⌒.

The file should now be gone from the window, and the Trash icon should be bulging. To complete the process, select the Empty Trash option from the Special pull-down menu.

5. Move the pointer to Special on the main menu.

6. Press and hold the ⌒.

7. Drag the pointer to the Empty Trash option (see Fig. 2.16).

8. Release the ⌒.

A dialog box will ask you if you are sure you want to remove it.

9. Move the pointer to [OK].

10. Click the ⌒.

The Trash should return to its normal size.

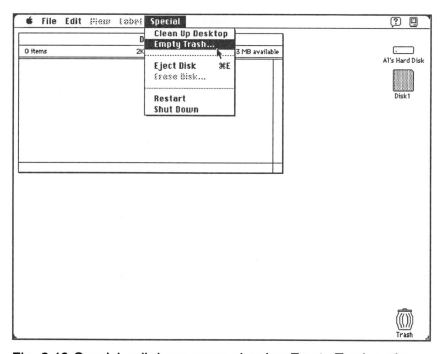

Fig. 2.16 Special pull-down menu showing Empty Trash option

Removing Disk1

Close the DISK1 window.

1. If the title bar of the DISK1 window is not highlighted, click on the window.

2. Move the pointer to the close box on the title bar.

3. Click the ⌒.

4. To make DISK1 inactive, move the pointer to the hard disk icon, and click the ⌒.

5. Move the pointer to the DISK1 icon.

6. Press and hold the ⌒.

7. Drag the pointer to the Trash icon.

8. Release the ⌒.

The disk should eject and the disk icon should be gone from the desktop.

Shutting Down the System

Before turning the computer off, you should always select the Shut Down option from the Special pull-down menu.

1. Move the pointer to the Special item on the main menu.

2. Press and hold the ⌒.

3. Drag the pointer to the Shut Down option (refer to Fig. 2.16).

4. Release the ⌒.

The system will display a message indicating it is safe to turn the computer off.

Summary

Integrated programs have an advantage over stand-alone programs because the integrated system has a consistent interface, and its application programs can easily share information.

Microsoft Works is an integrated program that contains word processing, spreadsheet, database, graphics, telecommunication, and draw capabilities. All applications in Works share the same menus and commands, and this reduces the learning time required to master the applications.

In addition, the most commonly used commands and procedures to manage files can be performed from the Macintosh desktop. Folders and files can be copied, renamed, or deleted by using the mouse.

Questions

1. How can a microcomputer help individuals and companies?

2. What are the differences between stand-alone and integrated programs?

3. What can a word processor be used for?

4. What is a spreadsheet?

5. What is a database?

6. Why should managers use computer graphics?

7. What are windows?

8. What is meant by file management?

9. What are the advantages of using Microsoft Works over other stand-alone programs?

10. What is the advantage of the Works interface?

11. What functions can you perform from the Works Opening dialog box?

Exercises

Exercise 1

1. Place a new disk in the floppy drive.

2. Format the disk in the floppy drive.

3. Label it WORKS DISK.

Exercise 2

1. Load Microsoft Works into memory.

2. Select the Word Processor icon.

3. Select New.

4. Type the following sentences: **This is my first document. It is going to be used for copying, deleting, and renaming a file.**

5. Save it under the name TEST (on Disk1 if you have it, or on any other disk).

6. Exit to the Macintosh desktop.

7. Copy the file (to Backup disk if you have it, or to any other disk) and name it FILE1.

8. Rename the file TEST as FILE2.

9. Make an additional copy of FILE1 and name it FILE3.

10. Delete the file FILE1.

Chapter 3

The Word Processing Tool

Objectives

After completing this chapter you will

1. Understand the benefits of automating word processing.

2. Recognize fundamental edit features of word processing.

3. Be able to position the pointer in Works documents.

4. Be able to create, save, and print a document in Works.

5. Be able to use the Works spelling checker.

6. Be able to insert and delete text.

7. Be able to move, copy, and delete blocks of text.

What Is Word Processing?

Traditionally, computers were used to process "data" that consisted primarily of numbers and involved computation. In the 1970s a new use emerged for the computer, involving the processing of text. Generally, word processing includes entering, editing, saving, and printing documents consisting primarily of text. The term "word processing" became common in the late 1970s, when word processing systems were sold to companies and when word processing programs became available for microcomputers in the home.

Word Processing in Industry

The creation of any document that uses written text is considered word processing. Interoffice memos, formal letters, proposals, manuals, and communication documents of all types were usually created on typewriters during the 1960s and 1970s. Secretaries and typing pools were commonplace in companies, and the typewriter could be found within easy access of any executive's office. Today's fast-paced society has replaced the typewriter with the microcomputer, and electronic word processing has become not only an accepted, but an expected way of processing text.

Characteristics of document processing include formatting the document, entering it, and editing it to ultimately provide an error-free copy as the end product. In both large and small companies, the process is the same. As the size and the complexity of the document increase, so does the complexity of formatting and editing it.

Consideration must be given to planning the document, regardless of its size. A memo should be formatted to fit company expectations. This includes spacing for any company logo, setting margins that conform to company guidelines, and providing any standardized heading information used by the company, such as company name or department name. Formal letters may include the company letterhead, requiring spacing considerations. They may require standard information at the top or bottom of each page, such as page numbers. Vertical lines per inch, horizontal characters per inch, and character font are common considerations. Training manuals and other large documents may include an index and a glossary, requiring special consideration when planning and typing the document.

Editing, or making changes to the document, is the most needed aspect of document processing. Even the shortest memo may have typing errors or require content changes after it is typed. Changing characters is a relatively simple process, but adding or deleting text involves rearranging the layout and sequence of the printed text. "Cut and paste" operations, involving the movement of large blocks of text from one place to another in the document, are common.

Word Processing in the Home

Document processing has been commonplace in the home for many years. Writing a letter to a friend, writing a paper for class, creating a personal resume, and producing documentation for clubs or organizations are all examples of word processing in the home.

Although formatting personal correspondence is often not as critical as formatting business documents, decisions pertaining to margins and headings must be made. As with any document processing, the editing process is a vital consideration. Any household making use of a typewriter appreciates the problem of adding or deleting text after the document has been created.

Automating Word Processing

The advent of the microcomputer and of word processing programs in the late 1970s provided a relatively low-cost solution to the editing problems associated with processing and printing documents. Because a document is entered and stored on the computer, text can be added or deleted before the document is printed. Changes can easily be made to the format of the document on the page by controlling the way it is printed by the computer. In the late 1970s and early 1980s, computerized word processing emerged as the first major category of application software. Today it is the most frequently used application.

Word processing programs now provide the ability to check for spelling errors, delete text, move text, and copy text within a document. Page formatting and document design are designated by the programs, and character enhancements can be included in the text. The editing features of word processing programs have made them cost effective to both business and personal users who have extensive text processing applications.

The process of typing the document still involves entering the text, saving it, printing it, and making changes, but the sophistication of the editing capabilities makes computerized word processing the ultimate solution to typing problems. The entering is done by using the keyboard rather than by using typewriter keys. The printing provides a paper copy, much the same as a typewriter would. However, the use of disk for interim storage and of the screen to view interim results provides a setting in which the text can be edited quickly and efficiently, using the word processing features available on the computer.

When reviewing word processing software programs, there are several editing features that are important to you. The program should provide adequate information, including current status, prompts, and help references, when entering and editing the document. This is done by using status lines, spacing indicators, and automated help features. The program should provide formatting features such as inserting text, deleting text, and automatic carriage return (wordwrap) at the end of each line. It should provide the ability to do cut and paste operations, which include moving, copying, or deleting segments of text within the document. Automatic spelling checkers are common, and one should be available for checking the spelling of the words in the document. Features that allow for changing margins, changing the line spacing, including heading and footing information, and enhancing the print should be available. These and many other features commonly included in word processing programs are what make word processing programs the text processing solution for today and for the future.

Creating a Document

The Word Processing Window

As seen in Chapter 2, Works is started the same way, regardless of which application is being used. When the Works Application is selected from the Opening System Disk window, the Microsoft Works 3.0 Folder window will display the folders and files pertaining to the Works program (see Fig. 3.1). To use the Works Application program, move the pointer to the icon containing the small pictures, and double click the mouse button. The desktop will then display the Works Opening dialog box (see Fig. 3.2).

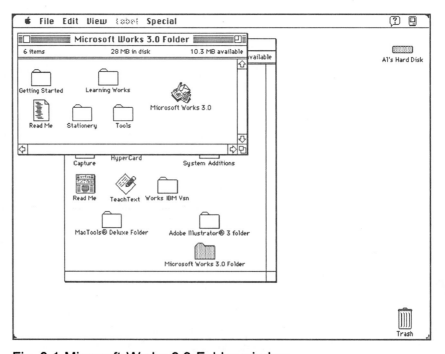

Fig. 3.1 Microsoft Works 3.0 Folder window

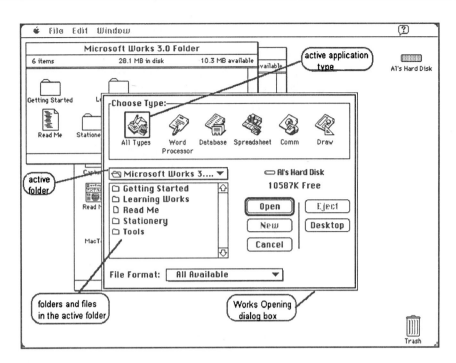

Fig. 3.2 Works Opening dialog box

The boxed icon at the top indicates the currently active application type and the list box on the lower left shows the folders and files in the active application. Remember that a folder is simply a compartment that can contain more files and folders. To open an existing folder or file, move the pointer to the desired name and double click the mouse button, or highlight the name by clicking the mouse button, and then select the Open button by clicking on it. The lower right portion of the dialog box includes options to open a highlighted folder or file or to cancel an operation. If the folder or file is on another disk, it can be referenced by selecting the Desktop button and then the appropriate disk name. To open a new file, move the pointer to the icon representing the type of new file desired (e.g., Word Processor), and double click the mouse button.

Whether you are using an existing file or creating a new one, the document window will appear and allow for entering and editing text. The word processing window is depicted in Fig. 3.3, and it shows several items that are provided for you. The top line of the desktop shows the menu options available.

The top line of the document window (the title bar) shows the name and type of the file that is in use. A new file will have the name "Untitled" until it is given a name. The "(WP)" following the name indicates that it is a word processing file. The box on the left end of the title bar is used to close the file. The box on the right end is called the zoom box and is used to change the size of the window. The title bar itself can be used to move the window on the screen. The lines on the bar indicate that the window is active.

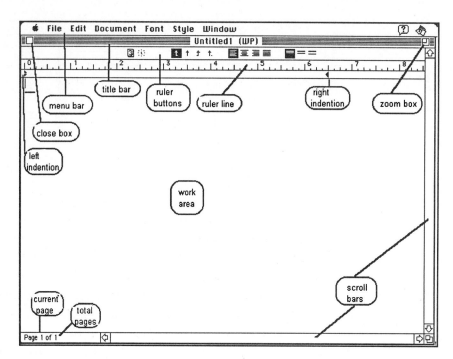

Fig. 3.3 Information provided on the word processing window

The second line of the window is the ruler line. It contains the ruler buttons, the ruler, and a distance indicator and markers for indentions and tabs.

The ruler buttons include buttons to insert the date or time, buttons to set tabs, and buttons to set justification and line spacing. The ruler indicates the spacing in inches. The tabs and indents are depicted by arrows underneath the ruler.

Default tab settings are at every half inch. Unless tabs are changed, they are not shown on the screen. The large open area (work area) displays text. The vertical scroll bar on the right side and the horizontal scroll bar on the bottom contain arrows that are used to scroll through the document. The number of pages currently in the document and the current page number are displayed in the lower left corner of the window. A vertical blinking line indicates the current position of the insertion point within the text. The arrow indicates the current position of the mouse pointer. The insertion point can be moved to a different location in the document by moving the pointer to the desired location and clicking the mouse. Review Chapter 2 as necessary for further information about window features.

Entering a Document

Assuming a new file is to be created, the insertion point will be in the upper left corner of the window. From that point, you can begin typing, just as you would on a typewriter. Begin typing text for block format, or use the TAB key to indent the first line. As the text nears the end of the line, you may be concerned about how to get to the next line. You should not press the RETURN key unless you are at the end of a paragraph. When the text passes the right margin, the wordwrap function in the program will automatically move the insertion point to the beginning of the next line and continue displaying text as it is typed. The break at the end of the line is referred to as a soft carriage return and always occurs between words and as close to the margin as possible.

You may continue typing as far as necessary to complete the sentence and then to complete the paragraph. At the end of the paragraph, press the RETURN key. This is referred to as a hard carriage return and signifies the end of the paragraph to the word processing program. If double spacing between paragraphs is desired, pressing the RETURN key again will produce a blank line containing only a hard carriage return. Once the window is filled with text, the top lines will begin to move off the window to make room for new lines at the bottom. This disappearing text is still in memory and remains a part of the file. It can be accessed by pointing to the arrow on the upper right corner of the vertical scroll box and pressing or repeatedly clicking the mouse button. As the document scrolls up, the text will reappear in the window. When learning to use the word processor, it is recommended that you practice entering short documents and learn the features of window control as you begin to create longer ones.

Saving and Continuing

Any document that is created should be saved from memory onto disk periodically to prevent loss or damage to the document if an error or system failure occurs during processing. Two options exist on the File pull-down menu, shown in Fig. 3.4, that allow for saving the document and continuing to work with it without needing to retrieve it again. The Save option allows for saving the document under its currently assigned name. The Save As option allows for changing or assigning the name of the document to be saved. With either option, the document remains in memory for continued processing.

When a document is created, the name area indicates "Untitled1" (or Untitled"n"). When the document is saved, a name must be assigned to it. The name must be unique from other files stored in the folder. Any previous file saved under that name is destroyed, and any future file saved under that name will destroy the current one. To assign a name to a file, use the Save As option (refer to Fig. 3.4). When that option is used, the dialog box displayed will allow for entering a name, as in Fig. 3.5. Once the name is typed, move the pointer to the Save button, and click the mouse button to save the file and return to the document.

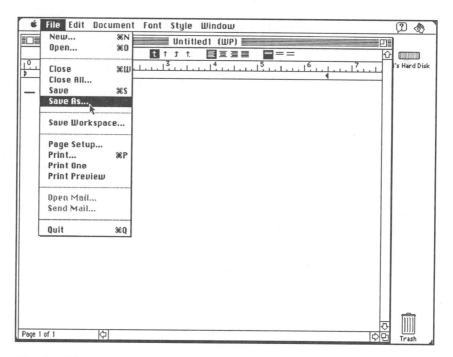

Fig. 3.4 File pull-down menu showing Save As option

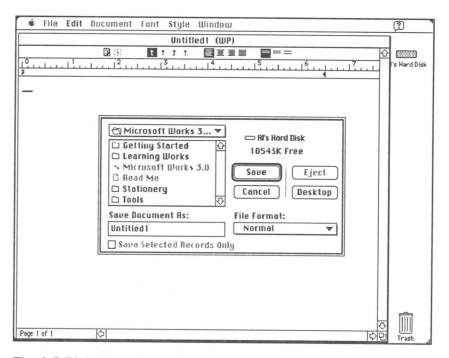

Fig. 3.5 Dialog box to assign a name to a file

If a document has already been assigned a name and you don't want to change it, the Save As option is not needed. Selecting the Save option will save the file under its current name and return the pointer to the document. Saving the memory copy of a document causes the system to replace any version previously saved under the same name. If a backup or duplicate copy is desired, it should be saved under a separate name with the Save As option or kept in a separate folder.

Spell Checking

Once the document is entered, it should be checked for spelling errors. This can be done with the Works program by selecting the Document pull-down menu and then selecting Spelling (see Fig. 3.6). The program will begin checking at the beginning of the document and check every word in the document against a dictionary. If you want to check only a portion of the document, highlight the segment prior to selecting the Spelling option. Then only that portion will be checked.

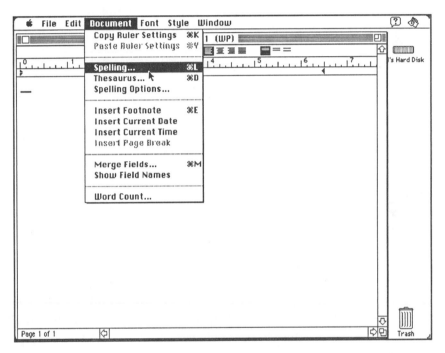

Fig. 3.6 Document pull-down menu showing the Spelling option

As the search is conducted, the program compares each word in the document to a dictionary file containing thousands of words. If a word in the document is not in the dictionary, it is identified as being not in the dictionary (see Fig. 3.7), and several options are offered to you. The word may not be misspelled. For example, it may be a proper noun, such as the name "McDonald's." For those words that are actually correct, move the pointer to the Ignore button, and click the mouse button. This will leave the word as it is and continue searching the document.

When the word is incorrectly spelled and needs to be changed, you can type the correct spelling in the highlighted area labeled "Change To." Then move the pointer to the Change button, and click the mouse button. You can also refer to the Suggestions box (see Fig. 3.7) to see the suggested words appearing in the list box. The highlighted word is the suggested change. Clicking on any word in the list will highlight it and cause it to appear in the Change To box. Double clicking the pointer on any word in the dictionary list box will replace the unknown word with that one and continue the search. You can terminate the checking at any time by moving the pointer to the Cancel button and clicking the mouse button.

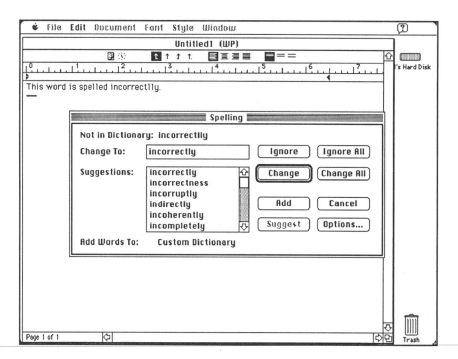

Fig. 3.7 Dialog box for processing words that are not in the dictionary

Once the checking is completed, a dialog box will indicate that the spelling check is finished. Then point to the OK button, and click the mouse button to return to the document.

Editing a Document

Moving the Insertion Point

Once a document is entered into the computer's memory, it is important to be able to move the insertion point to any area of the text, in order to review and make changes to the document. The insertion point can be positioned anywhere in the text on the window by moving the pointer to the desired position and clicking the mouse button. The vertical bar that represents the insertion point will appear between characters. The direction of movement from the keyboard commands or keys will determine which characters are affected.

If the text to be modified is not in the window, you can use the vertical scroll bar to scroll to the appropriate area. By placing the pointer on one of the arrows and pressing the mouse button, you can scroll through the text in the direction of the arrow, until the appropriate text is in the window. Clicking on the arrow will move a line at a time. You can also move through the document by dragging the box on the vertical scroll bar. When the appropriate text is in the window, move the pointer to the desired position, and click the mouse button. If the text is wider than the window, the arrows on the horizontal scroll bar at the bottom of the window can be used to scroll horizontally through the text, or the box can be dragged horizontally.

You can use the arrow keys to move the insertion point one character at a time in any direction. You can also use the HOME, END, PAGE UP, and PAGE DOWN keys to move through the text. The HOME key will move to the beginning of the text, the END key will move to the end of the text. The PAGE UP and PAGE DOWN keys will move up or down a page (window) at a time.

Inserting Text

When reviewing a document, it is common to need to add text within the document. This may be a character, a word, or a sentence. Insertion mode allows for adding text at the location of the insertion point without destroying the existing text. Move the pointer between the two characters where insertion is needed, and click the mouse button. The program will move the existing text to make room for the text being added. All text to the left of the insertion point will remain where it is. The text to the right will continue to move to the right as long as text is being added. Wordwrap will move text to subsequent lines automatically, and lines will be moved to subsequent pages automatically.

Deleting Text

You may discover, when reviewing text, that characters, words, or sentences need to be removed. Move the pointer to the right of the character to be deleted, and click the mouse button. Pressing the DELETE (or BACKSPACE) key will remove the character to the left of the insertion point. When the character is deleted, the text that follows will move left to fill the void.

If removal of characters causes the line to shorten significantly, the reformatting process will automatically reposition the text from the next line to fill the void created at the end of the line. As lines are drawn up by the process, lines on subsequent pages of the document will be drawn to the current page automatically.

Selecting Text

Some operations can be better performed by identifying and selecting segments of text prior to the operation. These operations are typically called block operations because they involve blocks of text.

Selecting a block of text is a four-step process. Place the pointer at the first character of the text segment. Press the mouse button. Drag the pointer to the end of the segment. Release the mouse button. The selected text should be highlighted. A block of text can be just one character long or an entire document, and it need not start or end on a word or sentence boundary. Typically a block involves a phrase, a sentence, or a paragraph.

Block Operations

Block operations involve moving (cut and paste), copying (copy and paste), or deleting (cut or clear) segments of text. The first step in the process is to select the text, as described above. (Note that if the RETURN key is accidentally pressed with text highlighted, the text will be deleted from the document.) The second step is to access the Edit pull-down menu, shown in Fig. 3.8, that contains the options of Cut, Paste, Copy, and Clear.

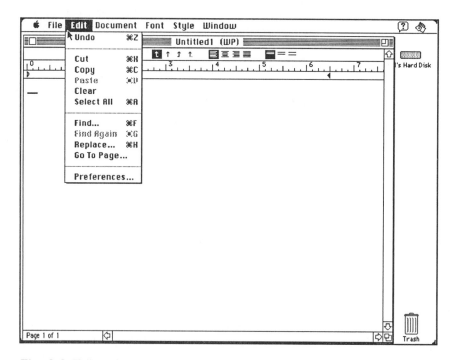

Fig. 3.8 Edit pull-down menu

If the block is to be deleted, simply select the Clear option on the pull-down menu, and the highlighted text will be removed from the document. The remaining text will be absorbed into the open space by the reformatting process. A selected block of text can also be deleted by pressing the DELETE (or BACKSPACE) key.

If the block is to be moved, select the Cut option from the Edit pull-down menu. This will remove the block from the document and store it in a temporary holding area called the clipboard. The program will reformat the document as necessary to remove the space where the text was. To put the text somewhere else, move the pointer to the destination location and click the mouse button to define an insertion point. Then select the Paste option from the Edit menu. The program will create space, as necessary, to insert the text. You can paste the text in multiple areas by repeating the process of creating an insertion point and selecting the Paste option. The text will remain on the clipboard until another operation is performed that requires use of the clipboard.

If the block is to be copied, use the Copy option from the Edit pull-down menu. This will leave the block where it is, but will also store it on the clipboard. To complete the copy process, move the pointer to the receiving location, and click the mouse button. Then select the Paste option from the Edit menu. You can paste the text in multiple areas by repeating the process of creating an insertion point and selecting the Paste option. As with using Cut, the text will remain on the clipboard until another operation is performed that requires use of the clipboard.

Printing

When preparing to print a document, turn on the printer and load paper as necessary. It is important to align the paper properly prior to printing and then control the printer from the Works program and from any external controls on the printer. Do not manually feed the paper during printing.

Select the Print option from the File pull-down menu (see Fig. 3.9). To do this, move the pointer to File, press the mouse button, drag the pointer to Print, and release the mouse button. A dialog box will then be displayed that has several options, including an option for the number of copies to be printed (see Fig. 3.10). Notice that the upper left line indicates DeskWriter. If you are using a different printer, the box may vary slightly, but the content is generally the same. Typically it is not necessary to change any of the items on this menu, although you should become familiar with them as time permits. The document can now be printed by moving the pointer to the OK button and clicking the mouse button. When printing is complete, Works will return to the document.

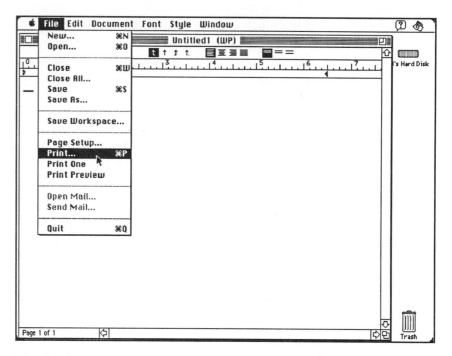

Fig. 3.9 File pull-down menu showing the Print option

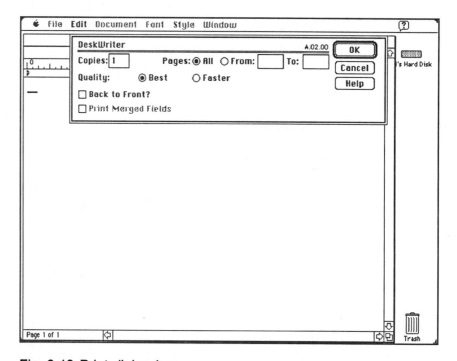

Fig. 3.10 Print dialog box

Saving and Exiting

Once the final copy of the document is completed, it is necessary to save it on the disk, as mentioned previously, prior to exiting the Works program. This can be done in one of three ways, all of which are found in the File pull-down menu shown in Fig. 3.9. The Save option will save the document under the current name. The Save As option will save the document under a newly specified name. The Close option will remove the document from the desktop and from memory and close the file.

If the Close option is selected, the program will check to see that all changes have been saved. If they have, the program will remove the file from memory and return control to the Microsoft Works 3.0 Folder window, with the option of accessing other files or exiting Works. If all changes have not been saved, a dialog box will appear that will provide the option of saving the modified document or not saving it. Any changes not saved to disk will be lost once the document is removed from memory.

To exit the Works program, select Quit from the File pull-down menu. This should return control to the Microsoft Works 3.0 Folder. Then select the close box on the left end of the title bar. This should return you to the Opening System Disk window.

You can now do other applications. When you have finished using the machine, close any windows still open on the desktop, and follow the shut down procedure for your system.

Before turning the computer off, you should select the Shut Down option from the Special pull-down menu. This will prepare the computer to be turned off.

Hands-on Word Processing

PART I

Typing a Letter

To begin typing the sample letter illustrated in Fig. 3.11, first enter Works and create a word processing file. To do this, follow the steps listed below.

Works should be properly installed and should access the appropriate disk drive. Refer to Chapter 2, as necessary, for instructions on accessing software on your disk.

1. From the Opening System Disk window, move the pointer to a folder icon labeled Microsoft Works 3.0 Folder (or something indicating the Works program), and double click the ⬭.

A Works Application window containing Microsoft Works programs and possibly other Works related software should appear (see Fig. 3.12). If it doesn't, refer to Chapter 2 and check the system.

Dear Fred,

I have been studying the use of word processing. The Microsoft Works program includs a spell checker that identifies words that are not in the dictionary. If a word is misspelled, I cah have the program suggest changes, or I can enter the corect spelling without suggestions. Not all words identified are actually misspelled. It may be that a word is spelled correctly, but is not ni the dictionary.

Sincerely,

Jane

Fig. 3.11 Sample letter

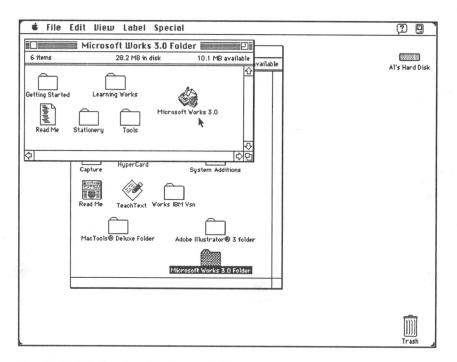

Fig. 3.12 Works Application window

The icon containing small pictures is used to access Works files created by the user.

> 2. Move the pointer to the Works icon containing the small pictures, and double click the .

The dialog box shown in Fig. 3.13 should now appear. If it doesn't, try the selection process again or get help.

You want to create a new word processing file.

3. Point to the icon labeled Word Processor at the top of the dialog box.

4. Click the 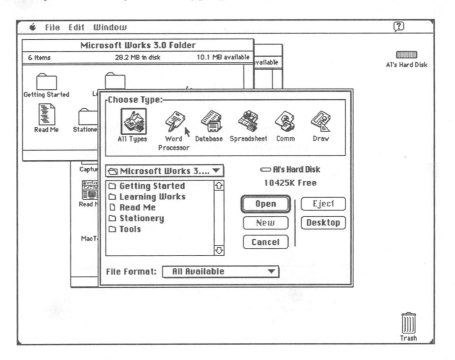.

The icon should now be boxed.

5. Move the pointer to [**New**].

6. Click the .

You should now see the window displayed in Fig. 3.14, with Untitled1 or Untitled"n" displayed on the title bar. If not, you may have selected the wrong type of file to create.

You are now ready to enter the document, displayed in Fig. 3.11. Type the letter as you see it. If you make typing errors, do not correct them yet.

Fig. 3.13 Works Opening dialog box

7. Type the letter exactly as it appears in Fig. 3.11, including the misspelled words. (Be sure to press the RETURN key after typing the word "Jane," as you do at the end of all paragraphs.)

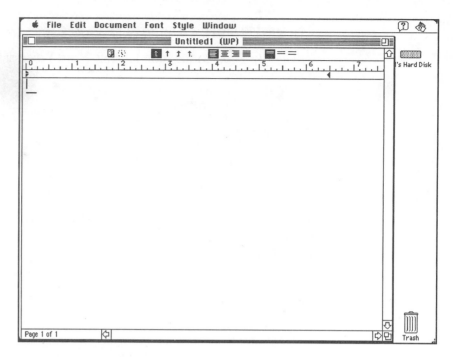

Fig. 3.14 Opened word processing file without text

Checking the Spelling

To check the spelling of the words in the letter, you want to select the Spelling option from the Document pull-down menu (see Fig. 3.15).

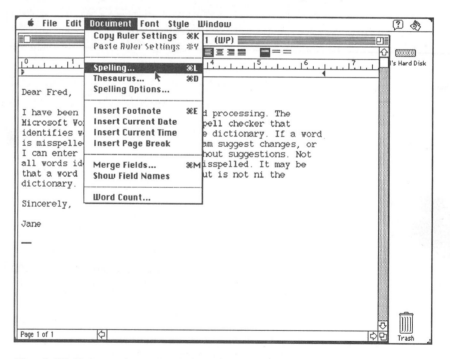

Fig. 3.15 Document pull-down menu showing Spelling option

The checking will start at the location of the insertion point. It will check words to the end of the document, then check from the beginning of the document to the point where it started (the original location of the insertion point). If a block is highlighted, only the highlighted area will be checked.

Begin the spell check at the beginning of the document.

1. Move the pointer to the left of the first character in the document (the "D" in "Dear").

2. Click the 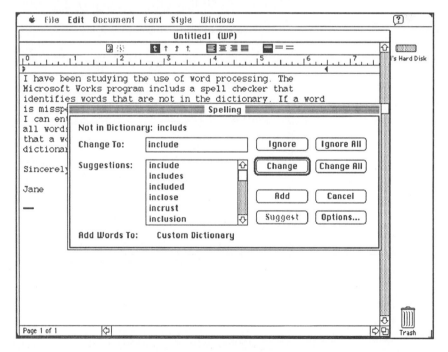 to create an insertion point.

3. Point to Document on the main menu.

4. Press and hold the ⌒.

5. Drag the pointer down until Spelling is highlighted, and release the ⌒.

As words are found that are not in the dictionary, you will encounter spelling errors that you made when entering the document. Type the correct spelling of the word in the "Change To:" box, and press the RETURN key or point to the Change button and click the mouse button.

You will encounter the word "includs" (see Fig. 3.16). You can change the spelling by typing the word correctly, or you can select the word "includes" from the "Suggestions:" box in the Spelling dialog box.

Fig. 3.16 Spelling dialog box for processing words that are not in the dictionary

6. Move the pointer to the word "includes" in the "Suggestions:" list box.

7. Click the ⬛.

The word "includes" should appear in the Change To box.

8. Move the pointer to [Change].

9. Click the ⬛ to make the change.

You will encounter the word "cah," which should be "can."

10. With the Change To box highlighted, type **can** and press [**return**] (or select the Change button).

You will encounter the word "corect."

The word "correct" should be displayed in the Change To box as the suggested change.

11. Move the pointer to [Change], and click the ⬛.

You will encounter the word "ni."

12. Type **in** and press [**return**].

When you see the dialog box indicating Finished checking document (see Fig. 3.17), it means the program has checked every word in the document. Selecting the OK button will leave the Spelling option and return you to the document.

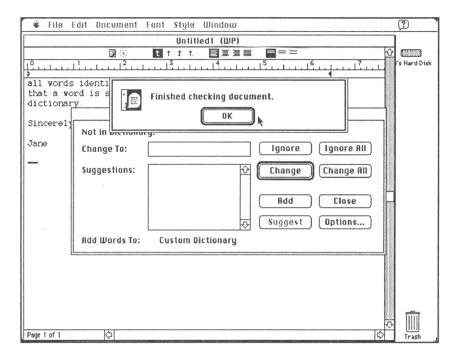

Fig. 3.17 Finished dialog box for Spelling check

13. Move the pointer to ⌈OK⌉, and click the ⌖.

14. Since the word "in" is still highlighted, move the pointer to an open area in the work area, and click the ⌖ to remove the highlighting.

Generally, you can leave the spelling checker at any time by selecting the Cancel button in the Spelling dialog box, which will return you to the document. If you are not sure of where you are in the spelling checker or what your options are, you can leave it, and then restart it from the beginning.

Saving the Letter

You now have a letter that has been entered and contains correctly spelled words. To protect it from the many things that can happen to the memory work area, it is necessary to save it on the disk.

On the File pull-down menu, the Save As option allows you to specify a new name prior to saving the file. The Save option will save the file under the current name specified. (The first time it is referenced with a new file, it will act like the Save As option.)

Since this is a letter, you can name it LETTER.

To save the document, select File on the main menu. Then select Save As on the pull-down menu (see Fig. 3.18).

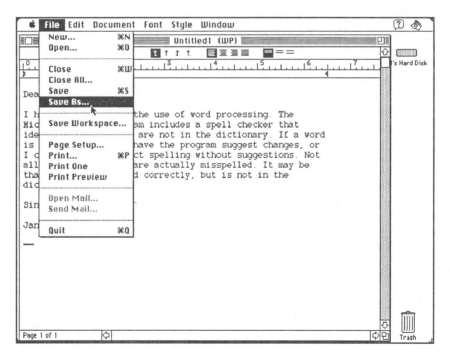

Fig. 3.18 File pull-down menu showing Save As option

1. Point to File on the main menu.

2. Press and hold the ⬲.

3. Drag the pointer to the Save As option on the pull-down menu.

4. Release the ⬲.

A dialog box similar to the one in Fig. 3.19 should appear.

To assign a file name, type in the name desired (or you can modify an existing name by adding or deleting characters).

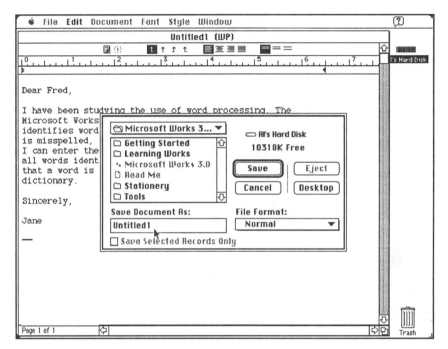

Fig. 3.19 Save As dialog box to assign a name to file being saved

5. Without moving the pointer, type **LETTER** to name the document.

6. If you are to save the file to a floppy disk, insert the disk, as necessary, and select the appropriate disk from the Desktop list box.

7. Press ‖ **return** ‖ (or select the Save button) to save the document you have named LETTER.

You should be returned to the document once the save operation is completed. If you encounter problems here, check your disk drive.

The document remains in memory for reference and editing, but a copy is now saved on disk as a permanent copy. As the document is updated, you can use the Save option to replace the existing file with a newer version of the document.

Printing the Letter

You have entered the letter and saved it on disk. If you want a copy on paper, you can also print it. Remember that you are printing the document that is in memory, not the one on disk. The print command is located on the File pull-down menu. When preparing to print, be sure that the printer is on and has paper loaded.

To print the document, select File on the main menu, then select the Print option on the pull-down menu (see Fig. 3.20).

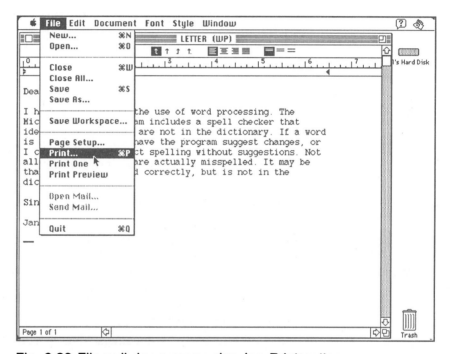

Fig. 3.20 File pull-down menu showing Print option

1. Move the pointer to the File item on the main menu.

2. Press and hold the .

3. Drag the pointer to the Print option.

4. Release the .

You will get a print options dialog box like the one in Fig. 3.21. If your printer is not a DeskWriter, the box may be slightly different. You don't need to change any options in this menu. To print the document, select the OK button.

5. Point to ⌈OK⌋.

6. Click the .

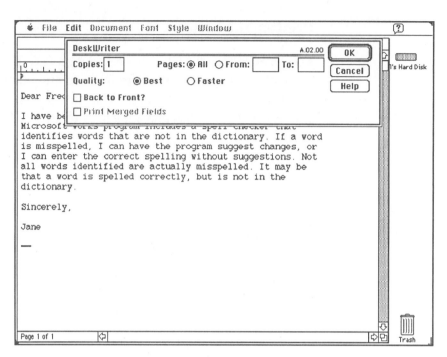

Fig. 3.21 Dialog box containing print options

Closing the File

Once you have completed the document, you are ready to close the file, which removes it from memory but leaves the saved copy on disk for later use. If you have made changes since the last time you saved it, the program will ask you if you want to save the changes prior to closing the file.

The Close option is on the File menu depicted in Fig. 3.20. It can be accessed by selecting File on the main menu, then selecting the Close option on the pull-down menu. Also, the file can be closed by selecting the close box on the left end of the title bar.

1. Point to the File item on the main menu.

2. Press and hold the ⌧.

3. Drag the pointer to the Close option.

4. Release the ⌧.

Exiting Works

To continue working on files once the file is closed, you would create a new file or open an existing one. Once you have completed the work session and are ready to leave Works, select the Quit option from the File pull-down menu (see Fig. 3.22) to exit Works.

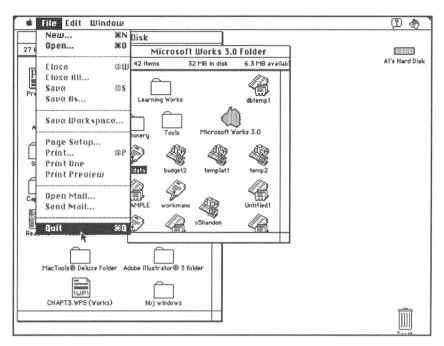

Fig. 3.22 File pull-down menu with Quit option selected

1. Point to the File item on the main menu.

2. Press and hold the ⌧.

3. Drag the pointer to the Quit option.

4. Release the ⌧.

This should return control to the Microsoft Works 3.0 Folder.

To close the Works folder, select the Close Window option from the File pull-down menu, or point to the close box on the left end of the title bar, and click the mouse button.

5. Point to the File item on the main menu.

6. Press and hold the ⌧.

7. Drag the pointer to the Close Window option.

8. Release the ⌧.

This should return you to the Opening System Disk window.

PART II

Retrieving the Document

You will now retrieve an existing document from the disk into memory. To start from the beginning, if the machine is off, turn it on. If you are in the Opening System Disk window, select the Microsoft Works 3.0 Folder from the folders on your disk. Then select the Works icon indicating Microsoft Works 3.0 to access the Works Opening dialog box.

You will retrieve the LETTER document created in PART I. (If you did not create the letter, refer to Fig. 3.23 and create the letter depicted; then save it in a file named LETTER.)

Dear Fred,

I have been studying the use of word processing. The Microsoft Works program includes a spell checker that identifies words that are not in the dictionary. If a word is misspelled, I can have the program suggest changes, or I can enter the correct spelling without suggestions. Not all words identified are actually misspelled. It may be that a word is spelled correctly, but is not in the dictionary.

Sincerely,

Jane

Fig. 3.23 Document to be changed

Retrieve the letter in the file named LETTER.

1. From the Opening System Disk window, move the pointer to the Microsoft Works 3.0 Folder icon, and double click the ⌒.

This should open the Works Application folder.

2. Within the Works Application folder, move the pointer to the icon representing Microsoft Works 3.0, and double click the ⌒.

You should now see a screen similar to Fig. 3.24.

3. Highlight the LETTER document name on the list of folder and document names in the lower left of the dialog box by pointing to it and clicking the ⌒. (It may already be highlighted.)

4. Move the pointer to [Open], and click the ⌒.

The LETTER file should be opened and displayed on the desktop. It is now available for use.

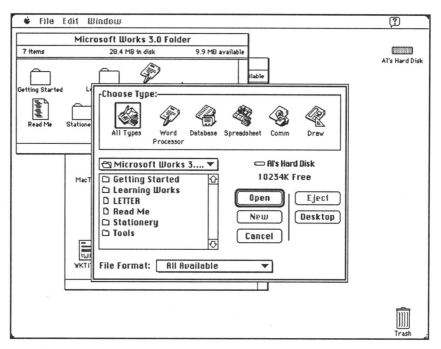

Fig. 3.24 Works Opening dialog box

Making Changes

Any changes made will be made to the copy of the document that is in memory. Once the editing is completed, the copy of the file on disk must be updated by saving the modified document to disk. It is also a good idea to periodically save the document as you are making changes, to protect yourself against problems that can occur during editing.

The document you currently have in memory should look like the document in Fig. 3.23. You will modify the document by adding text and then making further changes to it.

1. Move the pointer to the left edge of the letter "T" which begins the second sentence, and click the ⟨☐⟩.

2. Type in the following text exactly as it is written.

    It can be used to write documents, and changes cannot be made to the text without retyping the entire document. If I leave out a character when typing a letter, I can add it to the document later. If I include two too many characters or words in a document, I can remove them from the document.

3. Then press ⟨ return ⟩ twice, once to end the paragraph and again to produce a blank line before the next paragraph.

The document should now look like Fig. 3.25, with the insertion point positioned to the left of the first letter of the second paragraph. The last sentence of the first paragraph has too many "to"s ("two" and "too") in it. You should remove the "two."

Dear Fred,

I have been studying the use of word processing. It can be used to write documents, and changes cannot be made to the text without retyping the entire document. If I leave out a character when typing a letter, I can add it to the document later. If I include two too many characters or words in a document, I can remove them from the document.

The Microsoft Works program includes a spell checker that identifies words that are not in the dictionary. If a word is misspelled, I can have the program suggest changes, or I can enter the correct spelling without suggestions. Not all words identified are actually misspelled. It may be that a word is spelled correctly, but is not in the dictionary.

Sincerely,

Jane

Fig. 3.25 Modified letter

4. Move the pointer to the left of the "t" in the word "too."

5. Click the ⬡.

6. Press ‖**delete**‖ four times.

Notice that any extra space between the remaining words is gone and that wordwrap may have moved a word from the next line to fill the space at the end of the line.

In the third sentence, starting with "If I leave out," insert "or word" following the word "character."

7. Move the pointer to the left of the "w" in the word "when" in the third sentence.

8. Click the ⬡ to create an insertion point.

9. With the insertion point to the left of the "w" in "when," type **or word** . Make sure that you type a space after the "d" in "word."

Notice that as the line became longer, wordwrap may have moved text to the next line to maintain the appropriate margin.

The word "cannot" in the second sentence of the first paragraph (starting with "It can be used") should be changed to "can."

    10. Move the pointer to the right of the "t" in "cannot."

    11. Click the ⬠.

    12. Press `delete` three times.

Move the insertion point to the end of the second paragraph and add a third paragraph to the document.

    13. Press `end` to move the insertion point to the end of the document.

    14. Press `↑` until the insertion point is between the last paragraph and "Sincerely".

    15. Press `return` to provide double spacing between paragraphs.

    16. Type the text below. Be sure to press `return` at the end of the last sentence to conclude the paragraph and retain the blank line prior to "Sincerely,".

> If I want to reuse a segment of text, I can select a block of text and copy it to another area. If I no longer need a segment of text, I can remove it by selecting the block and deleting it from the document. To place a segment of text in a different area of the document, I can select the block and move it to another position in the document.

Block Changes

To use the block delete capability, highlight a block of text using the mouse. Delete the phrase "from the document" from the end of the second sentence of the last paragraph, which refers to removing text. Make sure that you include a space before the word "from" in the block selected.

    1. Move the pointer to the left of the space just before the "f" in the word "from" in the second sentence of the last paragraph.

    2. Press and hold the ⬠.

    3. Drag the pointer to the right of the "t" in "document" at the end of the sentence.

    4. Release the ⬠.

The words "from the document," including the space before the "f" in "from" should be highlighted.

5. Press ⌈delete⌉ to delete the text.

Reformatting automatically closes the open space caused by the deletion.

You can use the copy process to select a block of text and copy it to any other area of the document. Copy the phrase "If I want," including the space after "want," from the beginning of the first sentence of the last paragraph to the beginning of the third sentence, and replace the "T" with "t" in the word "To."

6. Move the pointer to the left of the "I" in the word "If" in the first sentence of the last paragraph.

7. Press and hold the 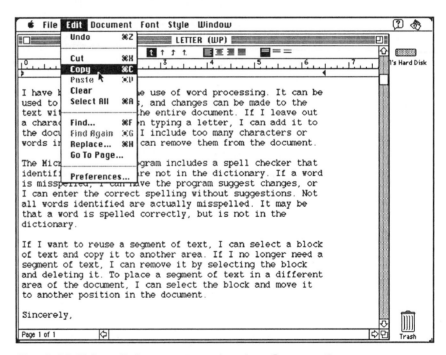.

8. Drag the pointer to the right of the space after "want."

9. Release the ⌐⌐.

The phrase "If I want," including the space after "want" should be highlighted.

The copy process requires placing the selected text onto the clipboard by selecting the Copy command (see Fig. 3.26), and then placing the text into the destination by using the Paste command (refer to Fig. 3.26).

10. Point to the Edit item on the main menu.

11. Press and hold the ⌐⌐.

12. Drag the pointer to the Copy option on the pull-down menu.

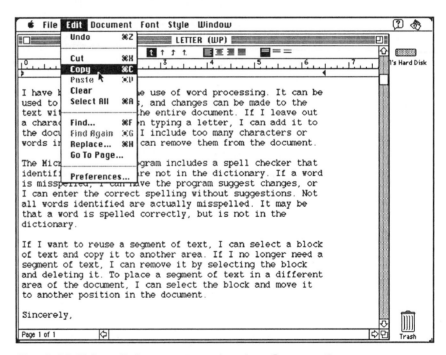

Fig. 3.26 Edit pull-down menu showing Copy option

13. Release the ⟨☁⟩.

The phrase is now stored on the clipboard.

14. Move the pointer to the left of the "T" in "To" at the beginning of the third sentence of the last paragraph.

15. Click the ⟨☁⟩ to define the insertion point.

16. Point to the Edit item on the main menu.

17. Press and hold the ⟨☁⟩.

18. Drag the pointer to the Paste option on the pull-down menu.

19. Release the ⟨☁⟩.

The phrase "If I want" should be at the beginning of the sentence. Change the "T" to a "t" in the word "To."

20. Press ⟨→⟩ to move to the right of the "T."

21. Press ⟨delete⟩ to remove the "T."

22. Type the letter **t**.

Notice that you used the Copy command, and the words "If I want" are now in both places in the text.

You can use the move capability to select a block of text and move it from one area of the document to another. You will move the third sentence of the last paragraph between the first and second sentences. Instead of using the Copy option on the Edit pull-down menu, use the Cut option (refer to Fig. 3.26), which removes the text from the source location and places it on the clipboard.

23. Move the pointer to the left of the space preceding "If" in the last sentence of the last paragraph.

24. Press and hold the ⟨☁⟩.

25. Drag the pointer to the right of the period at the end of the last sentence.

26. Release the ⟨☁⟩.

The sentence and the space preceding it should be highlighted.

27. Point to the Edit item on the main menu.

28. Press and hold the ⟨☁⟩.

29. Drag the pointer to the Cut option on the pull-down menu.

30. Release the ⟨☁⟩.

Notice that the sentence is no longer in the document. (However, it is on the clipboard.)

31. Move the pointer to the right of the period at the end of the first sentence in the last paragraph.

32. Click the ⬚.

The insertion point should now be at that position.

33. Point to the Edit option on the main menu.

34. Press and hold the ⬚.

35. Drag the pointer to the Paste option on the pull-down menu (refer to Fig. 3.26).

36. Release the ⬚.

The sentence should appear at the selected location, with the program reformatting the next sentence to make room for it.

The document should now look like the one shown in Fig. 3.27.

Dear Fred,

I have been studying the use of word processing.   It can be used to write documents, and changes can be made to the text without retyping the entire document.   If I leave out a character or word when typing a letter, I can add it to the document later. If I include too many characters or words in a document, I can remove them from the document.

The Microsoft Works program includes a spell checker that identifies words that are not in the dictionary.   If a word is misspelled, I can have the program suggest changes, or I can enter the correct spelling without suggestions.   Not all words identified are actually misspelled.   It may be that a word is spelled correctly, but is not in the dictionary.

If I want to reuse a segment of text, I can select a block of text and copy it to another area. If I want to place a segment of text in a different area of the document, I can select the block and move it to another position in the document. If I no longer need a segment of text, I can remove it by selecting the block and deleting it.

Sincerely,

Jane

Fig. 3.27 Modified document

Saving the Letter

You now have a letter that has been modified, but not re-saved. The copy of the document on disk has none of the additional text. You must now save the document again to replace the copy on disk with the currently modified copy.

You can use the Save As option to change the name or the Save option to keep the present name, both of which are found on the File pull-down menu (refer to Fig. 3.28). The Save As option, which allows you to change the name, is not needed, since you have already named the file LETTER. The Save option allows you to save the file to disk under the current name, replacing the previous version with the current one.

1. Point to the File item on the main menu.

2. Press and hold the ⬭.

3. Drag the pointer to the Save option.

4. Release the ⬭.

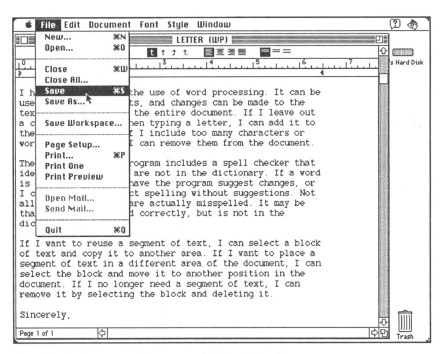

Fig. 3.28 File pull-down menu showing Save option

Printing the Letter

You have loaded the letter into memory, made several changes to it, and saved the updated letter to disk. If you want a copy on paper, you can also print it. The Print command is located on the File pull-down menu. When preparing to print, be sure that the printer is on and has paper loaded.

To print the document, select the Print option from the File pull-down menu (refer to Fig. 3.28).

1. Point to the File item on the main menu.

2. Press and hold the 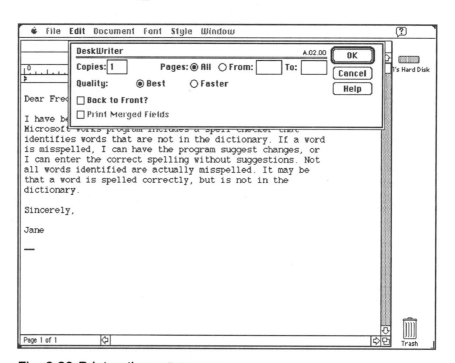.

3. Drag the pointer to the Print option.

4. Release the .

You will get a Print options dialog box like the one in Fig. 3.29. Depending on the type of printer you are using, the dialog box may be slightly different. You don't need to change any options in this menu. To print the document, select the OK button from the dialog box.

5. Point to [OK].

6. Click the .

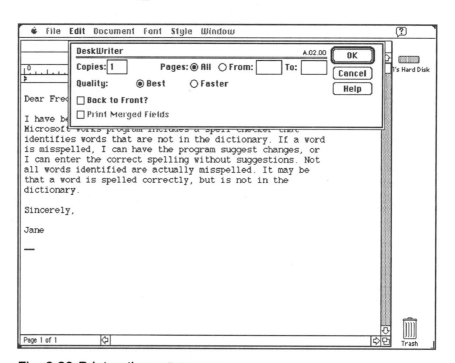

Fig. 3.29 Print options dialog box

Closing the File

Once you have completed the document, you are ready to close the file, which removes it from memory, but leaves the saved copy on disk for later use. If you have made changes since the last time you saved it, the program will ask you if you want to save the changes prior to closing the file.

The Close option is on the File pull-down menu depicted in Fig. 3.28. The file can be closed by selecting the option from the File pull-down menu. Also, it can be closed by placing the pointer in the close box on the left end of the title bar and clicking the mouse button.

1. Point to the File item on the main menu.

2. Press and hold the ⬛.

3. Drag the pointer to the Close option.

4. Release the ⬛.

Exiting Works

To continue working on files once the file is closed, you would create a new file or open an existing one. Once you have completed the work session and are ready to leave Works, select the Quit option from the File pull-down menu.

1. Point to the File item on the main menu.

2. Press and hold the ⬛.

3. Drag the pointer to the Quit option.

4. Release the ⬛.

This should close the Works application and remove the shading from the icon.

To close the Works folder, select the Close Window option from the File pull-down menu, or point to the close box on the left end of the title bar, and click the mouse button.

5. Point to the File option on the main menu.

6. Press and hold the ⬛.

7. Drag the pointer to the Close Window option.

8. Release the ⬛.

This should return you to the Opening System Disk window.

Summary

Word processing is one of the most practical applications of an integrated package. Everyone creates documents at one time or another, and the automated editing features provide significant advantages to you. Entering, saving, and printing the document are standard operations in word processing programs. Editing and enhancement features are also available in all word processing programs.

To edit a document effectively, you must be able to move the insertion point through the document and reference the appropriate text. Works provides insertion point control at the character, word, line, page, and document levels. Works allows you to insert, delete, copy, and move text. The spell checking feature has become commonplace in most word processing programs and is a standard feature of Works.

Questions

1. How long has automated word processing been available to the typical household?

2. Name at least three uses of word processing in industry.

3. Name at least three uses of word processing in the home.

4. Identify the purpose of the following keys in word processing with Works:

   RIGHT ARROW

   LEFT ARROW

   UP ARROW

   DOWN ARROW

   HOME

   END

   PAGE UP

   PAGE DOWN

5. What is the difference between saving a document and retrieving a document?

6. What is the benefit of automated spelling checkers?

7. What is the most important feature of using automated word processing?

8. List the steps in inserting a character in a document.

9. List the steps in deleting a character in a document.

10. List the steps in deleting a block of text.

11. List the steps in performing a copy operation.

12. List the steps in performing a move operation.

13. When should a document be saved?

Exercises

Exercise 1

Using the paragraph below, do the following:

1. Create a new word processing file.

2. Enter the paragraph below as it is written.

3. Run the Spelling option, changing any incorrectly spelled words.

4. In the first sentence, change the word "jig" to "jam" and change "carpentry" to "lumber." In the last sentence, change "construction" to "obstruction."

5. Save the document as JAM.

6. Print the document.

The expression "to be in a jig" originated from the carpentry industry. When timber was floated to the mill, often the logs became "jammed" and entangled. "To be in a jam" means that some construction halts personel progress.

Exercise 2

Using the paragraph below, do the following:

1. Create a new word processing file.

2. Enter the paragraph as it is written.

3. Run the Spelling option, changing any incorrectly spelled words.

4. Save the document as MUSTARD.

5. Close the file.

6. Open the existing file MUSTARD.

7. Block select the last sentence and delete it.

8. Block select the first sentence and move it to the end of the paragraph, making it the last sentence in the paragraph.

9. In the new first sentence, change "Gut" to "Cut" and "Custard" to "Mustard." In the new third sentence, change the word "provide" to "prove."

10. Save the document.

11. Print the document.

If, after three tries, he could not split the tiny mustard seed that was placed on a speck of wood, he was required to wait a year and try again. The term "Gut the Custard" dates to the ancient Middle East. It was used as a symbol of masculine power and was part of a prenuptial ritual. A prospective groom was forced to provide his masculinity prior to marriage by cutting a mustard seed with his sord. It may be that this ritual led to the expression "Third time is the charm."

Exercise 3

Using the paragraph below, do the following:

1. Create a new word processing file.

2. Enter the memo as it is written.

3. Run the Spelling option, changing any incorrectly spelled words. (The word "Hireme" is correct.)

4. Save the document as POSTING and continue processing.

5. Change "nerd" to "word" in the second sentence. Change "nature" to "mature" in the fourth sentence.

6. Move the first sentence so that it is just before the last sentence, which starts "An interview can be."

7. Save the document.

8. Print the document.

To whom it may concern:

Applicants should provide a current resume, including complete work history. A position will be available in the coming month for someone who can do nerd processing using a microcomputer. The job will require a working knowlege of Microsoft Works. The person who fills the opening must be nature minded. An interview can be sceduled by contacting George Hireme in the personnel office.

Problems

Problem 1

Write a memo at least two paragraphs in length to a business associate announcing a meeting to be held during the coming week. Save the memo to disk. Print the memo as a draft copy. Make at least three changes to the memo, using both insertion and deletion (add, delete, or change spelling of words). Correct any grammatical errors. Save the final copy to disk. Print the final copy.

Problem 2

Write a summary of what you hope to learn from this book. It should be at least a half page in length. Intentionally include at least five spelling errors. Save the document to disk. Print the document as a draft copy. Use the Spelling feature to identify and correct the spelling errors in the document. Correct any grammatical errors. Save the corrected copy to disk. Print the document.

Problem 3

Write a brief letter to a company indicating an interest in a job opening which it advertised in the local paper. Save the document to disk. Print the document as a draft copy. Use the Spelling feature to identify and correct any spelling errors in the document. Correct any grammatical errors. Save the document. Print the document.

Problem 4

Write a letter to a friend inviting him/her to a party (no more than half a page). Describe where the party will be, who will be attending, and other pertinent information. Include at least five spelling errors. Save the document. Print the document as a draft copy. Use the Spelling feature to identify and correct the spelling errors. Correct any grammatical errors. Save the document. Print the document.

Problem 5

In a half page or less, describe your favorite hobby. Include at least two spelling errors. Save the document. Print the document as a draft copy. Use the Spelling feature to identify and correct the spelling errors. Make at least two insertions and two deletions of characters or words. Correct any grammatical errors. Save the document to disk. Print the document.

Problem 6

Write a letter to a friend that is at least a page and a half in length. Include at least five spelling errors. Save the document after each half page of entry. Print a draft of the document as a draft copy. Use the Spelling feature to identify and correct any spelling errors. Select and delete a block of text containing at least one sentence. Select and move a block of text containing at least one paragraph. Make at least two insertion changes. Save the document. Print the document.

Problem 7

Write a speech on a topic of your choice (two pages long). Include at least ten spelling errors in the document. Save the document after each half page of entry. Print the document as a draft copy. Use the Spelling feature to identify and correct spelling errors. Identify a sentence or sentences that can be used in the summary and copy the block of text into the speech summary at the end of the document. Make at least three insertions/deletions of characters or words and at least two moves or deletions of blocks of text. Save the document. Print the document.

Problem 8

Write a summary (two pages long) of an article or book you have read recently. Include at least five spelling errors. Save the document after each half page of entry. Print the document as a draft copy. Use the Spelling feature to identify and correct the spelling errors. Make at least one block move and one block deletion in the document. Make at least five character or word insertions or deletions in the document. Save the document to disk. Print the document.

Chapter 4

Document Formatting with the Word Processor

Objectives

After completing this chapter you will

1. Understand the importance of planning the page layout.

2. Know the features generally used when planning the page layout.

3. Know several features used to enhance text.

4. Be able to review default margin settings in Works and modify them as necessary.

5. Be able to create document headers and footers using Works.

6. Be able to number pages in Works, using the automatic numbering feature.

7. Be able to use the justification, centering, and single or double line spacing options in Works.

8. Be able to use the boldfacing and underlining features of Works to enhance text.

Layout and Presentation Features

Planning a Document

When watching someone typing letters, it is easy to assume that he or she simply types through a stack of paper, producing document after document with little consideration for where things are positioned on the page or how text flows from one page to the next. Actually, many decisions are being made regarding the look of the text and the positioning of text on the page. Sometimes the decisions are avoided by labeling the document "draft," but this often creates problems instead of solving them.

A good typist finds out specific information prior to typing a document. The length of the document plays an important role in deciding such things as where margins will be and whether page numbering is needed. The user must know where the document is being sent in order to know if company letterhead paper is to be used. The degree of formality associated with the document may suggest a need for common header or footer information on each page. The content of the document may warrant such features as underlining or typing all caps. These decisions and others should generally be made prior to typing the document rather than after it is completed.

Automated word processing has provided the luxury of applying such specifications as the ones defined above after the document has been typed. The ease with which editing is done invites the typist to simply enter the text and then begin to consider such things as margin placement and header information. If, however, more planning is done prior to typing the document, it will reduce the need for modifications after the draft is entered, and it will inspire you to concentrate on refining the document rather than just entering data. Although changes in formatting may often be made after the document is entered, the quality of the product will be improved by prior planning.

Several sources of information can be used in defining the specifications of the document to be typed. If it is part of standard company correspondence, look at similar documents to identify formatting characteristics. If it has been requested by a person other than the typist, ask that source if he or she has some characteristics in mind, and if possible look at work previously done for that person. If standard settings have been designated by the department, review those settings and apply them as they are appropriate. Analyze the document content, its intended use, and commonly accepted style features.

Formatting a Document

Planning the formatting characteristics for a document is much like framing a picture. The margin area becomes the frame and should complement the size of text, the line spacing, and the enhancement of text within the document. Generally, decisions regarding the length of the page and the number of lines printed per inch will influence the size of the top and bottom margins. The width of the paper and the number of characters printed per inch will influence the left and right margin widths. If the document is to be placed in a binder, the margin on that edge (top or side) of the document may need to be wider to allow for the binding. The number of vertical lines per inch and the number of horizontal characters per inch may be influenced by the type of document being produced and its intended size. For example, a short memo may use large print, fewer lines per inch, and large side margins. A manual may use smaller print, more lines per inch, and narrow margins.

Header and footer considerations also are a factor in deciding on the page format. A standard header with the company name or other information may be required on each page. A footer area may contain such things as page numbering, which can be done automatically by the program. Paragraph indentation is also considered when deciding on the layout. Generally, all these factors are considered together, and a clearly defined page layout is the end result. A sample page layout is shown in Fig. 4.1. A sketch similar to this should be made when planning any document.

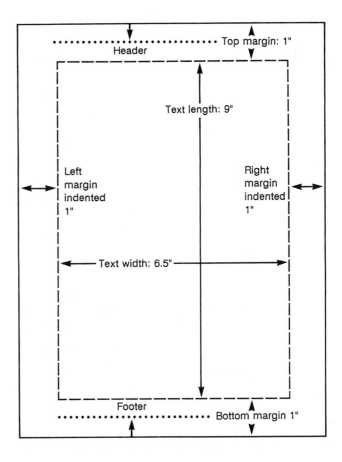

Fig. 4.1 Sample page layout

Enhancing a Document

Several features can be used to enhance the presentation of the text. Some of them emphasize words or phrases, while others simply add to the overall aesthetic quality of the document.

Justification can be used to give the text a "framed" appearance by aligning the printing on both the left and right margins. Textbooks typically use this technique, which provides cosmetic enhancement to the entire document.

Formatting segments of text is often used to distinguish them from the remainder of the document. This may be done by providing line spacing above and below the selected text and moving the margins in to clearly distinguish the segment from the rest of the document (see Fig. 4.2). A direct quote is sometimes enhanced this way. Paragraph indentation, also shown in Fig. 4.2, can be used to enhance the document. Indenting can be applied to the first line of the paragraph or to subsequent lines (in the case of hanging indents) by using the appropriate settings.

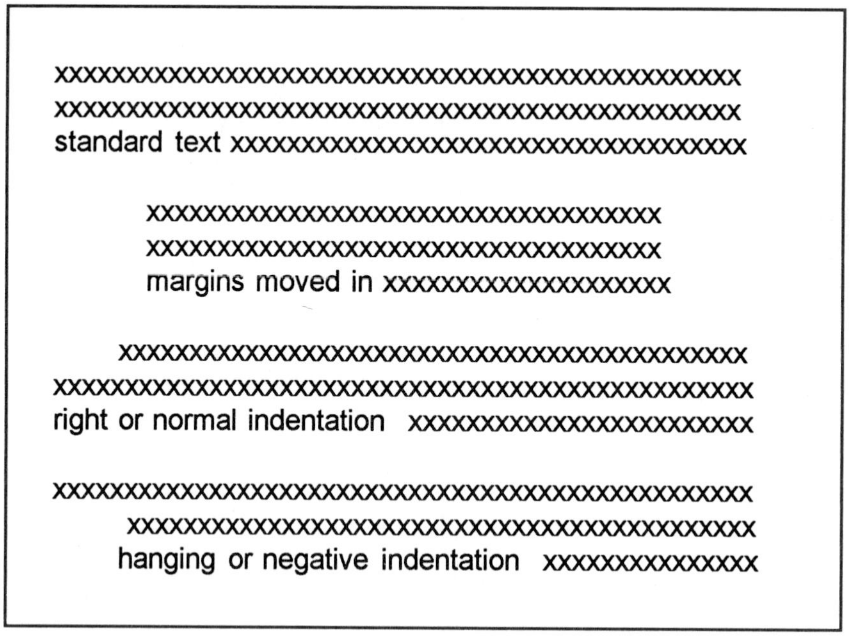

```
xxxxxxxxxxxxxxxxxxxxxxxxxxxxxxxxxxxxxxxxxxxxx
xxxxxxxxxxxxxxxxxxxxxxxxxxxxxxxxxxxxxxxxxxxxx
standard text xxxxxxxxxxxxxxxxxxxxxxxxxxxxxxxxxxx

    xxxxxxxxxxxxxxxxxxxxxxxxxxxxxxxxxxxxxx
    xxxxxxxxxxxxxxxxxxxxxxxxxxxxxxxxxxxx
    margins moved in xxxxxxxxxxxxxxxxxxxx

    xxxxxxxxxxxxxxxxxxxxxxxxxxxxxxxxxxxxxxxxx
xxxxxxxxxxxxxxxxxxxxxxxxxxxxxxxxxxxxxxxxxxxxxxx
right or normal indentation  xxxxxxxxxxxxxxxxxxxxxx

xxxxxxxxxxxxxxxxxxxxxxxxxxxxxxxxxxxxxxxxxxxxxxx
    xxxxxxxxxxxxxxxxxxxxxxxxxxxxxxxxxxxxxxxxxx
hanging or negative indentation  xxxxxxxxxxxxxx
```

Fig. 4.2 Inset margins and paragraph indentation

A centering feature is typically available, which allows for centering a line of text, such as a title. This eliminates the need for manually centering a line and ensures that, as margins are changed, the text will remain centered. *Boldfacing* and *underlining* can also be used to bring attention to specific words or phrases of text. Underlining such things as book titles appearing in the text is done with this feature. You can place emphasis on words or phrases by printing them in *italics*. Boldfacing important words causes them to print darker, which attracts the attention of the reader.

These features should be strategically employed to enhance rather than detract from the intended message. Overuse of these features can be as damaging as underuse. When possible, use writing guide materials in deciding when and how to best use the enhancement features available in word processing programs.

Page Layout and Formatting with Works

Margin Settings

When the document file is created, margin and spacing settings are assigned to the standard values stored in Works (default values). Items of particular importance are listed in the Page Setup section of the File menu. This is accessed by selecting the File pull-down menu, shown in Fig. 4.3, and then the Page Setup option. The Page Setup dialog box includes the page size, printer information, and a button to select a Document dialog box to display margin settings and other information. If you are using a printer other than a DeskWriter, the boxes may be slightly different, but the contents will be generally the same.

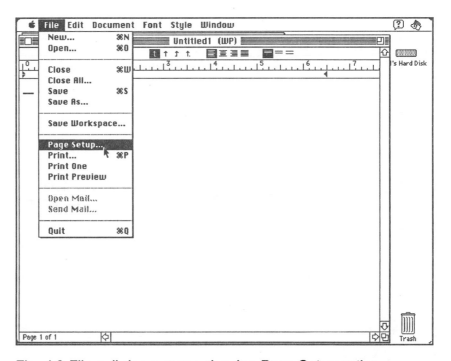

Fig. 4.3 File pull-down menu showing Page Setup option

Typically the paper is US Letter (8.5" by 11"). The standard Works margin settings are illustrated in Fig. 4.4, and include top, bottom, left, and right margins of 1 inch. Any of these settings can be changed by using the pointer to select the entry area and making the desired change. (You can also use the TAB key to reference any item and enter a different value.) Selecting the OK button will record all changes made. The Cancel button will leave values as they were when the dialog box was accessed. Enter new margin values in inches. The new settings entered will be used in the current document only. Each document contains its own settings once it is created. The appropriate settings should be assigned prior to typing the document, but can be modified at any time.

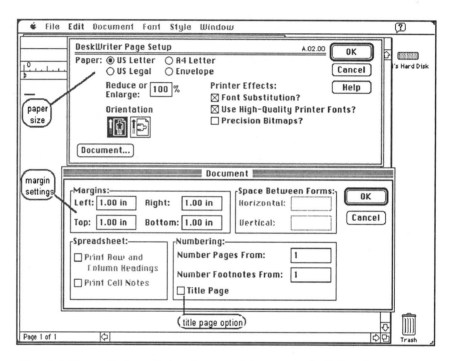

Fig. 4.4 Page Setup dialog box and Document dialog box

The indentation settings within the document should allow for the text to fit within the settings in the Page Setup dialog box (refer to the Indenting Text section in this chapter). Settings in the document are defined by the arrows on each end of the ruler line that point toward the middle. The default is typically zero on the left and 6.5 inches on the right. This means that the page setup parameters need to provide 6.5 inches of horizontal print area for the document, or else some of the text will not be printed. The indentation settings can be changed by selecting either arrow with the pointer and moving it to the desired location. To change the settings for existing text, move the insertion point anywhere in a paragraph, or highlight multiple paragraphs before moving the indentation arrow. Newly entered paragraphs will use the new settings.

Headers and Footers

Header and footer options are available for putting identical information at the top or bottom of each page. These are found in the Window pull-down menu (see Fig. 4.5). Either option can be selected, and a corresponding window will be displayed in which to enter the header or footer information (see Fig. 4.6, showing both windows). The header line is contained within the top margin spacing and the footer line within the bottom margin. One line is assigned for each header and footer, but more lines can be allocated if needed. If not specified, Works will left justify the header and footer on the appropriate line. Options exist for positioning header and footer information to the left, center, or right of the page by using the buttons in the toolbar (see Fig. 4.6). The TAB key can be used to have a three-part entry with the first part left justified, the second part centered, and the third part right justified. You can also include the date, time, and/or page numbers by using the corresponding buttons on the toolbar (see Fig. 4.6).

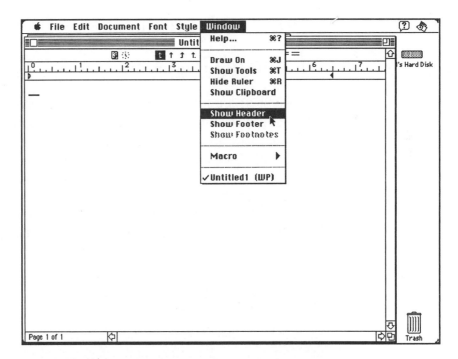

Fig. 4.5 Window pull-down menu showing Header option

It is often desired that a header and/or footer not appear on the first page of the document. By selecting the Title Page option from the Document dialog box (refer to Fig. 4.4), these elements will be on every page except the first one. When the option is on, you can see an X in the box to its left. To turn it off, simply select it again.

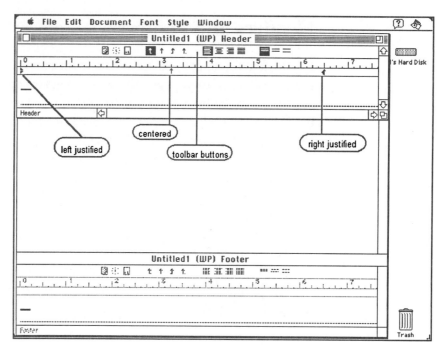

Fig. 4.6 Header and footer windows

Numbering Pages

Page numbers are sometimes included in the header or footer information. To include a page number in the header or footer, position the insertion point in the header or footer box and select the page numbering button on the toolbar (refer to Fig. 4.6). The page number will start at 1 unless otherwise specified. The starting value can be changed by changing the Number Pages From option in the Document dialog box (refer to Fig. 4.4). The number will increment automatically for each page printed. The page number can be positioned on either side or centered on the page by positioning the insertion point in the entry area prior to selecting the option.

Viewing the Layout

Once the document is entered, the Print Preview option allows the user to view the layout of the document on the desktop prior to printing. This is a time-saving alternative to printing the document to be able to see the general format of the final product. Adjustments can be made to the layout as necessary to achieve the desired results. The option is accessed by selecting Print Preview from the File pull-down menu (refer to Fig. 4.3). Works will display a miniature version of the document as it will be printed (see Fig. 4.7). The document can be previewed page by page, by using the Next or Previous icons. Once the previewing is complete, you can select Cancel to go back to the document, or Print to print the document. You can zoom into an area by pointing to it and clicking the mouse button, then return it to its original size by double clicking the mouse button.

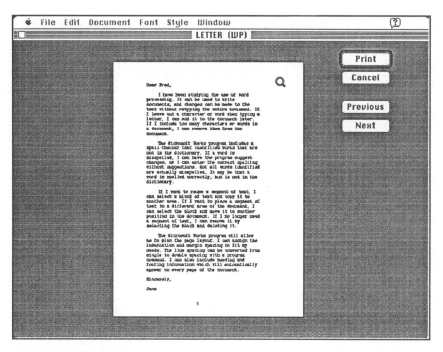

Fig. 4.7 Print Preview display

Formatting Text

In Works, formatting features can be applied to paragraphs or groups of paragraphs. Justification, line spacing, centering, and indentation are among the options. These features can be applied by setting them prior to entering text or modifying them after text is entered. To apply a feature after text is entered, the insertion point should be placed in the paragraph to be modified, or a block select should be used to identify multiple paragraphs to be modified. In either instance the changes will be made to the paragraph(s) identified, but the feature will not be changed on future data entered. To preset the feature, the insertion point should be in a file with no data or it should be positioned immediately after a hard carriage return and prior to entering any data in the current paragraph. The feature will remain changed for all new text entered.

Other features, like boldfacing and underlining, apply to selected text only, rather than to the entire paragraph in which the text exists. The procedure for applying a feature after the text is typed is to highlight the block and select the desired feature. A feature can be applied to text as it is entered by selecting the feature, typing the text, then selecting the feature again to turn it off.

97

Justification and Centering

Formal documents, and sometimes informal ones, are printed with the text aligned on both the left and right margins. Textbooks are typically printed this way. Paragraphs or the entire document can be justified this way.

The default in Works is to display and print text with the left margin aligned and the right margin as a "ragged edge." To activate justification, highlight the Alignment option on the Style pull-down menu. You will then see a submenu that contains the options Left, Center, Right, and Justified (see Fig. 4.8).

To justify multiple paragraphs or the entire document after entry, use the block select technique to highlight the segment, and then choose the Justified option from the Alignment submenu of the Style pull-down menu. To return text from justified to normal (left justified with ragged right edge), highlight the segment and select the Left option from the same submenu.

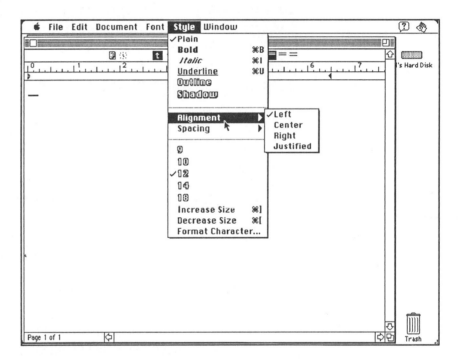

Fig. 4.8 Style pull-down menu with Alignment submenu displayed

Centering a large block or paragraph is uncommon. However, there are numerous situations where one or several lines of text need to be centered. An example would be the heading on the first page, which may not be included in the header line. Another example is the cover page for a document, and another is the name and address on a resume.

A single line can be centered by having the insertion point anywhere on the line and selecting the Center option from the Alignment submenu. Multiple lines are centered by using the block select to highlight them and then selecting the

Center option. It should be noted that centering will occur from each line to the end of the current paragraph, so the last line being centered must have a hard carriage return at the end (created by the RETURN key), or subsequent lines will be centered until a hard carriage return is encountered. This problem can also occur if the data prior to the first line being centered does not have a hard carriage return at the end of it. Centering can be removed by selecting the Left, Right, or Justified option.

Any of the options of Left, Center, Right, or Justified can be chosen prior to entering data by placing the insertion point in a file with no data or immediately after a hard carriage return. Then text entered will have the format specified, until you select another format.

Line Spacing

For a paragraph or a group of paragraphs, the program can automatically convert from single to double spacing or from double to single spacing between lines. You can also select one and one-half line spacing. The default is single spacing. A trick allows you to use single spacing between lines and double spacing between paragraphs. Simply press the RETURN key a second time at the end of each paragraph to create a blank line.

The desired paragraph, paragraphs, or entire document can be selected and highlighted by using the block select feature. Then one of the options can be selected from the Spacing submenu on the Style pull-down menu (see Fig. 4.9). A single paragraph can be changed simply by having the insertion point anywhere in the paragraph and selecting the option.

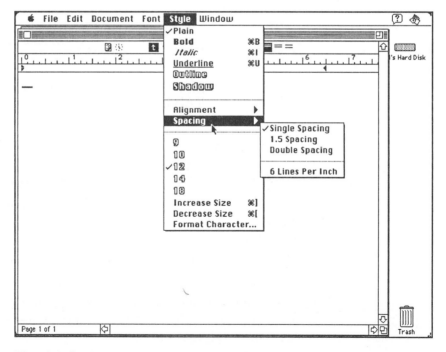

Fig. 4.9 Style pull-down menu with Spacing submenu displayed

Any of the options can be chosen prior to entering data by placing the insertion point in a file with no data or immediately after a hard carriage return and selecting the option. Then any text entered will use the assigned spacing.

Boldfacing and Underlining

These features are also found in the Style pull-down menu (refer to Fig. 4.9). An option can be used as the text is entered by simply selecting it at the point where the text will be entered, then selecting the option again to turn it off after the enhanced text is entered. The options can be applied to words or phrases, without affecting the entire paragraph. More than one of the options can be applied to the same text (e.g., bold and underline). To turn off multiple options, select the Plain option from the Style pull-down menu.

To use one or more of these options with text that is already in the document, use the block selection technique to highlight the block. Then select the Bold or Underline feature from the Style pull-down menu. You can apply both of these features to the same text if desired, by selecting one and then the other while the text is highlighted. After the insertion point is moved, the text will remain enhanced. A feature can be removed by again highlighting the block of text and choosing the option on the Style pull-down menu to remove it. Multiple items in this category can be removed by selecting the Plain option.

You can use other options on the Style pull-down menu, such as italics, to further enhance text (refer to Fig. 4.9). A different character size can also be selected prior to entering text or after the text has been entered (refer to Fig. 4.9). The Font pull-down menu can be used to enhance text by changing the text font (see Fig. 4.10). The size, font, and style features can be combined in many ways to enhance the text.

Indenting Text

The default tab stops are set at intervals of one-half inch and are not visible on the ruler line. The TAB key can be used to indent paragraphs or inset lines of text. A tab is entered as a single entry that assigns the correct number of blank spaces, and therefore the spaces for a tab can be removed by pressing the DELETE key only once. Indentation of one inch is achieved by pressing the TAB key twice.

To indent paragraphs automatically as text is entered or to add paragraph indentation to existing text, set the upper half of the left arrow on the ruler line to the desired location. The arrow appears split, because the upper half is used for first line indentation, and the lower half is used for indentation of subsequent lines in the paragraph. To apply the same indentation to all lines, move both the upper and lower parts of the arrow to the same location. The right arrow can be used to modify the indentation of text on the right side to do such things as inset a phrase or paragraph. It is important to remember that the actual

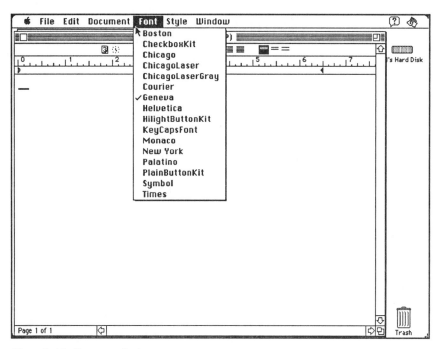

Fig. 4.10 Font pull-down menu

print margins are set in the Page Setup option of the File pull-down menu, and the text must fit within those margins when printed. Also remember that the value of the left indentation is added to the value of the left margin setting when positioning the text on the page. Examples of indentation are shown in Fig. 4.11.

This text is not indented and not justified. It will wordwrap at the right margin and be flush at the left margin, regardless of the actual line length. The arrows depict indentation of all lines on both sides.

This text has no indentation, but is justified. This will cause the indentation to be flush on both sides of the page, regardless of the actual line length. The indentation of every line is placed at the position of the arrows.

   This text has the first line of the paragraph indented. It will wordwrap to the bottom half of the left arrow, leaving only the first line indented. The upper half of the left arrow indicates the indentation of the first line.

This text has hanging or negative indentation. It leaves the first
   line of the paragraph at the position of the upper half of the
   left arrow and indents subsequent lines to the position of
   the lower half of the left arrow.

Fig. 4.11 Samples of indentation options

101

Hands-on Layout and Formatting with Works

Retrieving the Letter

To retrieve an existing document from the disk into memory, select the document icon from the window, select the folder icon of the folder containing the file, or select the file from a list of file names in the Works Opening dialog box. To continue our established sequence, if the machine is off, turn it on. If you are in the Opening System Disk window, first select the Microsoft Works 3.0 Folder from the folders on your disk. Then select the Works icon indicating Microsoft Works 3.0 to access the Works Opening dialog box.

You will retrieve the LETTER document created in Chapter 3. (If you did not create the letter shown in Fig. 3.27, do so now and save it in a file named LETTER.)

Retrieve the file named LETTER.

1. From the Opening System Disk window, move the pointer to the Microsoft Works 3.0 Folder icon, and double click the ⬭.

This should open the Works Application window.

2. From inside the Works Application folder, move the pointer to the icon representing Microsoft Works 3.0, and double click the ⬭.

You should now see a screen similar to Fig. 4.12.

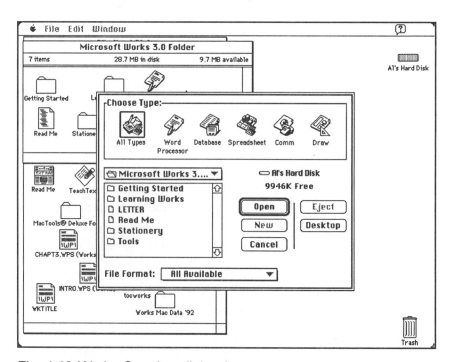

Fig. 4.12 Works Opening dialog box

3. Highlight the LETTER document name in the list of folder and document names on the lower left of the dialog box by pointing to it and clicking the ⟨⟩. (It may already be highlighted.)

4. Move the pointer to (Open) and click the ⟨⟩.

The Letter file should be opened and displayed on the desktop. It is now available for use. You can modify the letter or add new text if desired.

You will add the paragraph in Fig. 4.13 to the document.

The Microsoft Works program will allow me to plan the page layout. I can assign the indentation and margin spacing to fit my needs. The line spacing can be converted from single to double spacing with a program command. I can also include header and footer information which will automatically appear on every page of the document.

Fig. 4.13 Paragraph to be added to document

1. Move the insertion point to the left of the "S" in "Sincerely."

2. Type the paragraph in Fig. 4.13 into the letter.

3. At the end of the paragraph, press ‖ return ‖ twice, once to end the paragraph and again to create a blank line between paragraphs.

The letter should now have four paragraphs. Save the updated letter.

4. Select the Save option from the File pull-down menu.

Print a copy of the updated letter for reference.

5. Select the Print option from the File pull-down menu.

6. Select [OK] from the Print Options dialog box.

Indenting Text

It is important to remember that indentations and margins can be set prior to typing a document, as well as during the typing or after it is completed. The settings will remain in effect until they are modified. If you change the print margins to affect the printed output, you may have to change the indentations to keep the text within the desired width. If you change the indentations to affect the screen format, you may want to change the print margins to affect the printed output also. You will be changing the settings of the indentations in the LETTER document.

The document is now 6.5" wide on the screen. You will change the indentations from 0" and 6.5" to 1" and 6", making the text 5" across.

Highlight the text.

1. Press ⦊home⦉ to move the insertion point to the top left corner of the document.

2. Press and hold the ⌂.

3. Drag the pointer to the end of the document (the line containing "Jane").

4. Release the ⌂.

The entire document should be highlighted.

5. Move the pointer to the indentation arrow on the right side of the ruler line (probably at six and one half inches).

6. Press and hold the ⌂.

7. Drag the pointer to the 6" mark on the ruler line.

8. Release the ⌂.

The arrow should be under the 6" mark, and the text should reformat to the new marker location.

9. Move the pointer to the lower half of the indentation arrow on the left side of the ruler line.

10. Press and hold the ⌂.

11. Drag the pointer to the 1" mark on the ruler line (both parts of the arrow should move).

12. Release the ⌂.

If only the top half of the arrow moved, move it back over the bottom half and repeat the process as necessary to move both halves. If you accidentally create a tab marker, remove it by selecting it and moving it out of the ruler line.

The text should now be between the 1" mark and the 6" mark on the ruler line.

Now you will indent the first line of each paragraph of the document by 0.5" by moving the top half of the arrow to the 1.5" mark on the ruler line.

Highlight the four paragraphs, then move the indentation arrow on the ruler line.

13. Click the ⌂ to remove the highlighting from any text currently highlighted.

14. Move the pointer to the blank line above the first paragraph.

15. Press and hold the ⌂.

16. Drag the pointer to the blank line below the last paragraph.

17. Release the 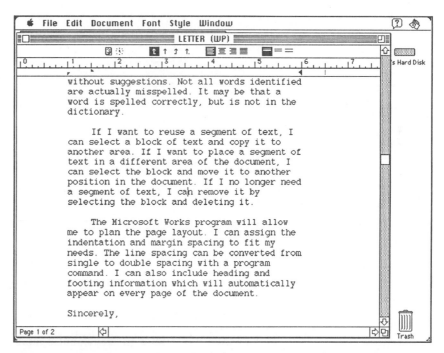.

The four paragraphs should be highlighted.

18. Move the pointer to the upper half of the indentation arrow on the left side.

19. Press and hold the 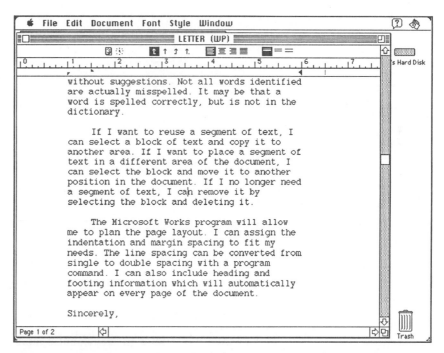.

20. Drag the pointer (moving only the top half of the arrow) to the 1.5" mark on the ruler line.

21. Release the 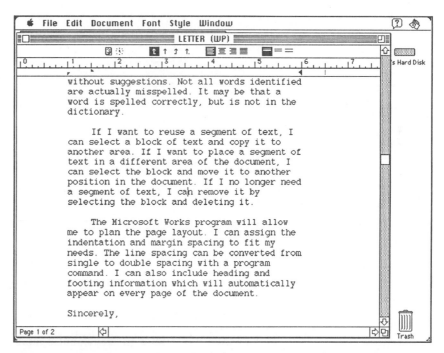.

The first line of each of the four paragraphs should now be indented to the 1.5" marker.

22. Click the 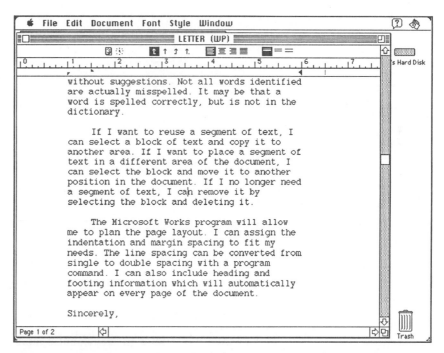 to remove the highlighting from the paragraphs.

The ruler line and the text should appear similar to the format shown in Fig. 4.14.

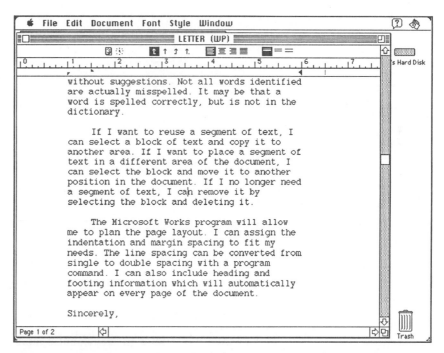

Fig. 4.14 Document with indentation moved in and paragraphs
indented

The indentations will be added to the margin settings when printing the document, so that with a 1" left margin the text will be 2" from the left edge of the paper.

105

Changing the Margins

The margin settings are found on the File pull-down menu as shown in Fig. 4.15, in the Page Setup option. The Page Setup dialog box is shown in Fig. 4.16. If your printer is not a DeskWriter, the box may be slightly different. From the Page Setup dialog box, select the Document button to display the Document dialog box (see Fig. 4.16). Once the option is selected, any or all margins can be modified.

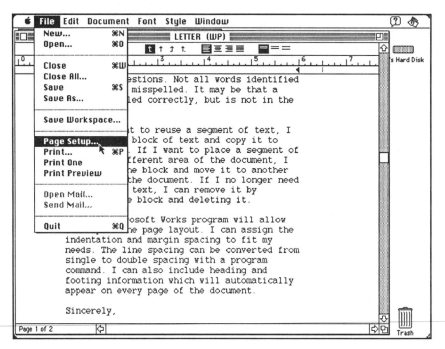

Fig. 4.15 File pull-down menu showing the Page Setup option

1. Move the pointer to the File item on the main menu.

2. Press and hold the ⌐.

3. Drag the pointer to the Page Setup option.

4. Release the ⌐.

5. Move the pointer to [Document...], and click the ⌐.

The dialog boxes shown in Fig. 4.16 should be on the screen (or something similar, depending on your printer type).

By moving the margins, you can control the positioning of the text on the printed page. It is important to remember that the left and right margin settings should provide enough distance to include the text and the left indentation. Change the left margin from 1" to .5", and change the top and bottom margins from 1" to 0.7". This will have the effect of moving the document up and to the left on the page.

6. Press **[tab]** until the Left Margin entry box is highlighted (it may already be highlighted).

7. Type **0.5**.

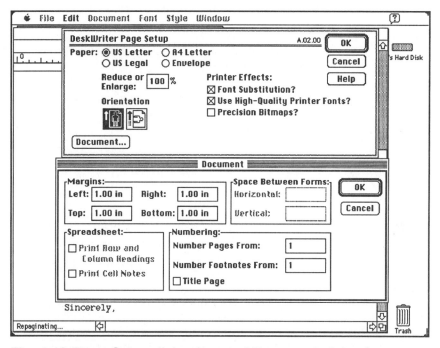

Fig. 4.16 Page Setup dialog box and Document dialog box

8. Press **[tab]** until the insertion point is at the Top Margin entry box (do not press the RETURN key).

9. With the Top Margin entry box highlighted, type **0.7**.

10. Press **[tab]** until the insertion point is at the Bottom Margin entry box (do not press the RETURN key).

11. With the Bottom Margin entry box highlighted, type **0.7**.

12. Press **[return]** to record the changes (or select the OK button with the mouse).

13. From the Page Setup dialog box, press **[return]** to return to the document (or select the OK button with the mouse).

This should return you to the document, with the margin changes recorded. Although no change is seen in the window, the difference will be seen when the document is printed.

Adding a Footer and Page Number

Footer information can be placed in the document with the footer option. The Footer dialog box is accessed by selecting the Show Footer option from the

Window pull-down menu (see Fig. 4.17), then entering the information in the Footer entry box (see Fig. 4.18). Header and footer information is printed on every page unless otherwise specified. You can automatically print page numbers on each page by selecting the button on the tool bar for including the page number in the header or footer.

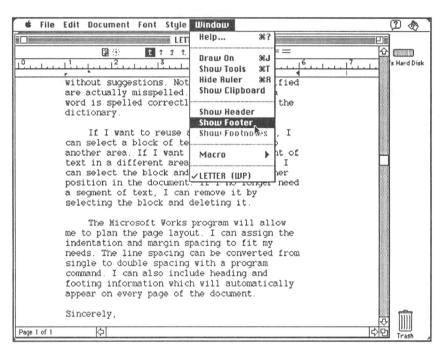

Fig. 4.17 Window pull-down menu highlighting Show Footer option

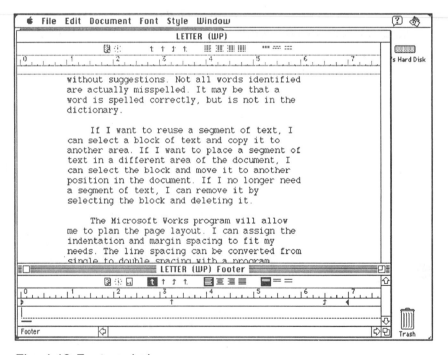

Fig. 4.18 Footer window

You will add the page number to this letter by including it in the footer information.

1. Point to Window on the main menu.

2. Press and hold the 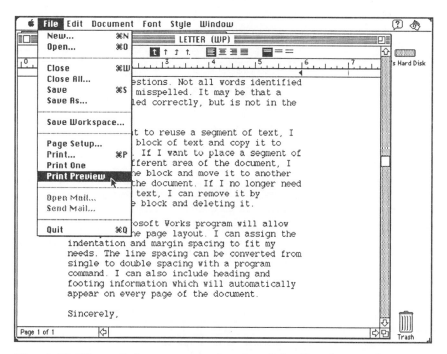.

3. Drag the pointer to the Show Footer option.

4. Release the 🖰.

5. With the Footer window displayed, press [tab] to move the insertion point to the middle of the entry line.

6. Move the pointer to the page number button on the toolbar (third button from the left), and click the 🖰.

You should see a "1" appear in the entry line.

7. Move the pointer to the close window box on the left end of the Footer title bar, and click the 🖰 to record the entry and close the window.

Viewing the Layout

Rather than print the document to review it each time you modify the layout, you can use the Print Preview option of the program, which shows the current print layout on the desktop. The Print Preview option is found in the File pull-down menu. To view the layout, select Print Preview from the File pull-down menu (see Fig. 4.19).

Fig. 4.19 File pull-down menu showing Print Preview option

1. Point to File on the main menu.

2. Press and hold the 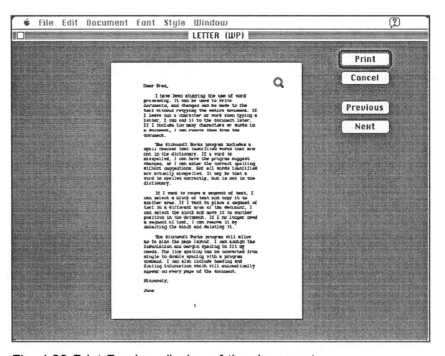.

3. Drag the pointer to the Print Preview option.

4. Release the ⌒.

You should see a picture of the output page on the desktop (see Fig. 4.20), including a magnifying glass (the pointer) to enlarge any portion of it.

5. Move the pointer to the middle of the second paragraph.

6. Click the ⌒.

You should see an enlarged display of that portion of the document, with a hand symbol as the pointer.

7. Move the pointer to the close box in the upper left corner of the window and click the ⌒. (You can double click the mouse button instead.)

This should return you to the full-page print preview display.

You could use the Previous and Next buttons to view any page in a multiple-page document. To print the document, you could select the Print button.

Fig. 4.20 Print Preview display of the document

8. Move the pointer to ⎡Cancel⎤, and click the ⌒.

This should return you to the document.

Adjusting the Line Spacing

The capability to automatically convert a single-spaced document to a double-spaced one is found in the Style pull-down menu, as seen in Fig. 4.21. The Double Spacing option in the Spacing submenu will convert the paragraph containing the insertion point or all paragraphs that have been block selected to double spacing. Since you may not want quadruple spacing between paragraphs, you can convert one paragraph at a time, which will create the effect of triple spacing between paragraphs.

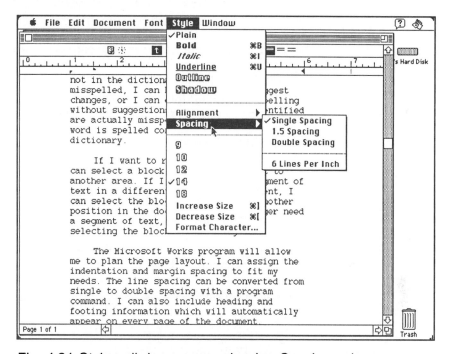

Fig. 4.21 Style pull-down menu showing Spacing submenu

If you want double spacing between paragraphs, you can delete the blank lines between paragraphs, and then double space the document by block selecting all the text and selecting the Double Space option.

To select a paragraph and convert the spacing, place the insertion point anywhere within the text of the paragraph, and select Double Spacing from the Spacing submenu on the Style pull-down menu.

1. Press **home** to move the insertion point to the top of the document.

2. Move the pointer to the second line of the first paragraph.

3. Click the ⟨⟩ to set the insertion point in the paragraph.

4. Point to the Style item on the main menu.

5. Press and hold the ⟨⟩.

111

6. Drag the ⬛ to the Spacing option.

7. Drag the pointer to the right to the submenu and then down to the Double Spacing option.

8. Release the ⬛.

The first paragraph should now appear double spaced. Triple spacing occurs between "Dear Fred," and the first paragraph, because double spacing adds a line above the first line of the paragraph.

9. Using the scroll bar as necessary, move the pointer to the second, third, and fourth paragraphs, and repeat steps 3 through 8.

The entire document should now appear double spaced.

By using the Print Preview option explained above, you can see that the document will now print on two pages, rather than one. Use the Previous and Next buttons to view both pages. Then select the Cancel button.

Now highlight the entire document and convert it back to single spacing.

10. Press ‖home‖ to move the insertion point to the beginning of the document.

11. Press and hold the ⬛.

12. Drag the pointer to the end of the document (the line below the line containing "Jane").

13. Release the ⬛.

14. Point to the Style item on the main menu.

15. Press and hold the ⬛.

16. Drag the pointer to the Spacing option, then to the Single Spacing option of the Spacing submenu.

17. Release the ⬛.

18. Click the ⬛ anywhere in the document to remove the highlighting.

By using the Print Preview option again, you can see that the document will now be single spaced and will print on one page.

Justifying the Text

Justification of text will cause the text to be aligned with the margins on both sides of the page. You can justify single paragraphs, or block select multiple paragraphs for justification.

112

You will block select the entire document. Then you will select the Alignment option on the Style pull-down menu, and select Justified from the Alignment submenu (see Fig. 4.22). This will justify the entire document.

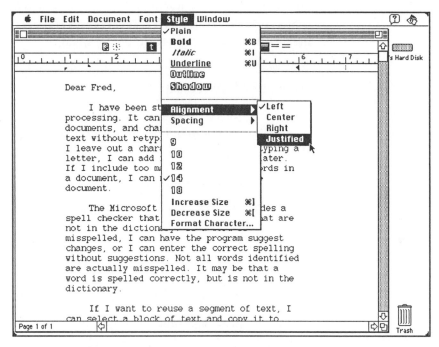

Fig. 4.22 Style pull-down menu showing Alignment submenu showing Justified option

1. Move the pointer to the beginning of the document.

2. Press and hold the .

3. Move the pointer to the end on the document (the line below the line containing "Jane").

4. Release the .

The document should be highlighted.

5. Point to the Style item on the main menu.

6. Press and hold the .

7. Drag the pointer to the Alignment option.

8. Drag the pointer to the right, then down to Justified.

9. Release the .

The entire document should now be justified. Use the scroll bar to move through the document to view it in the window.

10. Click the as necessary to remove the highlighting of text.

Centering Text

A paragraph or paragraphs can be centered within the left and right margins by highlighting the Alignment option on the Style pull-down menu, then selecting Center from the Alignment submenu. Usually the option is applied to individual lines (which technically form paragraphs).

You will center the lines containing "Sincerely" and "Jane," as well as the blank line between them.

1. Move the pointer to the line containing "Sincerely." (You can be anywhere on the line, but it's good policy to move to the left-most position.)

2. Press and hold the ⌒.

3. Drag the pointer to the line containing "Jane."

4. Release the ⌒.

The lines containing "Sincerely" and "Jane" should be highlighted.

5. Point to the Style item on the main menu.

6. Press and hold the ⌒.

7. Drag the pointer to the Alignment option (refer to Fig. 4.22).

8. Drag the pointer to the right and then down to Center.

9. Release the pointer.

"Sincerely" and "Jane" should now be centered on the lines.

10. Click the ⌒ to remove the highlighting.

Adding Formatted Text

Since Justification was applied to the entire document above the line containing "Sincerely" any new text entered after that point will be justified.

You will add the paragraph in Fig. 4.23. Prior to adding it, you must move the insertion point to the line just above the word "Sincerely."

1. Move the pointer to the line just above the line containing the word "Sincerely" and click the ⌒.

The insertion point should be at the position of the paragraph indentation box on the ruler line (1.5").

2. Press ⟦ return ⟧ to cause double spacing between paragraphs.

3. Type in the paragraph in Fig. 4.23. Be sure to press ⟦ return ⟧ after typing the period at the end of the last sentence to cause double spacing.

> I can enhance words or phrases of the text using features provided with the program. Boldfacing causes darker print. Underlining causes the text to be underlined when printed.

Fig. 4.23 Paragraph to be added to the document.

Notice that the paragraph appears indented and justified.

Using Boldfacing and Underlining

Notice in Fig. 4.22 that Bold and Underline are on the Style pull-down menu. One important distinction from spacing and justification is that these enhancement features operate on block selected text segments, not on paragraphs only. If a block of text is selected, the option chosen will apply the feature to the selected block. If a block is not selected, the feature will be activated for any new text being entered. To turn it off after it has been activated, select the feature again, or select the Plain option.

You will apply Bold to the word "Boldfacing" just added to the text.

1. Move the pointer to the left of the "B" in "Boldfacing" in the paragraph just entered.

2. Press and hold the ⌖.

3. Drag the pointer to the right of the "g" in "Boldfacing."

4. Release the ⌖.

The word "Boldfacing" should be highlighted.

5. Point to the Style item on the main menu.

6. Press and hold the ⌖.

7. Drag the pointer to the Bold option on the pull-down menu.

8. Release the ⌖.

9. The word "Boldfacing" should now appear bold.

You will underline the phrase "Underlining causes the text to be underlined" in the text just added.

10. Move the pointer to the left of the "U" in "Underlining."

11. Press and hold the ⌖.

12. Drag the pointer to the right of the "d" at the end of the word "underlined."

13. Release the ⌖.

The phrase "Underlining causes the text to be underlined" should be high-lighted.

> 14. Point to the Style item on the main menu.
>
> 15. Press and hold the ⌐.
>
> 16. Drag the pointer to the Underline option on the pull-down menu.
>
> 17. Release the ⌐.

The phrase should be underlined.

> 18. Click the ⌐ to remove the highlighting.

(If you notice a line across the text in this area, it is the page break, indicating the end of the first page and the beginning of the second. It does not relate to the underline feature being used.)

You will apply the Bold feature as you add a phrase to the sentence starting with the word "Boldfacing" in the paragraph just added to the text. Add the phrase "on the block of text selected" to the end of the sentence. You will turn on the Bold feature prior to adding the text and turn it off after the text is entered.

> 19. Move the pointer to the left of the period at the end of the sentence ending with "darker print."
>
> 20. Click the ⌐ to set the insertion point.
>
> 21. Point to the Style item on the main menu.
>
> 22. Press and hold the ⌐.
>
> 23. Drag the pointer to the Bold option on the pull-down menu.
>
> 24. Release the ⌐.
>
> 25. Type the phrase **on the block of text selected**. Be sure to type a space before the word "on."

The text entered should appear bold.

> 26. Point to the Style item on the main menu.
>
> 27. Press and hold the ⌐.
>
> 28. Drag the pointer to the Bold option on the pull-down menu.
>
> 29. Release the ⌐.

There should now be a check by Plain and not one by Bold on the pull-down menu.

Saving the Letter

You now have a letter that has been modified but not re-saved. The copy of the document on disk has none of the changes you have just made. You must now save the document to replace the copy on disk with the currently modified copy.

You can use the Save As option to change the name or the Save option to keep the present name, both of which are found on the File pull-down menu (see Fig. 4.24). The Save option allows you to save the file to disk under the current name, replacing the previous version with the current one.

1. Point to the File item on the main menu.

2. Press and hold the ⬭.

3. Drag the pointer to the Save option.

4. Release the ⬭.

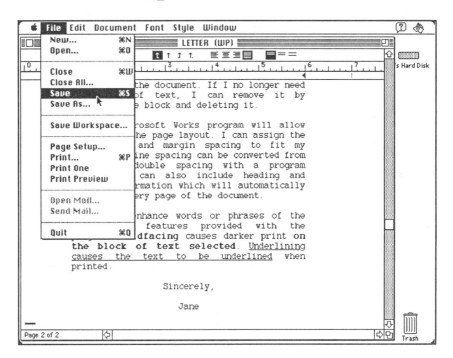

Fig. 4.24 File pull-down menu showing Save option

Printing the Letter

You have loaded the letter into memory, made several changes to it, and saved the updated letter to disk. If you want a copy on paper, you can also print it. Remember that you are printing the document that is in memory, not the one on disk. The Print command is located on the File pull-down menu. When preparing to print, be sure that the printer is on and has paper loaded.

To print the document, select the Print option from the File pull-down menu (refer to Fig. 4.24).

1. Point to the File item on the main menu.

2. Press and hold the 🖰.

3. Drag the pointer to the Print option.

4. Release the 🖰.

You will get a Print options dialog box. To print the document, select the OK button from the dialog box.

5. Point to OK.

6. Click the 🖰.

Closing the File

Once you have completed the document, you are ready to close the file, which removes it from memory but leaves the saved copy on disk for later use. If you have made changes since the last time you saved it, the program will ask you if you want to save the changes prior to closing the file.

The file can be closed by selecting the Close option from the File pull-down menu (refer to Fig. 4.24). It can also be closed by placing the pointer in the close box on the left end of the title bar and clicking the mouse button.

1. Point to the File item on the main menu.

2. Press and hold the 🖰.

3. Drag the pointer to the Close option.

4. Release the 🖰.

Exiting Works

To continue working on any other file once the file is closed, you would create a new file or open an existing one. Once you have completed the work session and are ready to leave Works, with the Microsoft Works 3.0 Folder active, select the Quit option from the File pull-down menu.

1. Point to the File item on the main menu.

2. Press and hold the 🖰.

3. Drag the pointer to the Quit option.

4. Release the 🖰

This should close the Works application and remove the shading from the icon.

To close the Works folder, select the Close Window option from the File pull-down menu, or point to the close box on the left end of the title bar, and click the mouse button.

5. Point to the File item on the main menu.

6. Press and hold the ⬡.

7. Drag the pointer to the Close Window option.

8. Release the ⬡.

This should return you to the Opening System Disk window.

Summary

Among the many automated features in document processing are those associated with page layout and text formatting. When planning the page layout, you should consider the specifications of all four margins around the document, and plan the use of headers and footers if needed. Automatic page numbering can be included in the header or footer of a document. Works will also allow the viewing and modification of a document layout prior to printing the document.

Many features are available for formatting the text within the document. Line spacing can be altered from single to double spacing. Justification can be used to align both sides of the text at the margins. Items can be centered automatically. Bold and underline features can be used to emphasize words or phrases within the document. Features used should enhance the document's appearance, rather than detract from it.

Questions

1. What does the term "page layout" refer to?

2. List at least three features associated with page layout.

3. Which pull-down menu includes the options to enter or change a header or footer?

4. Define the steps used to change the left and right margins in a document to 1.5" and 1.2" respectively.

5. Define the steps used to include page numbering centered in the footer of a document.

6. Explain the difference between justified and left aligned text.

7. Define the steps used to center a line of text.

8. Define the steps used to change the entire document from single spacing to double spacing.

9. Define the steps used to boldface a phrase as it is entered.

10. Define the steps used to underline a phrase which has already been entered.

Exercises

Exercise 1

Using the paragraph below, do the following:

1. Open a new word processing file.

2. Set the left margin to 1.4" and the right margin to .6", and set the top and bottom margins to 2.1" each.

3. Include the title "The Bull and the Bear" centered at the beginning of the paragraph.

4. Set the Justified option on.

5. Set the Double Spacing option on.

6. Enter the paragraph as it's written.

7. Run the Spelling option.

8. In the third sentence, change the word "novices" to "notices" and change "incompetent" to "bulletins."

9. Save the document, and name it BULLISH.

10. View the layout of the document using the Print Preview option.

11. Print the document.

The Bull and the Bear

The bull and bear symbols of the stock market do not originate from the strength and aggressiveness of the bull and the lumbering sluggishness of the bear. Instead, they date back to the eighteenth century stock exchange in London. Trading novices, called incompetent (or "bulls"), were posted every day on a large cork board (or bulletin board). If heavy trading occurred on a particular day, the board would contain many notices, indicating a "bullish" trend. If the board had few notices posted during the day, it would be referred to as bare or having "barish" activity.

Exercise 2

Using the paragraphs below, do the following:

1. Open a new word processing file.

2. Set the left margin to 1.3" and the right margin to .7". Set the top margin to 2.5".

3. Format a heading that is on the right side and contains the current date.

4. Add the heading "The Ringer" to the document, and center it after you type it in.

5. Enter the title and the two paragraphs. Single space the text, double space between paragraphs, and triple space between the title and the first paragraph.

6. Run the Spelling option.

7. Underline the word "ringer" in the first sentence, and underline the words "dead ringer" in the first sentence of the second paragraph.

8. Boldface the title.

9. Save the document, and name it RINGER.

10. View the layout of the document using the Print Preview option.

11. Justify the document.

12. Save the document.

13. Print the document.

The ringer is a term used in sports to refer to an expert player being discreetly placed on a team to give the team an unfair or unexpected advantage. This use of players by coaches and managers has been done for hundreds of years. But they have only been using the term ringer since the late 1800s. The ability to use the telephone to call or "ring up" a player in another city gave rise to the term ringer.

The term dead ringer, referring to someone who closely resembles another person, emerged during the same time period. The term dead in that time period meant absolute. Because of the logistics problems of campaigning across the country, political candidates often hired speakers to present themselves as the candidate, and duplicate their appearance and their message. Although audiences typically knew that the speaker was not the actual candidate, an extremely convincing stand-in was labeled as a "dead ringer" for the candidate.

Exercise 3

Using the paragraph below, do the following:

1. Open a new word processing file.

2. Enter the text.

3. Save the document to disk, and name it HORSE.

4. Run the Spelling option.

5. Print the document.

6. Change the left margin to 1.7", the right margin to .3", and the top margin to 2.8".

7. Format a header to include the phrase "The Horse Story" left justified in the header area.

8. Format a footer to include the current date, centered.

9. Center the title of the document, "The Color of the Horse."

10. Save the document.

11. Print the document.

The Color of the Horse

It is not common knowledge that dark horses generally run faster than light ones. In the 1870s, when horse racing on the frontier was common, an enterprising rider would sometimes whitewash his roan or black horse to give it the appearance of a bay or an Appaloosa. Newcomers to the races would often be fooled and were surprised when the light-colored horse won. This gave rise to the phrase "dark horse" in referring to an unexpected winner. The whitewashed horse, by the way, would typically "show its true colors" at the end of the race, when the sweat would cause the whitewash to streak.

Problems

Problem 1

Write a summary (at least a page and a half long) containing what you have learned from this book already. Correct any spelling errors. Place a centered page number in the footer. Use a left margin of 1.8" and a right margin of 1.6" for the entire document. Use a top margin of 2". Underline at least one word or phrase in the document. Indent the first line of each paragraph 0.5". Print the final copy.

Problem 2

Write a letter to a friend (at least a page and a half long). Correct any spelling errors. Use a top margin of 0.7" and left and right margins of 0.8". Use the boldfacing option on at least one word or phrase in the document. Include a header with the current date on the right side of the page. Print the final copy.

Problem 3

Write a one and one-half page document that includes your short-term and long-term plans, hopes and/or expectations for the future. Include the title "Planning for the Future." Use a top margin of 2", a left margin of 1.7", a right margin of 1.5", and a bottom margin of 2". Include a heading that contains the phrase "Planning Ahead" left justified and the current date right justified. Use a footer with the page number centered. Use the Title Page option in the Page Setup option to suppress printing of the header and footer on the first page. Print the final copy.

Problem 4

Write a two-page document to a prospective employer describing your background and explaining why you are the best person for the job. Use a top margin of 2", a left margin of 1.8", a right margin of 1.6", and a bottom margin of 2". Double space the document. Include a page number centered in the footer. Use the Title Page option in the Page Setup option to suppress printing of the page number on the first page. Boldface at least one word or phrase in the document. Print the final copy.

Problem 5

Write a two-page paper reporting on an article or book. Develop a draft copy with the default margin settings, then change the top, bottom, left, and right margins. Include at least one direct quote that is double spaced before and after the quotation and has indentations 0.5" in from the document margins. Underline or boldface at least one word or phrase. Include a page number in the header on the right side of the page.

Problem 6

Write a one-page resume. Include a centered title. Use boldfacing for section headings. Use hanging indentation to depict the subsections. Modify the margins to appropriately fit the information to the page.

Chapter 5

Spreadsheets

Objectives

After completing this chapter you will

1. Understand the common uses of a spreadsheet.

2. Be familiar with the characteristics of a worksheet.

3. Be able to explain spreadsheet terms, including *cell*, *active cell*, *row*, *column*, *label*, *value*, and *formula*.

4. Be able to distinguish among labels, values, and formulas as data types.

5. Be able to efficiently move the cell pointer to any cell in the worksheet.

6. Be able to create, save, and print a spreadsheet in Works.

7. Be able to edit cell entries of all types.

8. Be able to define and explain the term *range*.

9. Be able to use formulas in a spreadsheet.

10. Be able to use the SUM function in a spreadsheet.

What Is a Spreadsheet?

A spreadsheet is distinguished from other applications because it is associated primarily with number processing rather than text. However, it is not traditional number processing. A spreadsheet is usually a table of numerical data, which may be processed repeatedly while at the same time changing the entries to see the effect of the changes on the computed results. Spreadsheet use emerged in 1979 as a clearly discernable microcomputer application in the form of a program called Visicalc, and it quickly mushroomed in popularity. By 1985 Lotus 1-2-3, a sequel to Visicalc, had established itself as the leader in the spreadsheet market.

Numbers and Tables

While word processing involves the development and editing of text-oriented documents, spreadsheets primarily involve the development and editing of numerically oriented documents. The term *worksheet* will be used here to refer to the blank table before entries are made into it. The term *data* will refer to the entries made into the worksheet. The term *spreadsheet* will refer to the combination of the worksheet and the data in it.

The worksheet is characterized by having rows and columns in which data can be entered. Typical usage involves numeric entries that extend across the rows or down the columns. Each intersection of a row and column in the worksheet is referred to as a *cell*, or *location*. The location (called the address) is referenced by the row number and the column number; they form the inter-section point. (An accountant's ledger typically contains numbers identifying the rows and columns for reference.)

The cell can contain a number or a label entry. The numbers are the primary reason for using the spreadsheet, and the labels are used as titles to identify the numbers. Fig. 5.1 illustrates the use of numbers and labels in a worksheet, as well as identifying symbols used for each row and column.

Generally, any use of numerical data in a table format can be characterized as a spreadsheet application. The accountant's ledger can be called a spreadsheet. Retail sales information, such as that in the sample, is a spreadsheet. Inventory, payroll, payables, and receivables can all be characterized as spreadsheet applications. However, it is commonly the way that the data is used that will ultimately identify the most appropriate spreadsheet application. Tables of numbers that are periodically modified represent the most typical spreadsheet applications.

The spreadsheet is further characterized by the fact that computations are typically done on the numbers contained in it. The example in Fig. 5.1 includes total sales for each month, quarterly totals for each department's sales, and total quarterly sales for the company. These totals must be computed when data is entered into the spreadsheet. They must be recomputed if any adjustments are made to the data. In large manual spreadsheets, the computations can take hours, or even days, and may inherently contain some human error. Automating the spreadsheet incorporates both speed and accuracy to facilitate the calculations being processed.

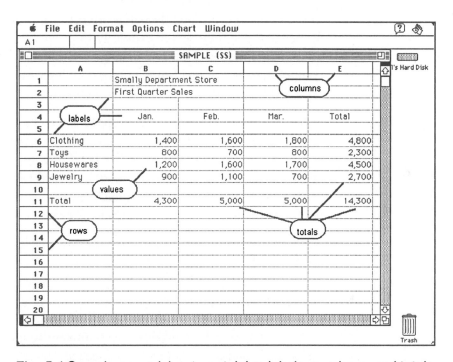

Fig. 5.1 Sample spreadsheet containing labels, numbers, and totals

Financial Applications

Accountants and financial managers have historically been heavy users of spreadsheets. The general ledger, used by the accountant as the primary record of the financial flow within the company, is a common example of a spreadsheet. Any subsidiary ledgers maintained are also spreadsheets. The bookkeeper commonly works from a book of worksheets in recording daily financial transactions that involve receipts or expenditures by the company.

Financial modeling, used to forecast the future, is commonly facilitated by the use of spreadsheets. Current trends can be analyzed in predicting future situations. Forecasts of various situations can be consolidated into a spreadsheet to provide a comprehensive picture of the future. Modeling of such things as income tax alternatives through a spreadsheet can provide the flexibility of reviewing alternatives and finding the most favorable choice.

One of the most practical uses of a spreadsheet is in preparing and implementing a budget. This incorporates the ability to use the spreadsheet as a planning tool, then as an implementation tool, and ultimately provides a historical record of financial transactions.

Automating the Spreadsheet

As computers became common in large businesses in the 1960s and 1970s, many accounting-related applications were automated. Automated applications in the 1960s were typically batch oriented, allowing little flexibility to the accountant, and they served primarily to provide historical data regarding the accounting function. Financial managers in that period had limited access to the computer and often had limited understanding of its potential. Most programs provided little flexibility and almost no interaction with the operator.

In the 1970s, as computer prices dropped and more companies automated, most of the accounting functions in medium- to large-sized companies were computerized. Accountants and financial managers generally became more computer literate. Computer systems moved in the direction of the user, providing more flexibility and interactive capabilities. This set the stage for the microcomputer and the automated spreadsheet.

The need for financial managers to have direct access to a spreadsheet tool was satisfied in 1979 when Dan Bricklin and Robert Frankston developed a program called Visicalc (VISIble CALCulator) to apply spreadsheet concepts on a microcomputer. The features emulated an accountant's ledger, allowing entry and updating of tables of numbers. Probably the most significant features of the automated spreadsheet program were the abilities to modify the worksheet, update data, and recompute totals as needed. Entry of data and labels is similar to a manual spreadsheet, but the abilities to change the structure of the spreadsheet, modify the values, and automatically recompute totals and other formulas have made manual spreadsheets virtually obsolete.

While more accounting and financial data processing was being moved into large computer processing systems, the ease and flexibility with which data could be manipulated attracted professionals to the desktop computer and the Visicalc spreadsheet program. By 1982 Lotus 1-2-3 was introduced with improved processing capabilities, and it added the applications of graphics and database processing. A major selling feature continued to be the ease in which a spreadsheet program could recalculate totals as changes were made to the data.

While file processing and database programs could handle much of the traditional data processing work load, spreadsheets became a major micro-computer application area of software during the 1980s, second only to word processing in market size. Spreadsheet programs became a mainstay for applications like budgeting and forecasting, which require many changes to the data after the spreadsheet is developed. The best two-word expression in describing spreadsheet usage is "What if?," referring to the ability to change data and immediately see its impact on the summary information in the spreadsheet. Although Lotus 1-2-3 has remained the leader in spreadsheet programs, there are many comparable spreadsheet packages available on the market, and Microsoft's Excel has become a primary competitor.

Creating a Spreadsheet with Works

The Spreadsheet Window

As seen in Chapter 2, Works is started the same way, regardless of which application is being used. When the Works Application is selected from the Opening System Disk window, the Microsoft Works 3.0 Folder window will display the folders and files pertaining to the Works program (see Fig. 5.2). To use the Works Application program, move the pointer to the icon containing the small pictures, and double click the mouse button. The desktop will then display the Works Opening dialog box (see Fig. 5.3).

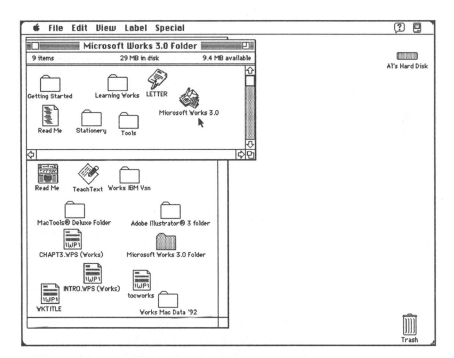

Fig. 5.2 Microsoft Works 3.0 Folder window

The boxed icon at the top indicates the currently active application type, and the list box on the lower left shows the folders and files in the active application. Remember that a folder is simply a compartment that can contain more files and folders. To open an existing folder or file, move the pointer to the desired name, and double click the mouse button. Alternatively, highlight the name by clicking the mouse button, and then select the Open button by clicking on it. The lower right portion of the dialog box includes options to open a highlighted folder or file or to cancel an operation. If the folder or file is on another disk, it can be referenced by selecting the Desktop button and then the appropriate disk name. To open a new file, move the pointer to the icon representing the type of new file desired (e.g., Spreadsheet), and double click the mouse button (or click on the type, and then click on the New button).

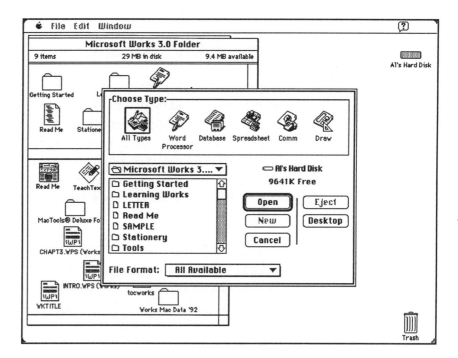

Fig. 5.3 Works Opening dialog box

Whether you are using an existing file or creating a new one, the spreadsheet window will appear and allow for entering and editing text. The spreadsheet window is depicted in Fig. 5.4, showing several items that are provided for you.

The top line of the desktop shows the menu options available. The second line contains three parts. The first part contains the address of the active cell. The second part (the box) is blank, but during data entry it contains a Cancel option, depicted by an X, and an Enter option, depicted by a check mark. When entering or editing data, the check mark can be used to record the entry, or the X can be used to cancel it. The third part of the line contains the contents of the active cell. When entering or editing data, it contains the changes being made prior to recording them in the cell.

The title bar (third line in the figure) is the top line of the document window, and it shows the name and type of file in use. A new file will have the name "Untitled1" (or Untitled"n") until it is given a name. The ("SS") following the name indicates it is a spreadsheet file.

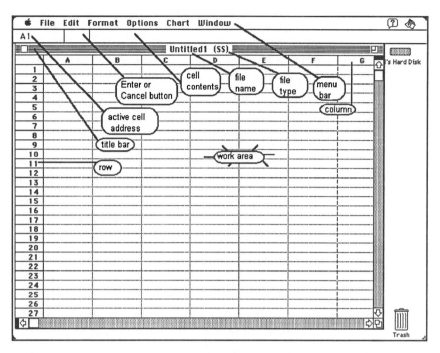

Fig. 5.4 Information provided with the spreadsheet window

The work area in the middle of the window is where data entry will occur. The pointer is called a cell pointer in a spreadsheet and will point to a cell location. Each cell is bordered by the lines between the rows and columns. The default cell width is 12 character positions. The work area is bordered on the left and upper sides by identifiers specifying the row and column. Works uses a typical identification system. It begins row identifiers with the number 1 and increments the number by one for each row. It begins column identifiers with the letter A and increments each consecutive column by a letter. The 27th column, following the one called Z, is identified by AA, column 28 by AB, 29 by AC, and so forth. Most spreadsheet programs, including Works, have more rows and columns available than you will ever need. Each cell is assigned an address or reference name, which is depicted by the column and then row identifier. For example, the cell in the second column and third row is referred to as cell B3.

The Cell Pointer and Cell Reference

In a spreadsheet file, the pointer highlights a cell rather than an insertion point. This is called the active cell. A cell can be made active by moving the pointer to the cell and clicking the mouse button, causing a highlighted border to appear around the cell. The four ARROW keys can be used to move the cell pointer in any of the four directions to make the adjacent cell the active cell. By repeatedly pressing the ARROW keys, movement will continue in the direction specified, one cell at a time.

Since the spreadsheet is typically much larger than the window, it is important to have more efficient ways of moving through the spreadsheet to the desired cell. The pointer can be used to move to any cell in the spreadsheet by pointing to the scroll bars at the right side and bottom of the window. The HOME key can be used to move the window to the upper left corner of the spreadsheet. The PAGE UP and PAGE DOWN keys can be used to move the window up or down one page (window size) at a time.

After entering data in a cell or editing a cell, you can have it remain the active cell or have any of the adjacent cells become the active cell. Pressing the ENTER key or selecting the check box on the edit line will enter the data and leave the current cell active. Pressing the RETURN key will enter the data and cause the cell below the current cell to become active. Pressing SHIFT/RETURN will enter the data and cause the cell above to be active. Pressing TAB will enter the data and cause the cell to the right to be active. Pressing SHIFT/TAB will enter the data and cause the cell to the left to be active. By using the appropriate keys when entering data, you can automatically position the active cell for the next entry.

Range

The use of a range provides flexibility in identifying multiple cells to be referenced in one operation. It is similar to a block in word processing, but it has a more rigid definition. A range is a group of contiguous (connecting) cells that form a rectangular shape. It can refer to several cells in a column, several cells in a row, or a series that includes multiple columns and rows of cells. Many of the operations involving formatting and data manipulation are made easier by referencing a range.

Ranges are typically represented by designating the upper left corner and the lower right corner of the series of cells. The two addresses are typically separated by a period or a colon. In Works, they are separated by a colon. Referring to Fig. 5.1, an example of a range is the cells B6 through B9 (B6:B9), which represent the sales data for the month of January. Another example is the range of B8 through D8 (B8:D8), which represents the sales of the Housewares Dept. for the months of January, February, and March. A third example is the range of B6 through D9 (B6:D9), which represents the sales entries for all items for the three months.

Data Labels

The term *data label* (or *label*) is used to refer to a series of characters that is treated as text rather than as a numeric value. Generally, these are words used to identify rows or columns of data, but they can also be specific data entries such as a person's name or a street address. The other types of data include values, formulas, and functions, all of which will be discussed in this chapter and in Chapter 6, and all of which require specific symbols as the first character entered to distinguish their presence. Any beginning character other than those that will be mentioned will indicate a label entry.

If an entry is to be specifically designated as a label, regardless of its contents, typing a double quote (") as the first character will designate the entry as a label. (The character will not be displayed as part of the output.) An example of when the quote is necessary would be a street address, which starts with a number but should be recorded as a label. Labels are left justified in the cell unless otherwise specified. They may be preceded by blanks as necessary, or the cell format may be changed to facilitate placement in the cell area.

Sometimes a label may have more characters than the number of positions in the cell. If the cell to the right is empty, the display will include the characters that extend into the next cell area. If the cell to the right contains data, the characters extending into that display area will not be shown on the screen. In either case, the complete label will be stored in memory, with a reference of the current address. Should the width of the cell be changed later, the display will adjust accordingly.

It is important to realize that even though a label is stored in memory, it may not all be displayed in the window, or it may appear to be stored in more than one cell. It is left to the designer of the spreadsheet and the person entering the labels to ensure the integrity between what is stored in memory and what is seen in the window.

Data Values

The term *data values* is used to refer to numeric entries in the spreadsheet which are stored as numeric values rather than as a series of characters. The typical distinction is that numeric values can have computations performed on them, whereas labels cannot. Numeric entries are stored right justified in the cell rather than left justified.

Numeric entries can have a first-character entry of a numeric digit, a decimal point, a plus sign, a minus sign, or a dollar sign. Any of these characters will designate the entry as a value and store it in numeric format.

Many entries containing numeric characters should be designated as labels rather than values. An obvious example is a street address. Less obvious examples are zip codes and telephone numbers. The numeric entry can be designated as a label by preceding it with the double quote (") symbol.

Sometimes a number is entered that is wider than the cell. In this situation, one of two things will happen. If the fractional portion of the number can be rounded to make the number of digits small enough to fit into the cell, it will be done. For example, 143.736 may be displayed as 143.74. In the second situation, the whole portion of the number may be too big to fit into the cell, in which case the number may be displayed in scientific notation (e.g., 1.4E+2), an error message may be displayed (e.g., *Error*), or ##### may be displayed in the cell. In any case, the number stored in memory and used in computations will be the actual number entered, rather than what is displayed in the cell.

Formulas

As stated previously, one of the major benefits of using spreadsheets is the calculation and recalculation of formulas. A formula entry is one that performs calculations on values and on the contents of cells in the spreadsheet. To ensure that the cell entry is designated as a formula entry, it should be preceded by an equal sign (=).

Formulas may be applied to all types of situations involving algebraic expressions. As with most spreadsheet programs, Works uses the standard rules of algebra when solving mathematic expressions. This is referred to as the operations hierarchy. The rules are covered here for review and for reference. As presented in Table 5.1, exponentiation is done first, followed by multiplication and division, then by addition and subtraction. Within each level, operations are performed left to right. The symbol commonly used for exponentiation is the caret (^). The asterisk (*) is used for multiplication and the slash (/) is used for division. The plus (+) and minus (-) are used for addition and subtraction. In the expression 87-6*3^2+5, the first step would be 3^2 (3 squared), then the result would be multiplied by 6, then the result would be subtracted from 87, then the result would be added to 5.

Parentheses can be used to change the priority of processing. Any portion of the expression in parentheses will be done first. In the example above, if you change it to read (87-6)*3^2+5, the first operation done is 87-6, which is 81, then the operation 3^2, which is 9, then 81*9, and then the result added to 5.

It is important to remember that in actual practice the expressions will typically have cell addresses rather than numbers. For example, the above expression might read (B4-D3)*E2^2+B8. This would subtract the contents of cell D3 from the contents of B4, then square the contents of E2, then multiply the results of the two operations, then add that to the contents of B8. In all the examples, the result would be stored in the cell containing the formula.

Hierarchy of Operations	Symbols Used
Parentheses	( )
Exponentiation	^
Multiplication and Division	* and /
Addition and Subtraction	+ and -
Left to right within any level	

Table 5.1 Hierarchy of mathematical operations

The user must be careful to write the expression consistent with the rules of computation to ensure accurate results. A common misconception is that multiplication is done before division, and addition is done before subtraction. This is not true. For example, the result of 8/4*2 is 4, not 1, and 12-4+3 is 11, not 5. No more than two values can be used in computation at any one time, so the size of the expression does not alter the procedure for solving it.

Unless otherwise specified, all formulas are recomputed each time a value is entered or changed in the spreadsheet. This means that any results displayed will reflect all changes made to the values in the spreadsheet.

It is important to realize that the displayed entry for any cell containing a formula will not be the formula, but the result of processing the formula. For example, if cell B4 contains a 3, cell B5 contains an 8, and cell B7 contains =B4+B5, the display in cell B7 will be 11, the total of the contents of cells B4 and B5. As is sometimes true with labels and values, what is seen on the display is not what is stored in memory. The contents of memory (=B4+B5 in the example) is what drives the spreadsheet. The display is what you see as the usable output information.

The SUM Function

Virtually all spreadsheet programs contain functions, which facilitate the ability to perform some operations. A function is a procedure that has been programmed into the application software. The procedure is given a name and is implemented by referring to the name. Functions must be entered in a specific format that has been defined by the author of the application software. The typical syntax (structure) of a function is a single character identifier, followed by the name of the function, followed by the argument, which is in parentheses.

The SUM function provides a way to add the contents of a list of cells. It is common, but not necessary, for the list to include a range of cells. In Works, the word SUM is preceded by an equal (=) sign. The argument, placed in parentheses, contains a list of cell addresses and/or values that will be totaled. The total will be displayed in the cell containing the function. For example, if the cell D8 contains =SUM(B6,C9,C12) and those cells contain the values 8, 9, and 3, cell D8 will display the number 20, the total of the contents of the three cells. A more common example would be =SUM(B6:B9) in cell B11 of the Sales spreadsheet in Fig. 5.1. This combines the use of a range and a function to total the January sales, and it is a simpler entry than =B6+B7+B8+B9. It can further be seen that the more cells that are being totaled, the more advantageous the SUM function becomes.

Saving a Spreadsheet

Any spreadsheet that is created should be saved from memory onto disk periodically to prevent loss or damage to it if an error or system failure occurs during processing. Two options exist on the File pull-down menu, shown in Fig. 5.5, that allow for saving the spreadsheet and continuing to work with it without needing to retrieve it again. The Save option allows for saving it under its currently assigned name. The Save As option allows for changing or assigning the name of the spreadsheet to be saved. With either option, the spreadsheet remains in memory for continued processing.

When a spreadsheet is created, the name area indicates "Untitled1" (or Untitled "n"). When the spreadsheet is saved, a name must be assigned to it. The name must be unique from other files stored in the folder. Any previous file saved under that name would be destroyed, and any future file saved under that name will destroy the current one. To assign a name to a file, use the Save As option (see Fig. 5.5). When that option is used, a dialog box will allow for entering a name (see Fig. 5.6). Once the name is typed, move the pointer to the Save button, and click the mouse button to save the file and return to the spreadsheet.

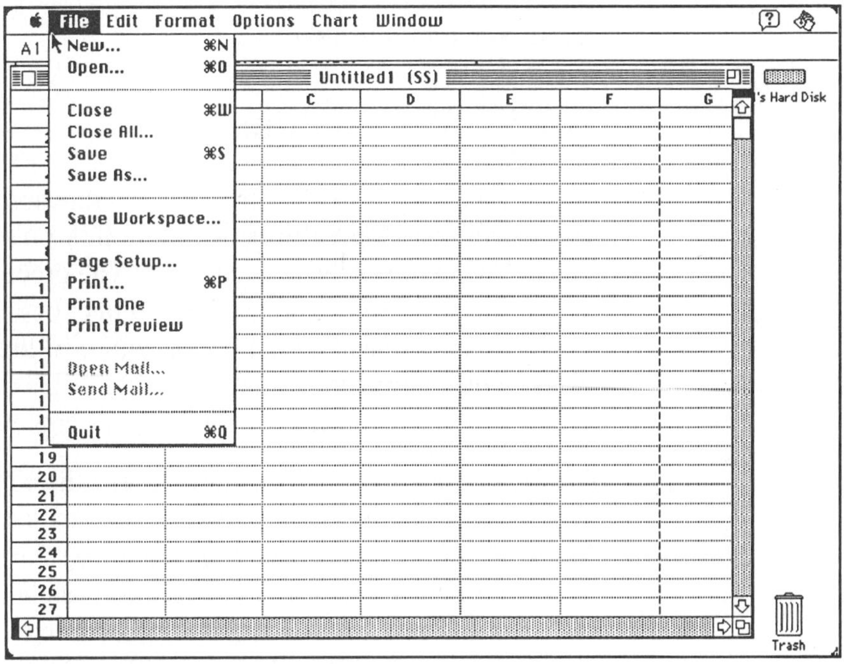

Fig. 5.5 File pull-down menu

If a document has already been assigned a name and you don't want to change it, the Save As option is not needed. Selecting the Save option will save the file under its current name and return you to the spreadsheet. Saving the memory copy of a spreadsheet causes it to replace any version previously saved in the folder under the same name. If a backup or duplicate copy is desired, it should be saved under a separate name with the Save As option or stored in a separate folder.

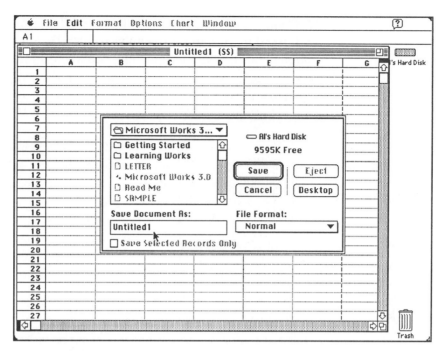

Fig. 5.6 Dialog box to assign a name to a file

Editing Data

The contents of a cell can be changed by moving the cell pointer to the cell and typing a new entry, which will replace the previous entry. This is not always the most practical way to make changes to the cell. The edit feature allows the user to make changes to a cell entry without retyping the entire value, label, formula, or function.

You can edit a cell entry by first making the cell active. Then click on the data in the edit line, creating an insertion point. Make the necessary changes to the cell, then use any of the appropriate movement keys to record the entry, or use the mouse to select the check button. More extensive cell editing can be done by using the Cut, Copy, and Paste options on the Edit pull-down menu.

Printing a Spreadsheet

When preparing to print a spreadsheet, the printer should be turned on, and the paper should be positioned properly. It is important to align the paper properly prior to printing and then control the printer from the Works program and from any external controls on the printer, rather than manually dragging paper through the printer.

Select the Print option from the File pull-down menu (see Fig. 5.7). A dialog box will then be displayed that has several options, including an option for the number of copies to be printed (see Fig. 5.8). If you are using a printer other than a DeskWriter, the dialog box may be slightly different. Generally it is not necessary to change any of the options on this menu. The spreadsheet can now be printed by moving the pointer to the OK button and clicking the mouse button. Once printing is complete, control will return to the spreadsheet.

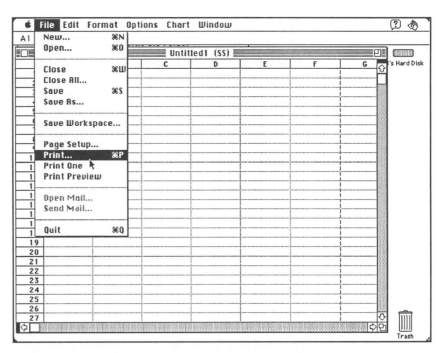

Fig. 5.7 File pull-down menu showing the Print option

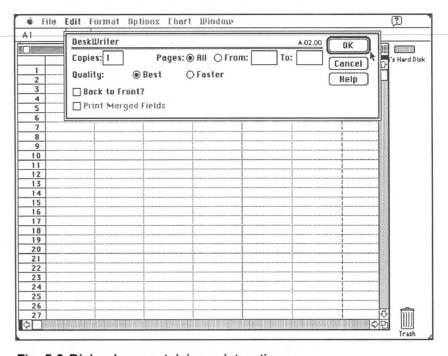

Fig. 5.8 Dialog box containing print options

Displaying Formulas

When developing a spreadsheet, it is important to review all formula entries to be sure that they are entered as intended. The display shows the result of the computation, but not how it was computed. To review the formula entries, you can select Show Formulas from the Options pull-down menu. This will cause the display to show the formulas rather than the computed results. Fig. 5.9 shows a formula display of the spreadsheet in Fig. 5.1. To get a printed copy of the formula data, print the spreadsheet with this option on. Once you have completed your review of the formulas, select the Show Values option from the Options pull-down menu to return to display mode.

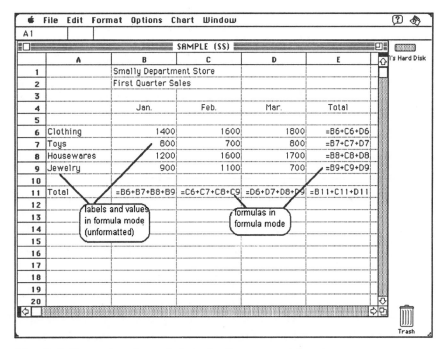

Fig. 5.9 Formula view of data in the spreadsheet

Saving and Exiting

Once the spreadsheet is completed, it is necessary to save it to disk, as mentioned previously, prior to exiting the Works program. This can be done in one of three ways, all of which are found on the File pull-down menu shown in Fig. 5.5. The Save option will save the document under the current name. The Save As option will save the document under a newly specified name. The Close option will remove the document from the desktop and from memory and close the file.

If the Close option is selected, the program will check to see that all changes have been saved. If they have, the program will remove the file from memory and return control to the Microsoft Works 3.0 Folder window, with the option of accessing other files or exiting Works. If all changes have not been saved, a dialog box will appear that will provide the option of saving the modified document or not saving it. Any changes not saved to disk will be lost once the document is removed from memory.

To exit the Works program, select Quit from the File pull-down menu. This should return control to the Microsoft Works 3.0 Folder. Then select the close box on the left end of the title bar. This should return you to the Opening System Disk window.

You can now do other applications. When you have finished using the machine, close any windows still open on the desktop, and follow the shut down procedure for your system.

Before turning the computer off, you should select the Shut Down option from the Special pull-down menu. This will prepare the computer to be turned off.

Hands-on with Spreadsheets

PART I

Creating the Spreadsheet

To begin typing the spreadsheet illustrated in Fig. 5.10, first enter Works and create a spreadsheet file. To do this, follow these steps.

	A	B	C	D	E	F
1	Personal Expense Budget					
2						
3		Quarter 1	Quarter 2	Quarter 3	Quarter 4	Total Expenses
4	Expenses					
5	Rent	1200	1200	1200	1200	4800
6	Utilities	500	300	600	400	1800
7	Auto	700	800	900	700	3100
8	Groceries	600	700	700	600	2600
9	Recreation	300	800	400	300	1800
10	Misc	300	300	300	300	1200
11						
12						
13						
14						
15						
16						
17						
18						
19						
20						
21						

Cell reference: A12. Menu bar: File Edit Format Options Chart Window. Window title: Untitled1 (SS)

Fig. 5.10 Expense budget spreadsheet containing values, labels, and formulas

Works should be properly installed and should access the appropriate disk drive. Refer to Chapter 2, as necessary, for instructions on accessing software on your disk.

1. From the Opening System Disk window, move the pointer to a folder icon labeled Microsoft Works 3.0 Folder (or something indicating the Works program), and double click the ⟨☁⟩.

A Works Application window containing Microsoft Works programs and possibly other Works related software should appear (see Fig. 5.11). If it doesn't, refer to Chapter 2 and check the system.

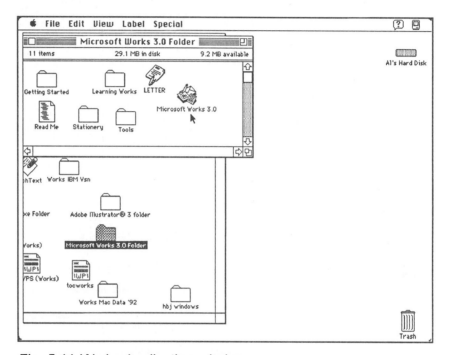

Fig. 5.11 Works Application window

The icon containing small pictures is used to access Works files created by the user.

2. Move the pointer to the Works icon containing the small pictures, and double click the ⟨☁⟩.

The dialog box shown in Fig. 5.12 should now appear. If it doesn't, try the selection process again or get help.

You want to create a new spreadsheet file.

3. Point to the icon labeled Spreadsheet at the top of the dialog box.

4. Click the ⟨☁⟩.

The icon should now be boxed.

5. Move the pointer to New.

6. Click the ⬭.

You should now see the window displayed in Fig. 5.13, with "Untitled1" (or Untitled"n") (SS) displayed on the title bar. If not, you may have selected the wrong type of file to create.

You are now ready to enter the data displayed in Fig. 5.10.

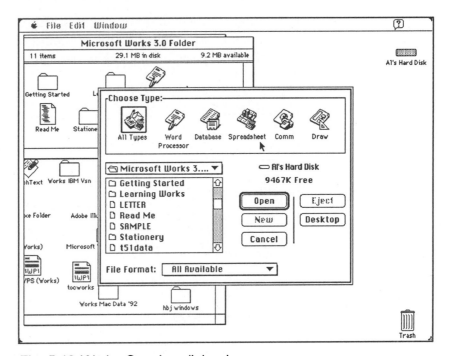

Fig. 5.12 Works Opening dialog box

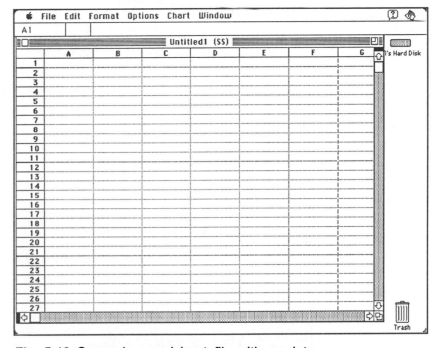

Fig. 5.13 Opened spreadsheet file with no data

Entering Labels

You are now ready to enter the labels in the spreadsheet (as displayed in Fig. 5.10). Enter the data as you see it. If you make typing errors, correct them by reentering the data.

1. If cell A1 is not active, move the pointer to cell A1 and click the mouse.

2. With cell A1 active, type **Personal Expense Budget**.

3. Press `return` to record the data and make A2 the active cell.

4. Press `↓` twice to make A4 the active cell.

5. Type **Expenses**.

6. Press `return` to record the entry and make A5 the active cell.

7. Type **Rent** and press `return`.

8. Type **Utilities** and press `return`.

9. Continue the process until all the labels in the A column have been entered.

10. Move the pointer to cell B3, and click the mouse to make it the active cell.

11. Type **Quarter 1**.

12. Press `tab` to record the entry and make cell C3 the active cell.

13. Type **Quarter 2**, and press `tab`.

14. Continue the process until all the labels in row 3 are entered.

15. Press `home`, if necessary, to display the upper left corner of the spreadsheet.

All the row and column labels should now be in the spreadsheet, and they will appear left justified.

Entering Values

You are now ready to enter the values from Fig. 5.10 into your spreadsheet. If you make errors when entering numbers, correct them by reentering any number containing an error.

1. Move the pointer to cell B5, and click the mouse.

2. Type **1200** in the cell, and press `return`.

3. With the cell pointer at cell B6, type **500**, and press `return`.

4. Continue entering all the numbers in column B.

5. Move the pointer to cell C5, and click the ⌒.

6. Enter the numbers in column C.

7. Enter the numbers in columns D and E using the same procedure.

Do not enter the numbers in column F yet.

Entering Formulas

You are now ready to enter the formulas from the spreadsheet in Fig. 5.10. Formula entries should be preceded by an equal sign to ensure that they are not designated as labels. Any numeric data that represents a computation of other values in the spreadsheet should be entered as a formula rather than as a value.

1. Move the pointer to cell F5 and click the ⌒.

2. Type in the formula **=B5+C5+D5+E5**, and press ⟦ return ⟧.

3. With the cell pointer at cell F6, type in the formula **=B6+C6+D6+E6**, and press ⟦ return ⟧.

4. Enter the remaining formulas in the same fashion.

Review the displayed totals to see that they are the same numbers shown in Fig. 5.10. If they are not, make corrections before going further.

Saving the Spreadsheet

You now have a spreadsheet. To protect it from the many things that can happen to the memory work area, it is necessary to save it on the disk. But don't close the file; you will continue to use it.

Since it is a new file, it must be named prior to saving it. On the File pull-down menu, the Save As option allows you to specify a new name prior to saving the file. Select the File pull-down menu, then select the Save As option (see Fig. 5.14). Since this is a budget, you can name it BUDGET1.

1. Point to the File item on the main menu.

2. Press and hold the ⌒.

3. Drag the pointer to the Save As option on the pull-down menu.

4. Release the ⌒.

A dialog box similar to the one in Fig. 5.15 should appear.

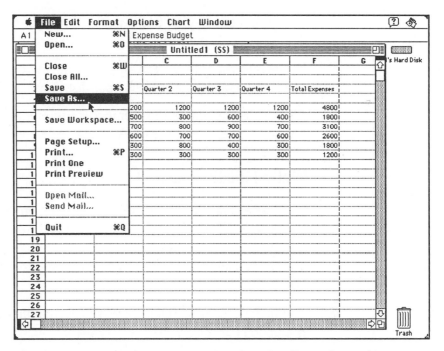

Fig. 5.14 File pull-down menu showing the Save As option

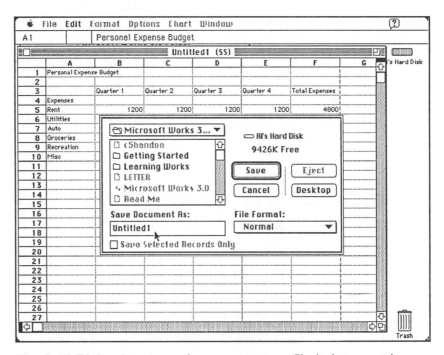

Fig. 5.15 Dialog box to assign a name to a file being saved

Type in the name desired. (You can modify an existing name by adding or deleting characters.)

> 5. Without moving the pointer, type **BUDGET1** to name the spreadsheet.

6. Press ⌸ **return** ⌸ to save the spreadsheet named BUDGET1. (You could have selected the Save button.)

You are returned to the spreadsheet once the save operation is completed. If you encounter problems here, check your disk drive.

The spreadsheet remains in memory for reference and editing, but a copy is now saved on disk as a permanent copy.

Printing the Spreadsheet

You have entered the spreadsheet and saved it on disk. If you want a copy on paper, you can also print it. Remember that you are printing the spreadsheet that is in memory, not the one on disk. The Print command is located on the File pull-down menu. When preparing to print, be sure that the printer is on and has paper loaded.

To print the document, select the File item from the main menu, then select the Print option (see Fig. 5.16).

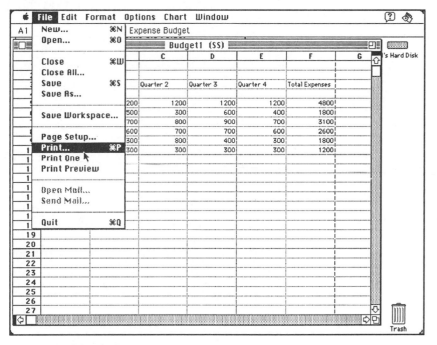

Fig. 5.16 File pull-down menu showing Print option

1. Point to the File item on the main menu.

2. Press and hold the .

3. Drag the pointer to the Print option.

4. Release the .

146

You will get a Print Options dialog box like the one in Fig. 5.17. If your printer is not a DeskWriter, the box may be slightly different. You don't need to change any options in this box. To print the document, select the OK button.

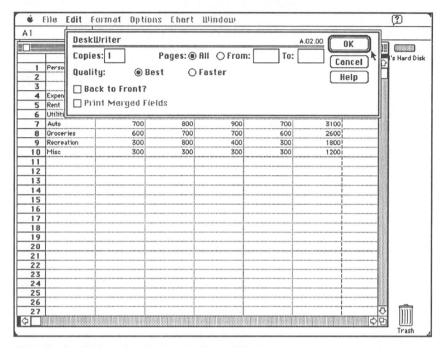

Fig. 5.17 Dialog box containing print options

     5. Move the pointer to ⌈ OK ⌋.

     6. Click the ⌁ to print the spreadsheet.

You are returned to the spreadsheet.

Displaying and Printing the Formulas

To review the formula entries, you will change the display to Show Formulas to show the actual cell entries rather than the result of the calculations. The Show Formulas option is on the Options menu (see Fig. 5.18).

     1. Point to the Options item on the main menu.

     2. Press and hold the ⌁.

     3. Drag the pointer to the Show Formulas option.

     4. Release the ⌁.

You should now see the formula entries for the Total Expenses column. Cell F10 may display #s because the formula is too long to be displayed. You could widen the column at this point to see all the formula, or you could make F10 the active cell and see the formula on the edit line.

     5. Point to cell F10, and click the ⌁ to make it active.

6. Review the formula on the edit line and change it if necessary.

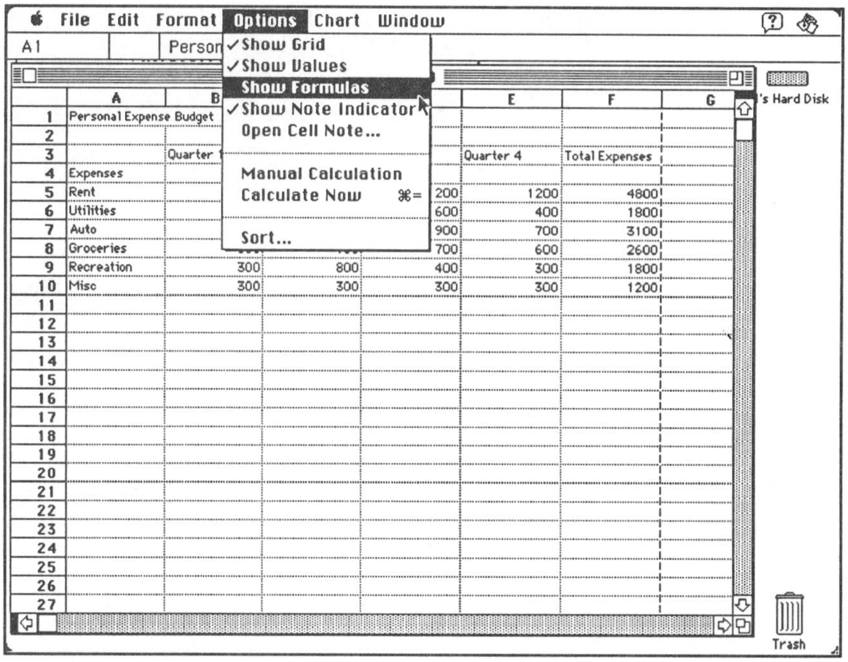

Fig. 5.18 Options pull-down menu showing the Show Formulas
option

To print a hard copy of the formula information for review, follow the print procedure specified above for printing the spreadsheet. Since formulas are displayed, they will be printed.

7. Using the print procedure in the preceding section, print the spreadsheet.

Once the formula entries have been reviewed, the option used to display formula entries should be turned off. This is done by selecting the Show Values option on the Options pull-down menu.

8. Point to the Options item on the main menu.

9. Press and hold the ⬚.

10. Drag the pointer to the Show Values option (refer to Fig. 5.18).

11. Release the ⬚.

Notice that a check indicates which of the two options is active. The check will be on the Show Values option after it is selected.

The spreadsheet should return to display mode.

Closing the File

Once you have completed the document, you are ready to close the file, which removes it from memory, but leaves the saved copy on disk for later use. If you have made changes since the last time you saved it, the program will ask you if you want to save the changes prior to closing the file.

The Close option is on the File pull-down menu depicted in Fig. 5.19. The file can be closed by selecting the File item from the main menu, then selecting the Close option, or by selecting the close box on the left end of the title bar.

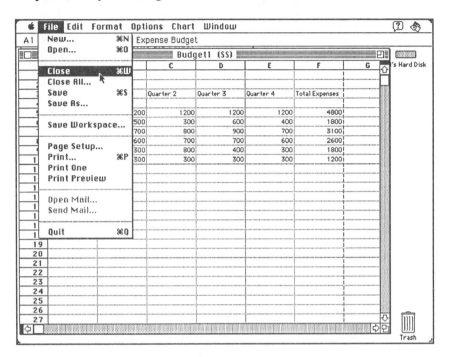

Fig. 5.19 File pull-down menu showing Close option

1. Point to the File item on the main menu.

2. Press and hold the .

3. Drag the pointer to the Close option.

4. Release the .

5. If you are prompted to save changes, select [Yes].

Exiting Works

To continue working on files once the file is closed, you would create a new file or open an existing one. Once you have completed the work session and are ready to leave Works, with the Microsoft Works 3.0 Folder active, select the Quit option from the File pull-down menu (see Fig. 5.20). (If this option is not available, reopen BUDGET1 by double clicking on the BUDGET1 file icon, and close it again.)

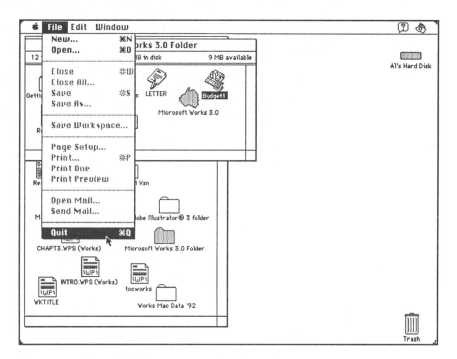

Fig. 5.20 File pull-down menu showing Quit option

1. Point to the File item on the main menu.

2. Press and hold the ⬤.

3. Drag the pointer to the Quit option.

4. Release the ⬤.

This should close the Works application, thus changing the icon to a picture rather than a shaded image.

To close the Works folder, select the Close Window option from the File pull-down menu, or point to the close box on the left end of the title bar, and click the mouse button.

5. Point to the File item on the main menu.

6. Press and hold the ⬤.

7. Drag the pointer to the Close Window option.

8. Release the ⬤.

This should return you to the Opening System Disk window (see Fig. 5.21).

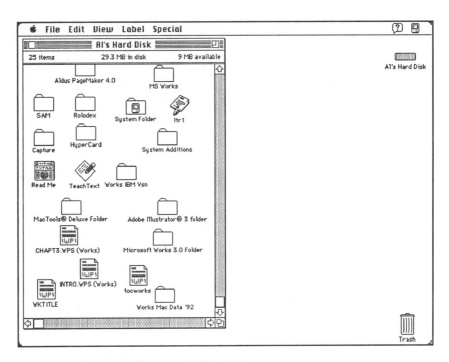

Fig. 5.21 Opening System Disk window

PART II

Retrieving the Spreadsheet

To retrieve an existing spreadsheet from the disk into memory, select the document icon from the window, select the folder icon of the folder containing the file, or select the file from a list of file names in the Works Opening dialog box. To continue our established sequence, if the machine is off, turn it on. If you are in the Opening System Disk window, first select the Microsoft Works 3.0 Folder from the folders on your disk. Then select the Works icon indicating Microsoft Works 3.0 to access the Works Opening dialog box.

You will retrieve the BUDGET1 spreadsheet created in PART I. If you did not create the spreadsheet, refer to the data in Fig. 5.10 and create a spreadsheet including the information depicted, and then save the spreadsheet in a file named BUDGET1.

Retrieve the spreadsheet in the file named BUDGET1.

> 1. From the Opening System Disk window, move the pointer to the Microsoft Works 3.0 Folder icon, and double click the ⌒.

This should open the Works Application window.

> 2. Referencing the Microsoft Works 3.0 Folder, move the pointer to the icon representing Microsoft Works 3.0, and double click the ⌒.

You should now see the Works Opening dialog box depicted in Fig. 5.22.

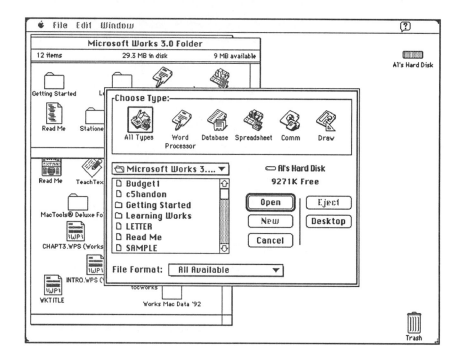

Fig. 5.22 Works Opening dialog box

3. Move the pointer to the Spreadsheet icon, and click the ⌂.

The spreadsheet files should now be displayed in the list box.

4. Highlight the BUDGET1 name in the list box of folder and document names by pointing to it and clicking the ⌂. (It may already be highlighted.)

5. Move the pointer to ⌈Open⌉ and click the ⌂.

The BUDGET1 file should be opened and displayed on the desktop. It is now available for use.

Editing the Spreadsheet

Any changes made will be made to the copy of the spreadsheet currently in memory. Once the editing is completed, the copy of the file on disk must be updated by saving the modified spreadsheet to disk. It is also a good idea to periodically save the spreadsheet as you are making changes, to protect yourself against problems that can occur during editing.

The spreadsheet you currently have in memory should look like the spreadsheet in Fig. 5.23. You will modify the spreadsheet by adding data and making further changes to it. You will add a total row that includes totals for each quarter and a total for the year. You will then modify some of the existing budget amounts.

	A	B	C	D	E	F
	File Edit Format Options Chart Window					
A2						
			Budget1 (SS)			
1	Personal Expense Budget					
2						
3		Quarter 1	Quarter 2	Quarter 3	Quarter 4	Total Expenses
4	Expenses					
5	Rent	1200	1200	1200	1200	4800
6	Utilities	500	300	600	400	1800
7	Auto	700	800	900	700	3100
8	Groceries	600	700	700	600	2600
9	Recreation	300	800	400	300	1800
10	Misc	300	300	300	300	1200
11						
12						
13						
14						
15						
16						
17						
18						
19						
20						
21						

Fig. 5.23 Sample spreadsheet containing labels, values, and formulas

You will first move the cell pointer to cell A12 and enter the label "Total" into the cell. Then you will use the SUM function to create totals for each of the columns, including the total column, by entering the function in the appropriate column of row 12.

1. Move the pointer to cell A12.

2. Click the ⊂⊃ to make the cell active.

3. Type the word **Total**.

4. Press [tab]. (Notice that you recorded the data and moved to the next desired cell with a single key.)

5. Type the function =**SUM(B5:B10)** and press [tab].

(You should see 3600 in the display of cell B12.)

6. In cell C12, type the function =**SUM(C5:C10)**, and press [tab].

7. In cell D12, type the function =**SUM(D5:D10)**, and press [tab].

8. In cell E12, type the function =**SUM(E5:E10)**, and press [tab].

9. In cell F12, type the function =**SUM(F5:F10)**, and press [return].

The additional row of totals is now complete.

You will make two changes to data values using the Edit feature. You will change the second quarter Auto expense to 1200, projecting a major repair. You will change fourth quarter Utilities to 500, projecting an earlier winter.

10. Move the pointer to cell C7.

11 Click the ⬿ to make the cell active.

12. Move the pointer to the right of the 8 in 800 on the edit line.

13. Click the ⬿ to designate the insertion point.

14. Press ‖ delete ∎ to remove the 8.

15. Type **12** to make the entry 1200.

16. Press ‖ return ∎.

You should see 1200 in cell C7, and the totals should change accordingly.

17. Move the pointer to cell E6.

18. Click the ⬿ to activate the cell.

19. Move the pointer to the right of the 4 in 400 on the edit line.

20. Click the ⬿ to designate the insertion point.

21. Press ‖ delete ∎ to remove the 4.

22. Type **5** to make the entry 500.

23. Press ‖ return ∎.

Cell E6 should now contain 500.

As the two values were changed, the spreadsheet automatically recalculated the totals relating to them. The spreadsheet should now look like Fig. 5.24. If it doesn't, review your entries and correct them as necessary.

	A	B	C	D	E	F
1	Personal Expense Budget					
2						
3		Quarter 1	Quarter 2	Quarter 3	Quarter 4	Total Expenses
4	Expenses					
5	Rent	1200	1200	1200	1200	4800
6	Utilities	500	300	600	500	1900
7	Auto	700	1200	900	700	3500
8	Groceries	600	700	700	600	2600
9	Recreation	300	800	400	300	1800
10	Misc	300	300	300	300	1200
11						
12	Total	3600	4500	4100	3600	15800
13						
14						
15						
16						
17						
18						
19						
20						
21						

Menu bar: File Edit Format Options Chart Window — A2 — Budget1 (SS)

Fig. 5.24 Sample spreadsheet with SUM function and value changes

Saving the Spreadsheet

You now have a spreadsheet that has been edited. You want to save it on the disk. Since the spreadsheet is already named BUDGET1, you will use the Save option rather than the Save As option.

Select the File pull-down menu, then select the Save option (see Fig. 5.25).

1. Point to the File item on the main menu.

2. Press and hold the ⬿.

3. Drag the pointer to the Save option on the pull-down menu.

4. Release the ⬿.

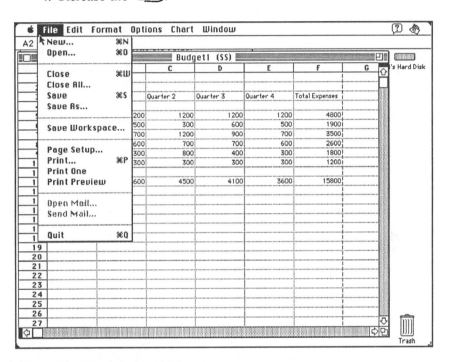

Fig. 5.25 File pull-down menu

You are returned to the spreadsheet when the save operation is completed. The spreadsheet remains in memory for reference and editing, but a current copy is now saved on disk as a permanent copy.

Printing the Spreadsheet

You have entered the spreadsheet and saved it on disk. If you want a copy on paper, you can also print it. Remember that you are printing the spreadsheet that is in memory, not the one on disk. The Print command is located on the File pull-down menu (refer to Fig. 5.25). When preparing to print, be sure that the printer is on and has paper loaded.

1. Point to the File item on the main menu.

2. Press and hold the ⌒.

3. Drag the pointer to the Print option.

4. Release the ⌒.

You will get a Print Options dialog box. To print the document, move the pointer to the OK button and click the ⌒.

5. Move the pointer to [OK].

6. Click the ⌒ to print the spreadsheet.

You are returned to the spreadsheet.

Closing the File

Once you have completed the document, you are ready to close the file, which removes it from memory, but leaves the saved copy on disk for later use. If you have made changes since the last time you saved it, the program will ask you if you want to save the changes prior to closing the file.

The Close option is on the File pull-down menu (refer to Fig. 5.25). You can close the file by selecting the close option or by selecting the close box on the left end of the title bar.

1. Point to the File item on the main menu.

2. Press and hold the ⌒.

3. Drag the pointer to the Close option.

4. Release the ⌒.

Exiting Works

To continue working on files once the file is closed, you would create a new file or open an existing one. Once you have completed the work session and are ready to leave Works. With the Microsoft Works 3.0 Folder active, select the Quit option from the File pull-down menu. (If this option is not available, reopen BUDGET1 by double clicking on the BUDGET1 file icon, and close it again.)

1. Point to the File item on the main menu.

2. Press and hold the ⌒.

3. Drag the pointer to the Quit option.

4. Release the ⌒.

This should close the Works application.

To close the Works folder, select the Close Window option from the File pull-down menu, or point to the close box on the left end of the title bar, and click the mouse button.

5. Point to the File item on the main menu.

6. Press and hold the ⬜.

7. Drag the pointer to the Close Window option.

8. Release the ⬜.

This should return you to the Opening System Disk window.

If you have completed the work session, use the shut down procedure to terminate the machine operation.

Summary

Spreadsheets are widely used in applications involving tables of numbers, particularly if changes and recalculations are involved. The automated worksheet can be designed to look like its manual counterpart. It can include rows and columns of data, labels to identify the entries, and formulas to provide calculated results. The entry and printing of the spreadsheet on the computer do not provide significant enhancement over manual alternatives. However, the ability to add and change data and to have results recalculated automatically provides a useful tool for financial modeling.

The worksheet is comprised of rows and columns, with each intersection of a row and a column referred to as a cell, which has an identifier name. The active cell is the one currently referenced by the cell pointer. The cell pointer can be moved anywhere in the worksheet to add, modify, or delete labels, values, or formulas in the worksheet. The completed worksheet, containing data, is referred to as a spreadsheet.

Questions

1. Describe the general characteristics of a spreadsheet.

2. What is a cell? A cell address? An active cell?

3. What is the difference between a worksheet and a spreadsheet?

4. Contrast label, value, and formula, and give an example of each.

5. Identify the purpose of each of the following keys when moving the cell pointer in a spreadsheet.

   RIGHT ARROW

LEFT ARROW

UP ARROW

DOWN ARROW

HOME

PGUP

PGDN

RETURN

TAB

SHIFT/RETURN

SHIFT/TAB

6. What happens when a label is too large to fit into a cell?

7. What happens when a value is too large to fit into a cell?

8. Explain the process used to edit a cell in Works.

Exercises

Exercise 1

Create a table of personnel information including name, status, department, and salary using the data below:

	A	B	C	D
1	EMPLOYEE INFORMATION FOR MY COMPANY			
2				
3	Name	Status	Dept.	Salary
4				
5	Brown	PT	R&D	22000
6	Carter	FT	R&D	38000
7	Jeffcoat	FT	ADMIN	44000
8	Saunders	PT	R&D	26000
9	Thompson	FT	MKT	34000

1. Enter the title in cell A1.

2. Enter the labels identifying each column into row 3 of columns A, B, C, and D.

3. Enter the data into rows 5 through 9.

4. Save the spreadsheet onto disk as EMPLOYEE.

5. Print the spreadsheet.

Exercise 2

Create a table of salary budget information using the data below:

	A	B	C	D	E	F
1		My Company				
2		Salary Budget				
3						
4	Name	Qtr1	Qtr2	Qtr3	Qtr4	Total
5						
6	Brown	8000	6000	6000	2000	22000
7	Carter	9500	9500	9500	9500	38000
8	Jeffcoat	11000	11000	11000	11000	44000
9	Saunders	2000	6000	9000	9000	26000
10	Thompson	8500	8500	8500	8500	34000
11						
12	Total	39000	41000	44000	40000	164000

1. Enter the title "My Company" in cell B1.

2. Enter the title "Salary Budget" in cell B2.

3. Enter the column labels in cells A4 through F4.

4. Enter the names in cells A6 through A10.

5. Enter the quarterly data into cells B6 through E10.

6. Enter formulas for employee totals into cells F6 through F10.

7. Enter the label "Total" in A12.

8. Enter the SUM function to total columns into cells B12 through F12.

9. Save the spreadsheet as SALBUDGT.

10. Print the spreadsheet.

11. Print the spreadsheet in formula mode.

Problems

Problem 1

Create an income statement similar to the one shown below. Put the labels in columns A and B, and put the numbers in column C. Use the SUM function to get Total Revenue. Use the SUM function to get Total Expense. Use a formula to get Net Income (Total Revenue - Total Expense). Save the spreadsheet. Print the spreadsheet in both display and formula mode.

	A	B	C
1	My Company		
2	Income Statement: March, 1994		
3			
4	Revenue:		
5	Dept. A		14000
6	Dept. B		22000
7	Dept. C		11000
8	Total Revenue		47000
9			
10	Expenses:		
11	Dept. A		9000
12	Dept. B		12000
13	Dept. C		8000
14	Admin.		9000
15	Total Expense		38000
16			
17	Net Income		9000

Problem 2

Create a spreadsheet showing the following repayment schedule for a loan of $1,000 for one year (repaying $1140 including the interest).

Enter the third column for months 1 through 12 by using a formula. For example, if the month 1 balance is in cell C6, the formula C5 - B6 would subtract the payment from the previous balance, leaving the new balance. The formula in C7 would be C6 - B7, and so on.

Save the spreadsheet. Print the spreadsheet in both display and formula modes.

	A	B	C
1	Loan Payment Schedule		
2			
3	Month	Payment	Balance
4			
5	0	0	1140
6	1	95	1045
7	2	95	950
8	3	95	855
9	4	95	760
10	5	95	665
11	6	95	570
12	7	95	475
13	8	95	380
14	9	95	285
15	10	95	190
16	11	95	95
17	12	95	0

Problem 3

Starting with the EMPLOYEE spreadsheet in Exercise 1, print a copy of the spreadsheet, and then make the following changes. Save the updated spreadsheet and print a display copy of it.

Saunders is converted from a part-time (PT) to a full-time (FT) employee.

Saunders' salary is increased from 26000 to 32000.

Carter's salary is increased from 38000 to 42000.

Jeffcoat's salary is increased from 44000 to 48000.

Add an employee named Dawson, who is part-time in the R&D Department and makes a salary of 16000.

Problem 4

Starting with the SALBUDGT spreadsheet in Exercise 2, print a copy of the spreadsheet and then make the following changes.

Change Saunders' salary to 8000 in each quarter.

Change Carter's salary to 10500 in each quarter.

Change Jeffcoat's salary to 12000 in each quarter.

Notice that the totals should recompute automatically.

Add an employee named Tyson who is budgeted to make 0 in the first quarter, 6000 in the second quarter, 6000 in the third quarter, and 4000 in the fourth quarter. Make adjustments in the spacing, formulas, and functions as necessary to complete the spreadsheet.

Save the updated spreadsheet.

Print a display and a formula copy.

Chapter 6

Managing the Spreadsheet

Objectives

After completing this chapter you will

1. Be able to distinguish between developing and maintaining a spreadsheet.

2. Be able to explain the significance of worksheet modification features such as adding rows and columns, deleting rows and columns, and formatting cells.

3. Be able to explain the significance of copying, moving, and deleting data in a spreadsheet.

4. Be able to define and explain the concept of range definition and usage.

5. Be able to define and explain the concepts of relative and absolute addressing.

6. Be able to insert and delete rows and columns in Works.

7. Be able to format worksheet cells to include fixed decimal places, commas, dollar signs, percent signs, or scientific notation.

8. Be able to format worksheet cells to include left, center, or right placement of data.

9. Be able to format worksheet cells to include date format.

10. Be able to copy a cell or range of cells in a worksheet.

11. Be able to move a cell or range of cells in a worksheet.

12. Be able to delete the contents of a cell, a range of cells, or all the entries in a worksheet.

Managing the Spreadsheet

Applying the Spreadsheet

As we have seen in Chapter 5, the spreadsheet consists of a worksheet and data. The worksheet is the rows and columns of cells that form the foundation for the spreadsheet. The data consists of labels, values, formulas, and functions entered into it that provide information to the user.

As you will see in this chapter, both the worksheet and the data can be modified in order to maintain and improve the ability of the spreadsheet to provide desired results. Changes can be made to the structure and format of the cells. The data can be modified and manipulated within the cells.

Manipulating the Worksheet

In looking at a handwritten worksheet, it is typical to have all cells exactly the same size. This is true of automated worksheets also, until they are modified. It is common when building or maintaining a spreadsheet to want columns to be narrow when small values are entered or wide when large values are entered.

Spreadsheet programs provide the ability to adjust the width of all cells in the worksheet or to adjust the width of only specified columns of cells. The typical starting size of worksheet cells in a program is 8, 9, 10, or 12, meaning that this is the number of character positions in each cell. When planning the worksheet, it is important to review samples of the data that will be placed in it, and plan the cell widths accordingly. If the data will contain no more than four or five characters, the default cell width will leave more space between the values than desired, unless the width of the cells is reduced. If the data will contain 12 or more characters, the cells must be widened in order for the data to be stored in them. Columns containing labels commonly need to be wider than columns containing the other types of data to hold long names, while columns containing numeric data may be of varying widths, depending on the size of the values. It is common to have some columns wide and others narrow in a spreadsheet.

In the course of developing and using a spreadsheet, it is common to want the displayed data to have characteristics that enhance its presentation and utility. Formatting of worksheet cells can cause numeric data to include such formats as fixed (which specifies a number of decimal places), currency (which adds a dollar sign), percentage (which adds a percent sign), and scientific notation (which uses exponential format).

Global commands in a spreadsheet are commands that apply to all the cells or all the data. A global command is typically available in a spreadsheet program to change the width of all cells in the spreadsheet to a specified size. A local command is also available, which will change the width of a single column to a specified size. Also, by using the range selection capability, a series of column widths can be adjusted at one time, using the command to change cell widths. Range commands take precedence over global commands. The commands to adjust cell width can be applied before entering data or after the spreadsheet is completed. It is important to realize that cell sizes within a single column cannot vary.

Once the spreadsheet is developed, it is inevitable that changes will be made that involve adding or removing a row or column of data. For example, if each row contains data for one employee, then adding an employee will warrant the need for adding a row of data, and terminating an employee will warrant the need to delete a row of data. To add a row of data requires a blank row of cells in the worksheet. To delete a row of data without deleting the cells would leave an unwanted blank row of cells within the data. In a manual spreadsheet, this process is accomplished by cutting the spreadsheet and pasting it back together with the desired rows (referred to as a "cut and paste" operation), or the spreadsheet data must be put into a new worksheet.

Spreadsheet programs provide the ability to automatically add rows and columns to the worksheet. This is typically done by a command that will insert a row between two existing rows or insert a column between two existing columns. Commonly the command will allow for specifying the number of rows or columns to be inserted, facilitating the addition of multiple rows or columns with one command.

Programs also provide the ability to remove rows and columns from the worksheet, whether or not they contain data. This is typically done by a command that will delete a row or column from between two other rows or columns. Commonly the delete command will allow for specifying the number of rows or columns to be deleted, facilitating multiple row or column deletions in one command.

The distinction between data in memory (referred to as formula format) and data displayed on the monitor (referred to as display format) is significant. It is not important that the data in memory have a dollar sign to indicate dollars, or consistency in the number of decimal places. But data displayed on the monitor or printed on a printer should be readable and aesthetically pleasing to the user. Typical business reports include a fixed number of decimal places and often include dollar signs.

Other formatting characteristics include the placement of commas after every third digit, since commas are not entered with the data and not stored in memory. A number that is to represent a percentage can be displayed with a percent sign following it. Percentage format also will multiply the stored value by 100 (0.03 would be displayed as 3%). Very large or very small numbers can be stored in scientific notation, which depicts a number and an exponent factor. The value of the exponent will adjust the decimal point to its true position

(3.4E+8 will move the decimal place 8 positions to the right and is actually the number 340000000). A negative exponent will move the decimal point to the left (2.6E-4 will convert to 0.00026).

Placement of data within cells is also a consideration. Although text is typically written from left to right and numbers are typically aligned to the right, there are times when it is practical to position data differently in the cells. A typical example is the positioning of column headings over the data by aligning the labels to the center or right side of the cells. Spreadsheet programs provide the capability of having the data left, center, or right aligned in the worksheet cells, regardless of data type. Date formatting can also be used to format calender dates in a cell.

Worksheet manipulation features provide flexibility in planning and maintaining the structure of the worksheet. They should be used when appropriate to facilitate the development and maintenance of spreadsheets.

Manipulating the Data

It is common to copy, move, or delete the contents of a single cell or range of cells, both in developing and in maintaining a spreadsheet. It is also necessary at times to erase the entire contents of the spreadsheet in memory in order to create a new one.

Removing the contents of a cell from the spreadsheet might need to be done either because of entering data in the wrong place or because it is no longer needed. It is not appropriate to replace the cell contents with spaces. A delete command should be used that will remove the cell contents from the spreadsheet and leave the cell empty, as if it had not contained a data value at all. Removal of a range of cells is accomplished by identifying the range and then applying the delete command. This is practical when a particular segment of the spreadsheet is no longer needed. A command is commonly available that will delete the contents of the entire spreadsheet. This is appropriate when the current spreadsheet is no longer needed and the worksheet needs to be erased in order to begin developing a new one.

Moving data from one cell to another is sometimes done during development of a spreadsheet because of a change in overall structure or simply to rearrange the data. Moving data may be done during maintenance for essentially the same reasons. Generally, movement of a single cell or a range of cells should be possible.

Copying cell contents provides a way to enter a series of identical values or to replicate a process, such as a formula or function. Generally, data can be copied from one cell to another cell, from one cell to a range of cells, or from a range of cells to another range of cells. For example, in an expense budget, the January car payment amount might be copied into the February car payment cell. The January car payment might be copied into the other 11 months of the year, or the January car payment, rent, and groceries might be copied into the other 11 months in one command. A formula or function to compute the total might be copied from one cell into another cell. The copy feature facilitates entry of large amounts of similar data, including functions and formulas.

The concepts of relative and absolute addressing are applied during copy and move operations. Relative addressing refers to the adjustment of address references as cells containing formulas or functions are copied. For example, if cell B7 contains A5 + B6 and it is copied to D10, then B7 contains A5 + B6, and D10 will contain C8 + D9. If the same copy had been done with B7 containing absolute rather than relative references, the contents of both B7 and D10 would be A5 + B6. This is a complicated concept for the beginning spreadsheet user, but a significant one.

The above-mentioned features and others make the entry and maintenance of data faster and more effective. Without the ability to manipulate existing data, the utility of spreadsheet programs would be reduced significantly.

Modifying Worksheets and Manipulating Data with Works

Worksheet Modification

Worksheets can be modified by adding or deleting rows or columns. Cell characteristics can also be set to have the data displayed in a specific format.

Adding Rows and Columns

During development and maintenance of a spreadsheet, it may be found that an additional row or column is needed between rows or columns of data already entered. In the Works program, you can insert a row or column between two existing rows or columns. Highlight the row or column where insertion is to take place by moving the pointer to the row or column label (e.g., B for column B or 6 for row 6) and clicking the mouse button. Then select the Insert command from the Edit pull-down menu (see Fig. 6.1). If a column label is highlighted, that column and all columns to its right are moved to the right one column, and a new column is inserted. If a row label is highlighted, that row and all rows below it are moved down a row, and a new row is inserted.

Deleting Rows and Columns

When removing data from a spreadsheet, it is often desirable to remove the row or column that contains the data. To do this in Works, move the pointer to the row or column label, and click the mouse button to highlight it. Then select the

Cut option from the Edit pull-down menu (refer to Fig. 6.1). The highlighted row or column will be deleted, along with any data in it. If a column is deleted, all columns to its right will move to the left one column to close the gap. If a row is deleted, all rows below it will move up a row to close the gap.

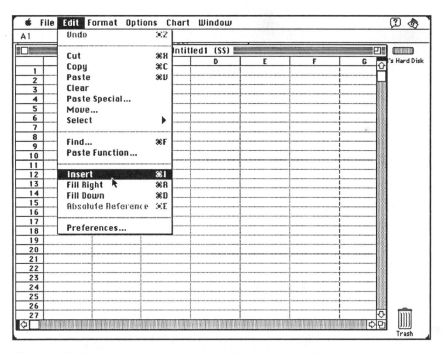

Fig. 6.1 Edit pull-down menu showing Insert option

Adjusting Column Width

The Works spreadsheet has a default column width of 12 character positions for each cell. In planning the layout of the spreadsheet, it is commonly necessary to modify the width of one or more columns of the worksheet. To change the column width, select the column by moving the pointer to the column label and clicking the mouse button to highlight the column. Then select the Column Width command found on the Format pull-down menu (see Fig. 6.2). Once the command is selected, a dialog box will be displayed that allows you to specify the number of character positions to allocate to the highlighted column.

The cell width of multiple columns can be adjusted by selecting the range of column labels to modify. Move the pointer to the label of the first column of the range, press and hold the mouse button, drag the pointer to the last column, and then release the mouse button. Then select the Column Width command. The number of character positions specified will then apply to the range of columns selected rather than to a single column.

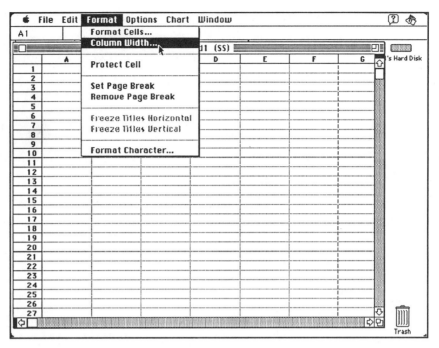

Fig. 6.2 Format pull-down menu showing Column Width option

Formatting Cells

The display format of data within cells can be enhanced by specifying the format of the cell in the worksheet. Individual cells or ranges of cells can be assigned a specific format. If more than one cell is to be formatted by a single command, select the range prior to implementing the format option. Once the cell is active or the range is highlighted, the formatting options can be applied by choosing Format Cells from the Format pull-down menu (see Fig. 6.3). The Format Cells dialog box provides options to include left, center, or right placement in the cell and number, date, or time format (see Fig. 6.4). Number format provides an Appearance list box of options for general, fixed, comma, currency, percentage, or scientific format, with an option to specify the number of decimal places to include in a value. Date or Time format provides a list of formatting options in the Appearance list box for displaying the date or time.

Character alignment within a cell can be applied to both numeric and label (text) data. The entry can be left, center, or right justified. The default alignment for text is left justified and the default alignment for numbers is right justified. Alignment of data in the cells can be specified before or after data is entered and can pertain to one cell or a range of cells. First highlight the cell or cells, then select the appropriate option.

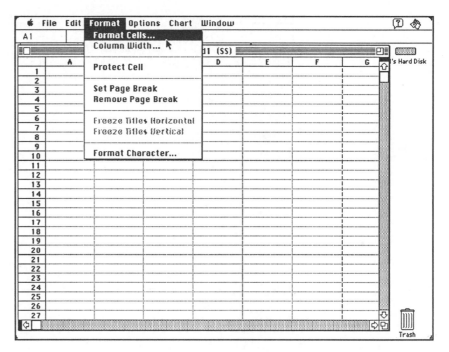

Fig. 6.3 Format pull-down menu showing Format Cells option

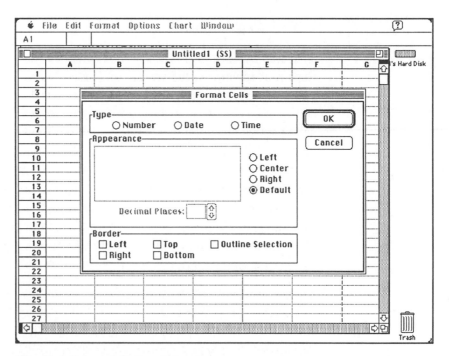

Fig. 6.4 Format Cells dialog box

Numeric data can appear exactly as it is typed in or have enhancements added
to its display by selecting the Number button in the Format Cells dialog box
and then selecting the appearance option desired. Once an option is selected
from the Appearance list box, the number of decimal places can be specified
(see Fig. 6.5). Appearance options for numeric data include general, fixed,
comma, currency, percent, and scientific notation.

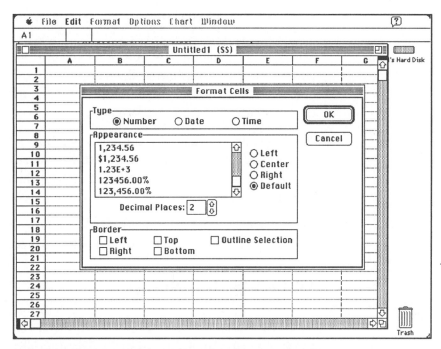

Fig. 6.5 Format Cells dialog box showing Number list box and
        Decimal Places box

General is the default number appearance, and it displays the data exactly as it is entered. It will use exponential notation or #s for a large number or round fractional positions of a long fraction if the number of digits is too large to fit in the cell. Negative numbers are displayed with a minus sign.

Fixed format assigns a specific number of decimal places to the value by adding decimal places or rounding off extra decimal places to express the desired number. Negative numbers are displayed with a minus sign.

Comma format is the same as fixed format, but includes a comma before every third whole number position, as appropriate. This option is found in the list box as a number containing four whole number positions with a comma between the first and second number from the left. The number of decimal places is selected after the option is chosen.

Currency format is chosen by selecting an option with a dollar sign ($) to its left. It includes the specified number of decimal places as in fixed format and a $ to its left. Depending on the currency option chosen, it can also include commas as in comma format. Negative dollar amounts are placed in parentheses.

Percent format is selected by highlighting one of the options with a percent sign (%) to its right. It multiplies the number by 100 and displays a percent sign following it. The number of decimal places is specified as in fixed format, and commas can be included if the item containing a comma is selected. A negative percentage is preceded by a minus sign.

171

Scientific format displays the number in scientific notation. For example, 3261000 would be displayed as 3.26E+06. Small numbers will have a negative exponent. For example, 0.00000172 would be displayed as 1.72E-06. Negative numbers are preceded by a minus sign. For example, -61740000 would be displayed as -6.17E+07. The number of decimal places is selected once the option is chosen, as in fixed format.

The Date option in the Format Cells dialog box (refer to Fig. 6.4) displays the contents of a cell in date format. The date can be displayed in a variety of formats, all of which are displayed in the Appearance list box when the Date button is selected.

The Time option in the Format Cells dialog box displays the contents of a cell in time format. The desired format is selected from the Appearance list box.

Data Manipulation

The data stored in cells can be moved, copied, and deleted as necessary. Functions can also be applied to the data to produce information.

Deleting Cell Contents

It is often necessary to delete the contents of a cell, either to clear the area or to replace it with something else. The cell should be highlighted. Then select the Clear option from the Edit pull-down menu (see Fig. 6.6). To delete the data from a range of cells, highlight the range, then select the Clear option from the Edit pull-down menu. The data can be erased from the entire spreadsheet by choosing the Select option on the Edit pull-down menu (see Fig. 6.6) and the All option on the Select submenu to highlight the entire spreadsheet, then selecting the Clear option.

Moving Cell Contents

Once data is entered into the spreadsheet, it may be necessary to move it to a different location. This could occur because of a design error, an entry error, or through normal maintenance of the spreadsheet.

To move the contents of a single cell, place the cell pointer on the cell, select the Cut command from the Edit pull-down menu (see Fig. 6.6), move the cell pointer to the new location, and select the Paste command from the Edit menu (see Fig. 6.6). The original (source) location should then be empty and the new (target or destination) location should contain the data. If the entry contains references to other cells (i.e., a formula or function), the effect of the move should be reviewed to be sure that it is referencing the appropriate locations after the move is completed.

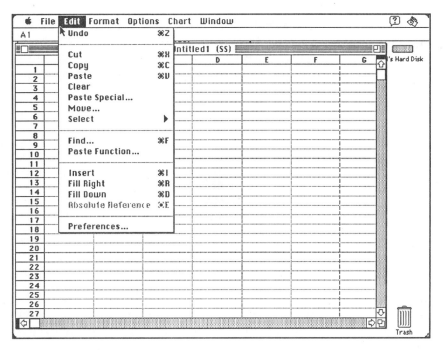

Fig. 6.6 Edit pull-down menu

When moving a range of cells, the first step is to highlight the range. Once the range is highlighted, select the Cut command from the Edit menu. Then move the cell pointer to the upper left corner of the destination area and select the Paste command. The original range of cells (the source location) should then be empty and the new range (target location) should contain the data. You should verify any addresses contained in the data for accuracy.

Copying Cell Contents

It is often practical to copy the contents of one or more cells into other locations of the spreadsheet. This facilitates entry of identical data into many cells. It also allows for repeating formulas that have identical or relatively identical references.

To copy the contents of a cell from one address to another one (called a "one to one" copy), move the cell pointer to the source location, select the Copy command from the Edit pull-down menu (see Fig. 6.6), move the cell pointer to the target (destination) location, and select the Paste command from the Edit pull-down menu. Both cells should now contain the same data, although any relative cell address will change during the copy. For example, if cell B5 contains the number 16 and it's copied to cell C5, cell C5 will contain 16 after the copy. If cell B5 contains =$A$2+$A$3 and is copied to cell C5, cell C5 will also contain =$A$2+$A$3 after the copy, since the $ indicates absolute addressing. But if cell B5 contains =B2+B3 and is copied to cell C5, C5 will contain =C2+C3 after the copy, because of relative addressing.

Sometimes it is practical to copy the contents of one cell into several adjacent cells. For example, the projected car payment for January may be identical for

173

February through December. To copy the contents of a single cell into several cells (a "one to many" copy), first place the cell pointer on the source cell. Select the range into which the data entry is to be repeated (with the source cell being the first cell in the range). Then select the Fill Down or Fill Right option, depending on the direction of the range. Copying into a noncontiguous series or into multiple rows or columns is more complicated, and will not be discussed in detail here. However, a common situation is to copy one cell into several noncontiguous locations. This can be done by copying the contents into the clipboard, then repeating the paste process into each of the destination cells.

It is common to copy the contents of a range of cells into another range of cells of equal size and shape. For example, the February budget entries may be identical to the entries for January. You can select the range of cells to be copied. Then select the Copy command from the Edit menu. Move the pointer to the upper left corner of the destination range and click the mouse button. Then select the Paste option from the Edit menu. The contents of the source range of cells should now be in both the source and destination ranges. Be sure to check any addresses that were in the cells to verify that they reference the desired area.

Functions

Works has a number of functions that are available for use with spreadsheets. The SUM function, already presented, is one example. The general characteristics of a function include the function name, followed by parentheses that contain what is called the "argument." If two or more argument entries are required for a function, they will be separated by commas. When entered, the function is preceded by the equal sign. The value produced by the function will be displayed in the cell. Table 6.1 contains several commonly used functions and their purposes.

Display and Print Options

Two additional printing options can be used to enhance the spreadsheet output. The Show Grid option is found on the Options pull-down menu. The default setting is on. Selecting it turns it off, displaying the spreadsheet without grid lines. This allows you to print the data without grid lines by selecting the option prior to printing. Selecting it again will cause grid lines to be displayed.

The second option allows you to rotate the print 90 degrees on the page to print the spreadsheet sideways. The feature is applicable when the spreadsheet is wider than the page width, and the length is short enough to fit within the page width after rotating it. The option, when available, is found in the Page Setup dialog box. Select the Page Setup option from the File pull-down menu, then look for an Orientation icon indicating the print will be facing the side rather than the top of the page. Select the icon to activate the option.

Function Name	Purpose
ABS	Absolute value
AVERAGE	Average of a list of values
COS, SIN, TAN	Trigonometry functions
COUNT	Counts the cells in a range
DATE, TIME, YEAR	Displays the date, time, or year
HLOOKUP, VLOOKUP	Searches a table
IF	Logical comparison
IRR	Internal rate of return
LN	Natural logarithm
LOG10	Base 10 logarithm
MAX, MIN	Largest or smallest value
MOD	Remainder
NPV	Net present value
PV	Present value
STDEV	Standard deviation
VAR	Variance

Table 6.1 Commonly used functions in Works

Hands-on Spreadsheet Manipulation

Retrieving the Spreadsheet

In this section, you will be modifying the BUDGET1 spreadsheet developed in Chapter 5. Prior to retrieving the spreadsheet from disk, you may want to make a backup copy into a different folder or onto a different disk. If you are not familiar with the process of copying documents in Works, refer to Chapter 2.

To retrieve an existing spreadsheet from the disk into memory, select the document icon from the window, select the folder icon of the folder containing the file, or select the file from a list of file names in the Works Opening dialog box. To continue our established sequence, if the machine is off, turn it on. If you are in the Opening System Disk window, first select the Microsoft Works 3.0 Folder from the folders on your disk. Then select the Works icon indicating Microsoft Works 3.0 to access the Works Opening dialog box.

You will retrieve the BUDGET1 spreadsheet created in Chapter 5. If you did not create the spreadsheet, refer to the data in Fig. 6.7 and create a spreadsheet including the information depicted. Use formulas for column F and functions for row 12 totals. Then save the spreadsheet in a file named BUDGET1.

🍎 File Edit Format Options Chart Window						
A1		Personal Expense Budget				
Budget1 (SS)						
	A	B	C	D	E	F
1	Personal Expense Budget					
2						
3		Quarter 1	Quarter 2	Quarter 3	Quarter 4	Total Expenses
4	Expenses					
5	Rent	1200	1200	1200	1200	4800
6	Utilities	500	300	600	500	1900
7	Auto	700	1200	900	700	3500
8	Groceries	600	700	700	600	2600
9	Recreation	300	800	400	300	1800
10	Misc	300	300	300	300	1200
11						
12	Total	3600	4500	4100	3600	15800
13						
14						
15						
16						
17						
18						
19						
20						
21						

Fig. 6.7 Sample spreadsheet containing labels, values, formulas, and functions

Retrieve the spreadsheet in the file named BUDGET1.

1. From the Opening System Disk window, move the pointer to the Microsoft Works 3.0 Folder icon, and double click the 🖱.

This should open the Works Application window.

2. From a reference to the Microsoft Works 3.0 Folder, move the pointer to the icon representing Microsoft Works 3.0, and double click the 🖱.

You should now see the Works Opening dialog box.

3. Move the pointer to the spreadsheet icon, and click the 🖱.

4. Highlight the BUDGET1 name on the list of folder and document names on the lower left of the dialog box by pointing to it and clicking the 🖱. (It may already be highlighted.)

5. Move the pointer to [Open] and click the 🖱.

The BUDGET1 file should be opened and displayed on the desktop. It is now available for use.

You will be modifying the spreadsheet to include actual expenses, along with the budgeted expenses already in it. When completed, it will look like Fig. 6.8.

Personal Expense Budget

EXPENSES	Quarter 1 Budget	Quarter 1 Actual	Quarter 2 Budget	Quarter 2 Actual	Quarter 3 Budget	Quarter 3 Actual	Quarter 4 Budget	Quarter 4 Actual	Total Expenses Budget	Total Expenses Actual
Rent	1,200	1,200	1,200	1,200	1,200		1,200		4,800	2,400
Utilities	500	450	300	320	600		500		1,900	770
Auto	700	650	1,200	1,100	900		700		3,500	1,750
Groceries	600	630	700	740	700		600		2,600	1,370
Recreation	300	370	800	700	400		300		1,800	1,070
Misc	300	300	300	350	300		300		1,200	650
Total	3,600	3,600	4,500	4,410	4,100	0	3,600	0	15,800	8,010

Fig. 6.8 Sample spreadsheet modified to include columns for actual expenditures

Moving the Data

First you will move the Expenses data down to provide space for headings for "Budget" columns and "Actual" columns. To do this, select the range A5 through F12 and move the data down one row, so that the data will be in rows 6 through 13.

    1. Place the pointer on cell A5.

    2. Press and hold the ⬚.

    3. Drag the pointer to cell F12.

    4. Release the ⬚.

The range from A5 through F12 should now be highlighted.

    5. Move the pointer to the Edit item on the main menu.

    6. Press and hold the ⬚.

    7. Drag the pointer to the Cut option (see Fig. 6.9).

    8. Release the ⬚.

The data should now be gone from the spreadsheet.

    9. Move the pointer to cell A6.

    10. Click the ⬚.

This highlights cell A6 and indicates the upper left corner of the destination (target) range.

11. Move the pointer to the Edit item on the main menu.

12. Press and hold the ⬚.

13. Drag the pointer to the Paste option (see Fig. 6.9).

14. Release the ⬚.

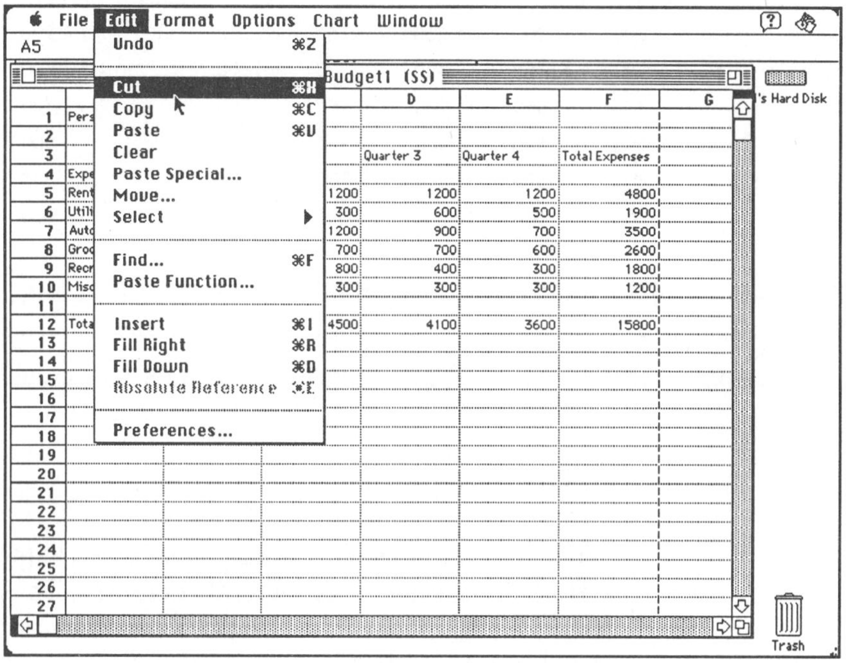

Fig. 6.9 Edit pull-down menu showing Cut option

The Move operation is now complete. Row 5 should now be blank. Note that this modification could have been accomplished by inserting a row between the original rows 4 and 5.

Adding New Columns

To make space for the "Actual" data for each quarter, you will add a column after each of the columns containing Quarter 1, Quarter 2, Quarter 3, and Quarter 4 data. A column does not need to be added for the Actual Total, since space is available to the right of the existing Total Expenses column. You will move the cell pointer to each of the columns containing second, third, and fourth quarter data and insert a column. Then move the cell pointer to the Total Column and insert a column.

1. Move the cell pointer to the top of column C (the box containing the letter C), and click the ⬚.

The entire column should now be highlighted.

2. Move the pointer to the Edit item on the main menu.

3. Press and hold the ⟨◯⟩.

4. Drag the pointer to the Insert option (refer to Fig. 6.9).

5. Release the ⟨◯⟩.

A new column C should now be on the window, between the Quarter 1 data and the Quarter 2 data.

You will notice that the formulas in the Total Expenses column and the functions in the Total row will adjust automatically as the columns are changed.

6. Move the pointer to the top of column E (now containing Quarter 3 data), and click the ⟨◯⟩.

The entire column should now be highlighted.

7. Move the pointer to the Edit option on the main menu.

8. Press and hold the ⟨◯⟩.

9. Drag the pointer to the Insert option.

10. Release the ⟨◯⟩.

A new column should now exist between Quarter 2 data and Quarter 3 data.

11. Repeat the above process to insert a column between Quarter 3 and Quarter 4.

12. Repeat the above process to insert a column between Quarter 4 and the Total Expenses column.

Copying Data

You need to add headings under the Quarter headings to depict Budget and Actual. The headings will be placed in row 4. Begin by placing the cell pointer in B4 and entering "Budget." Then enter "Actual" in C4. Then copy those entries into the other heading positions.

1. Place the pointer in cell B4.

2. Click the ⟨◯⟩ to highlight the cell.

3. Type **Budget**, and press ⌷tab⌷.

Cell C4 should now be highlighted.

4. Type **Actual**, and press ⌷shift⌷ ⌷tab⌷.

Cell B4 should now be highlighted.

Now highlight both cells to copy them into cells D4 and E4.

5. With the pointer in B4, press and hold the ⟨◯⟩.

    6. Move the pointer to cell C4.

    7. Release the ⌁.

Cells B4 and C4 should be highlighted.

Now copy the contents into cells D4 and E4.

    8. Move the pointer to the Edit item on the main menu.

    9. Press and hold the ⌁.

    10. Drag the pointer to the Copy option (refer to Fig. 6.9), and release the ⌁.

The two cell entries are now on the clipboard. You can see this by selecting the Show Clipboard option from the Window item on the main menu. Then select the close box on the left end of the Clipboard title bar to remove it from view.

    11. Now move the pointer to cell D4.

    12. Click the ⌁ to highlight cell D4.

It is not necessary to highlight both cells, since the highlighted cell depicts the upper left corner of the target area.

    13. Move the pointer to the Edit item on the main menu.

    14. Press and hold the ⌁.

    15. Drag the pointer to the Paste option on the Edit pull-down menu (refer to Fig. 6.9) and release the ⌁.

Cells D4 and E4 should now contain Budget and Actual. Copy the same labels into cells F4 and G4.

    16. Now move the pointer to cell F4.

    17. Click the ⌁ to highlight the cell.

    18. Move the pointer to the Edit item on the main menu.

    19. Press and hold the ⌁.

    20. Drag the pointer to the Paste option, and release the ⌁.

Cells F4 and G4 should now contain Budget and Actual.

    21. Repeat steps 16 through 20 in cell H4 and then in cell J4 to include headings in the Quarter 4 columns and the Total Expenses columns.

Since the Actual column totals will use the same function as the Budget column totals, and since the totals are in the same relative cell locations, you can copy the column total function into the appropriate locations in row 13.

    22. Move the pointer to cell B13, and click the ⌁ to highlight the cell.

23. Move the pointer to the Edit item on the main menu.

24. Press and hold the ⬡.

25. Drag the pointer to the Copy option, and release the ⬡.

26. Move the pointer to cell C13.

27. Click the ⬡ to make it the active cell.

28. Move the pointer to the Edit item on the main menu.

29. Press and hold the ⬡.

30. Drag the pointer to the Paste option, and release the ⬡.

The function =Sum(C6:C11) should be displayed on the edit line, and a zero should be displayed in cell C13.

31. Move the pointer to cell E13, and click the ⬡.

32. Select Paste from the Edit pull-down menu.

The edit line should show =Sum(E6:E11), and a zero should be displayed in cell E13.

33. Repeat steps 31 and 32 to put the function in cells G13, I13, and K13.

The Actual totals of the four quarters for each expense item (e.g., Rent) are found by adding the amounts for each of the four quarters. Note that this is the same formula as the one for the Total Expenses budgeted amounts, which is obtained by adding the budgeted amounts for the four quarters. Notice also that the data being added is in the same relative positions. Therefore, formulas in column J can be copied into column K.

34. Place the pointer on cell J6.

35. Press and hold the ⬡.

36. Drag the pointer to cell J11.

37. Release the ⬡.

Cells J6 through J11 should be highlighted.

38. Move the pointer to the Edit item on the main menu.

39. Press and hold the ⬡.

40. Drag the pointer to the Copy option, and release the ⬡.

41. Move the pointer to cell K6, and click the ⬡ to highlight the cell.

42. Select the Paste option from the Edit pull-down menu.

The formulas in column K now contain addresses referencing the Actual columns, and cells K6 through K11 should now contain zeros.

Changing Column Width

To provide more appropriate spacing within the spreadsheet, you will now modify the column width to match the data more closely. The Total Expenses columns can be narrowed, and the quarterly data columns can be narrowed even more. Begin by narrowing the Total Expenses columns to 10 positions.

1. Move the pointer to column J (any cell in column J).

2. Press and hold the 🖰.

3. Drag the pointer to the cell to the right (in column K), and release the 🖰.

Two cells should be highlighted, one in column J and one in column K.

4. Point to the Format item on the main menu.

5. Press and hold the 🖰.

6. Drag the pointer to the Column Width option (see Fig. 6.10), and release the 🖰.

You will now see a dialog box containing the current column width of the selected columns (see Fig. 6.11).

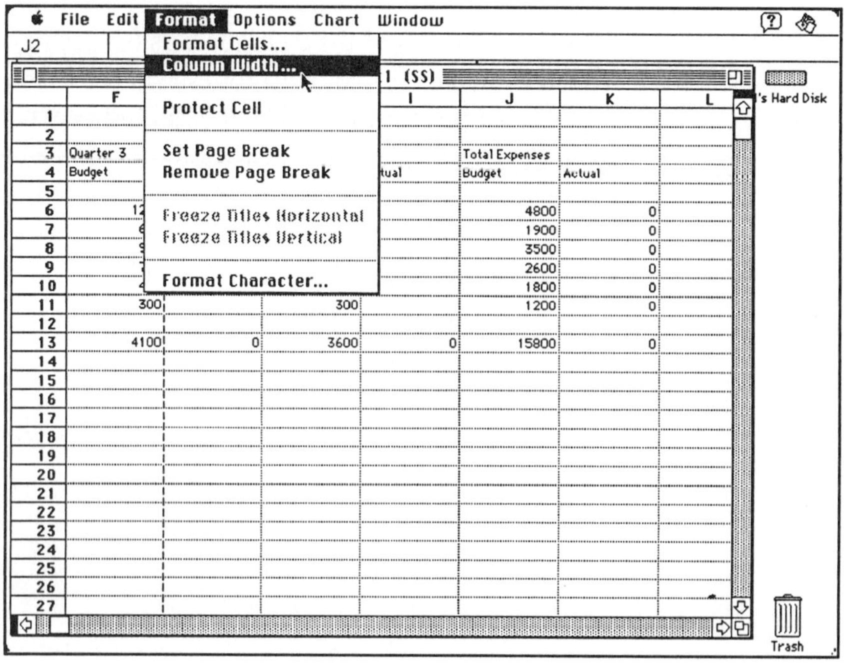

Fig. 6.10 Format pull-down menu showing Column Width option

7. Type **8** to change the value.

8. Move the pointer to [OK], and click the 🖰.

Columns J and K should be 8 positions wide.

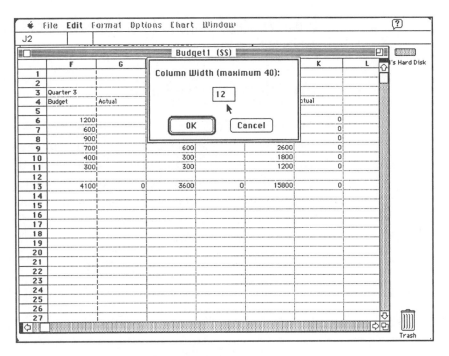

Fig. 6.11 Column Width dialog box

9. Move the pointer to column B (any cell in the column).

10. Press and hold the ⌐⌐.

11. Drag the pointer to column I in the same row, and release the ⌐⌐.

A row of cells from column B through column I should be highlighted.

12. Select the Column Width option from the Format pull-down menu (refer to Fig. 6.10).

13. Type **7** into the dialog box entry area (refer to Fig. 6.11).

14. Move the pointer to ⎡ OK ⎤, and click the ⌐⌐.

Columns B through I should now be 7 positions wide.

15. Move the pointer to column A (any cell in the column).

16. Click the ⌐⌐ to make the cell active.

17. Select the Column Width option from the Format pull-down menu (refer to Fig. 6.10).

18. Type **11** into the dialog box entry area.

19. Move the pointer to ⎡ OK ⎤, and click the ⌐⌐.

A vertical page boundary indicator (dashed line) should be between the Quarter 4 "Actual" column and the Total Expenses "Budget" column. If it is not, adjust column widths to position the page boundary between quarters, as indicated in Fig. 6.12. This is important because of the title overlap between columns. Refer to the "Printing the Spreadsheet" section near the end of this chapter for further explanation.

Formatting the Cells

The current format of all cells is general (as they were entered), which means that the numeric values are displayed without any enhancements. To improve readability, you will add commas before every third whole number digit, as appropriate. Since there are only whole numbers (no pennies), it is not necessary to display fractional decimal places. You can use comma format with zero decimal places for all numeric cells to maintain consistency during future spreadsheet maintenance.

1. Move the pointer to cell B6.

2. Press and hold the 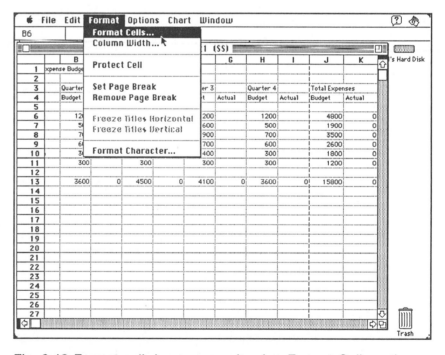 to begin selection of the range.

3. Drag the pointer to cell K13.

4. Release the ⌐.

5. Point to the Format item on the main menu.

6. Press and hold the ⌐.

7. Drag the pointer to the Format Cells option (see Fig. 6.12), and release the ⌐.

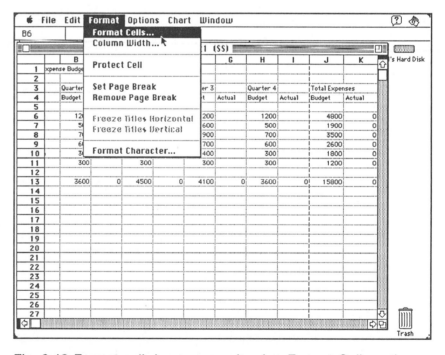

Fig. 6.12 Format pull-down menu showing Format Cells option

You should now have a dialog box displayed on the desktop, similar to the one in Fig. 6.13.

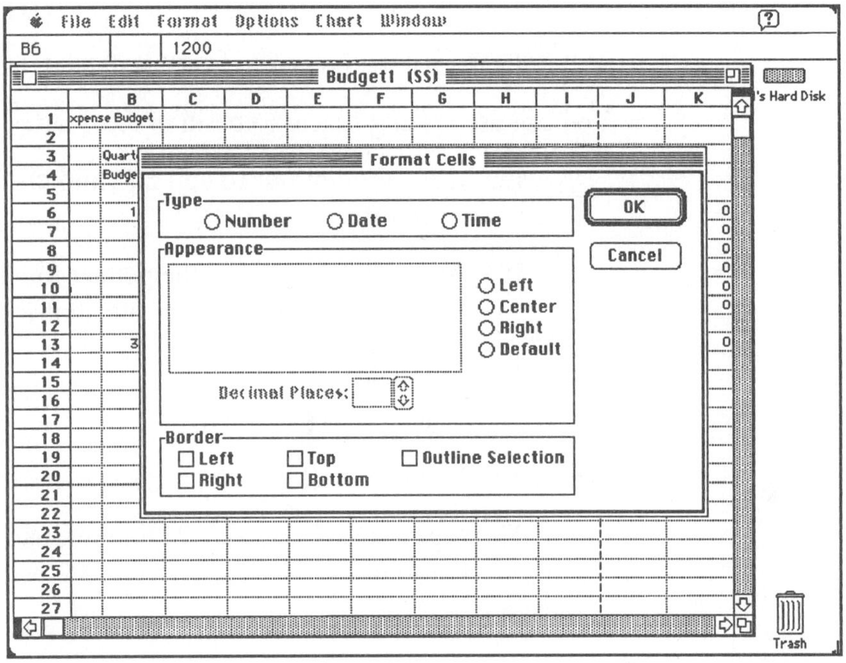

Fig. 6.13 Format Cells dialog box

First, select the Number option.

> 8. Move the pointer to the Number ⃝ , and click the ☁ .

A dot should appear in the button, and the Appearance list box should now have options in it.

> 9. Move the pointer to the item in the list containing a sample number with a decimal point and comma (1,234.56), and click the ☁ to highlight it.

Set the decimal places to zero.

> 10. With the Decimal Places box highlighted, type **0** (zero).

A zero should appear in the Decimal Places box.

> 11. Move the pointer to OK , and click the ☁ to record the entry.

The numbers with four digits should now have commas in them.

You can use the format options to position the column headings.

> 12. Move the pointer to cell B4.

> 13. Press and hold the ☁ .

> 14. Drag the pointer to cell K4, and release the ☁ .

15. Select the Format Cells option from the Format pull-down menu (refer to Fig. 6.12).

16. Move the pointer to the Center ○, and click the ⌒⌒ (refer to Fig. 6.13).

17. Move the pointer to [OK], and click the ⌒⌒.

You can use leading spaces to position the quarter headings over the cells.

18. Move the pointer to cell B3, and click the ⌒⌒ to make it the active cell.

19. On the edit line, move the pointer to the left of the "Q" in Quarter 1, and click the ⌒⌒ to create an insertion point.

20. Press ‖ space ‖ 8 times.

21. Press ‖ return ‖.

The heading Quarter 1 should now be centered over the Budget and Actual columns.

22. Repeat steps 18 through 21 for the Quarter 2, Quarter 3, and Quarter 4 headings.

23. Repeat steps 18 through 21 for the Total Expenses heading, pressing ‖ space ‖ 5 times.

Adding Data

You are now ready to add the Actual expenditures for the first two quarters of the year. Enter the data from Table 6.2 into the spreadsheet.

1. Move the pointer to cell C6.

2. Click the ⌒⌒ to make it the active cell.

3. Type **1200**, and press ‖ return ‖.

Actual Expenses for Quarters 1 and 2

	Quarter 1	Quarter 2
Rent	1200	1200
Utilities	450	320
Auto	650	1100
Groceries	630	740
Recreation	370	700
Misc	300	350

Table 6.2 Actual expense data for Quarter 1 and Quarter 2

4. In cell C7, type **450**, and press ⬚return⬚.

Notice that the column total, row total, and grand total are all being updated as each entry is made because of automatic recalculation. Notice that the 1200 in cell C6 is formatted with a comma because of previous formatting of the cells.

5. Complete the remaining entries of actual expenses for the first two quarters of the year.

The spreadsheet now contains the actual expenditures for the first half of the year. They can be compared to the budgeted (or planned) expenditures. The spreadsheet should now look like Fig. 6.14.

🍎 File Edit Format Options Chart Window										②
A15										
▱ Budget1 (SS)										
	A	B	C	D	E	F	G	H	I	J	K
1	Personal Expense Budget										
2											
3		Quarter 1		Quarter 2		Quarter 3		Quarter 4		Total Expenses	
4	Expenses	Budget	Actual	Budget	Actual	Budget	Actual	Budget	Actual	Budget	Actual
5											
6	Rent	1,200	1,200	1,200	1,200	1,200		1,200		4,800	2,400
7	Utilities	500	450	300	320	600		500		1,900	770
8	Auto	700	650	1,200	1,100	900		700		3,500	1,750
9	Groceries	600	630	700	740	700		600		2,600	1,370
10	Recreation	300	370	800	700	400		300		1,800	1,070
11	Misc	300	300	300	350	300		300		1,200	650
12											
13	Total	3,600	3,600	4,500	4,410	4,100	0	3,600	0	15,800	8,010
14											
15											

Fig. 6.14 Sample spreadsheet with modifications

Saving the Changes

You now have a spreadsheet that has been edited. You want to save it on the disk. You will use the Save As option to allow you to change the name and save the spreadsheet as BUDGET2.

Select the File pull-down menu, then select the Save As option.

1. Point to the File item on the main menu.

2. Press and hold the 🖱.

3. Drag the pointer to the Save As option on the pull-down menu.

4. Release the 🖱.

5. In the dialog box (see Fig. 6.15), change the name to BUDGET2.

6. Move the pointer to ⬚ Save ⬚, and click the 🖱.

The spreadsheet will be saved with the name BUDGET2.

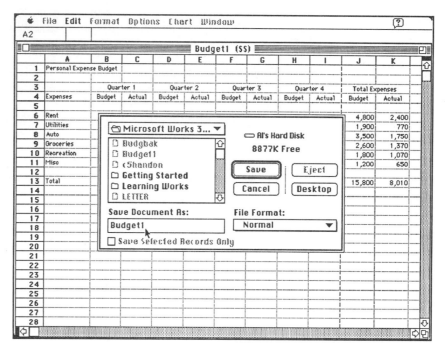

Fig. 6.15 Dialog box to assign a name to a file

You are returned to the spreadsheet when the save operation is completed. The spreadsheet remains in memory for reference and editing, but a current copy is now saved on disk as a permanent copy.

Printing the Spreadsheet

You have entered the spreadsheet and saved it on disk. If you want a copy on paper, you can also print it. Remember that you are printing the spreadsheet that is in memory, not the one on disk. The print command is located on the File pull-down menu. When preparing to print, be sure that the printer is ready and has paper.

1. Point to the File item on the main menu.

2. Select the Print option from the File pull-down menu.

3. Select [OK] on the Print dialog box.

Notice that the spreadsheet is printed on two pages. The heavy dashed line in the window between columns I and J indicates where the page break will be. When printing a spreadsheet, be careful to ensure that headings that cross column boundaries, such as the quarter headings, do not cross the page boundary, or they will not be printed properly. If necessary, you can add a blank column, change the cell width, or use condensed printing to avoid the problem. Or simply don't allow headings to cross column boundaries. The multiple-page spreadsheet can be taped together, if necessary, to read the information.

Often it is desirable to print the spreadsheet without the grid lines. Remove the grid lines and print the spreadsheet.

4. Point to the Options item on the main menu.

5. Select the Show Grid option from the Options pull-down menu (to remove grid lines).

6. Point to the File item on the main menu.

7. Select the Print option from the File pull-down menu.

8. Select $\boxed{\text{OK}}$ from the Print dialog box.

The spreadsheet will print without grid lines.

Although this spreadsheet extends onto two pages, it could fit on one page if rotated 90 degrees. Select the Orientation icon to rotate the printout and print the spreadsheet again.

9. Point to the File item on the main menu.

10. Select the Page Setup option from the File pull-down menu.

11. Select the side view Orientation icon to rotate the output.

12. Select $\boxed{\text{OK}}$ from the dialog box.

13. Point to the File item on the main menu.

14. Select the Print option from the File pull-down menu.

15. Select $\boxed{\text{OK}}$ from the Print dialog box.

The spreadsheet should print sideways on one page.

16. Select the Show Grid option from the Options pull-down menu (to display the grid lines).

17. Select the Page Setup option from the File pull-down menu.

18. Select the front view Orientation icon to position output in the standard position.

The grid control and the sideways orientation can be used when appropriate to enhance the output.

Deleting Cells

You have completed the update process and saved the spreadsheet to disk. You have finished the job.

There is one other benefit that can be gained from this assignment. You can remove the data entries and save the heading and formula entries for later use in developing a budget for you or someone else. This information is generally referred to as a template and can be stored on disk for future use.

To remove the existing data from the spreadsheet, select the range that includes value entries and delete the data.

1. Point to cell B6.

2. Press and hold the ⬜.

3. Drag the pointer to cell H11.

4. Release the ⬜ to complete the range selection.

5. Select the Clear command from the Edit pull-down menu.

6. Click the ⬜ anywhere in the spreadsheet to remove the highlighting.

The headings, formulas, functions, and all formatting remain in the spreadsheet, but the data is removed.

Saving the Template

Now save the template to disk under the name TEMPLAT1.

1. Select the Save As option from the File pull-down menu.

2. Type the name **TEMPLAT1** in the name box.

3. Select ⌐ **Save** ⌐ to save the spreadsheet.

The template file is now on disk.

Closing the File

You are now ready to close the file.

You can use the Close option on the File pull-down menu, or move the pointer to the close box on the left end of the title bar, and click the ⬜.

1. Move the pointer to the close box.

2. Click the ⬜.

The spreadsheet should be gone from the desktop.

Exiting Works

To continue working on files once the file is closed, you would create a new file or open an existing one. Once you have completed the work session and are ready to leave Works, select the Quit option from the File pull-down menu. (If this option is not available, reopen BUDGET2 by double clicking on the BUDGET2 file icon, and close it again.)

1. Point to the File item on the main menu.

2. Press and hold the ⌫.

3. Drag the pointer to the Quit option.

4. Release the ⌫.

This should close the Works application.

To close the Works folder, select the Close Window option from the File pull-down menu, or point to the close box on the left end of the title bar, and click the ⌫.

5. Point to the File item on the main menu.

6. Press and hold the ⌫.

7. Drag the pointer to the Close Window option.

8. Release the ⌫.

This should return you to the Opening System Disk window.

If you have completed the work session, use the shut down procedure to terminate the machine operation.

Summary

Entering the data into the worksheet is only the beginning of using a spread-sheet effectively. Modifying the worksheet characteristics and manipulating the data are important aspects of spreadsheet usage.

The worksheet can be modified in several ways. Rows and columns can be added or deleted. Column width can be modified to conform to the size of the data. Cells or ranges of cells can be formatted to include such characteristics as fixed decimal point, a dollar sign before the number, a comma before every third digit as appropriate, a percent sign after the number, or exponentiation format (scientific notation). Entries can be left justified, right justified, or centered in the cell. Date and time can be displayed in several ways.

The data can be manipulated in several ways. The contents of one cell, a range of cells, or the entire spreadsheet can be deleted. Data can be moved from one or more cells into other cells in the worksheet. Data can be copied from one cell to one or more cells, and data in a range of cells can be copied to another range of cells.

Questions

1. Explain the difference between changing the worksheet and manipulating the data.

2. Explain what is meant by a range of cells.

3. What is the difference between a global command and a local command?

4. Why is it important to be able to add a row or column?

5. Why is it important to be able to delete a row or column?

6. List five ways in which cells can be formatted to enhance the display of data.

7. Why is it important to be able to adjust column widths in a worksheet?

8. How many data items in cells can be deleted at one time?

9. What is the difference between relative and absolute addressing?

10. What is the difference between the Move and Copy commands?

Exercises

Exercise 1

1. Create an empty spreadsheet.

2. Widen column A to 16 character positions.

3. Narrow columns B and C to 7 positions.

4. Format cells D5 through D9 to currency format with zero decimal places.

5. Create a table of personnel information, including Name, Status, Dept., and Salary, using the data below.

6. Save the spreadsheet onto disk as EMPSTATS.

7. Print the spreadsheet.

8. Insert a row between Carter and Jeffcoat.

9. Add Dawson, Joe, PT, R&D, 16000 as a new employee.

10. Delete the row containing Saunders as a terminated employee.

11. Save the spreadsheet.

12. Print the spreadsheet without grid lines.

EMPLOYEE INFORMATION FOR MY COMPANY

Name	Status	Dept.	Salary
Brown, Fred	PT	R&D	22000
Carter, Nancy	FT	R&D	38000
Jeffcoat, Tom	FT	ADMIN	44000
Saunders, Harold	PT	R&D	26000
Thompson, Betty	FT	MKT	34000

Exercise 2

1. Create an empty spreadsheet.

2. Widen column A to 17 character positions.

3. Narrow columns B through E to 9 character positions.

4. Format cells B6 through F10 to fixed format with zero decimal places, and include commas.

5. Format cells B12 through F12 to currency format with zero decimal places, and include commas.

6. Using the following information, create a salary budget.

My Company
Salary Budget 1994

Name	Qtr1	Qtr2	Qtr3	Qtr4	Total
Brown	8000	6000	6000	2000	22000
Carter	9500	9500	9500	9500	38000
Jeffcoat	11000	11000	11000	11000	44000
Saunders	2000	6000	9000	9000	26000
Thompson	8500	8500	8500	8500	34000
Total	39000	41000	44000	40000	164000

7. Enter the function =SUM(B6:E6) in cell F6.

8. Copy the contents of cell F6 into cells F7 through F10.

9. Enter the function =SUM(B6:B10) into cell B12.

10. Copy the contents of cell B12 into C12 through F12.

193

11. Save the spreadsheet as COMPBUDG.

12. Print the display output with sideways orientation.

13. Print the formula output.

Problems

Problem 1

Create an income statement similar to the one shown below. Use the SUM function to get Total Revenue and Total Expenses. Use a formula to get Net Income. Put labels in column A and numbers in column C. Format cells containing numeric data to fixed format with two decimal places, and include commas. Format the cell containing Net Income to currency format with zero decimal places, and include commas. Save the spreadsheet. Print the spreadsheet in both display and formula mode.

My Company
Income Statement

Revenue:

Dept. A	14000
Dept. B	22000
Dept. C	11000
Total Revenue	47000

Expenses:

Dept. A	9000
Dept. B	12000
Dept. C	8000
Administrative	9000
Total Expenses	38000
Net Income	9000

Problem 2

Create a spreadsheet showing the following payment schedule for a loan of $1,000 for one year (repaying $1140, with interest). Enter 0 into cell A5 and =A5+1 into cell A6. Then copy cell A6 (Fill) into cells A7 through A17. Enter 0 into cell B5 and 95 into cell B6. Then copy (Fill) cell B6 into cells B7 through B17. Enter 1140 into cell C5 and =C5-B6 into cell C6. Copy cell C6 (Fill) into cells C7 through C17. Format cells B5 through C17 to currency format with two decimal places. Save the spreadsheet, and print both display and formula mode.

The display should look like the spreadsheet shown below.

Loan Payment Schedule

Month	Payment	Balance
0	0	1140
1	95	1045
2	95	950
3	95	855
4	95	760
5	95	665
6	95	570
7	95	475
8	95	380
9	95	285
10	95	190
11	95	95
12	95	0

Problem 3

Starting with the spreadsheet in Problem 1, print a display output of the spreadsheet, then make the following changes. Following the changes, save the spreadsheet and print a formula output, and then a display output rotated 90 degrees and without grid lines.

1. Widen column A to 16 character positions.

2. Delete column B (numeric data should then be in column B).

3. Move the contents of cells containing Expense labels and data to columns C and D beside the Revenue data. Adjust formatting and references as necessary to be consistent with the Revenue data.

4. Move the contents of cells containing the label and function data for Net Income to the top of columns E and F, and correct the Net Income formula to reflect the proper cells.

Problem 4

Starting with the original spreadsheet created in Exercise 2, print a display output of the spreadsheet, and then make the following changes. Save the spreadsheet, and print a display and a formula output.

Incorporate actual salary expenditures into the spreadsheet by doing the following:

1. Add a column after each Quarter, 1 through 4. Label them Actual Qtr1 through Actual Qtr4. Label the column after Total as Actual Total.

2. Modify the functions in the Total column to contain formulas which add the four budget columns. Change the first one and copy it down.

3. Add actual salary expenses into the spreadsheet.

Name	Q1	Q2	Q3
Brown	7400	5800	6200
Carter	9500	9500	9500
Jeffcoat	10400	10700	10900
Saunders	1500	7100	8600
Thompson	8500	8200	8700

4. Add formulas in the Actual Total column to reflect total year-to-date expenditures.

5. Add the following employee between Jeffcoat and Saunders.

Richardson, Budget, 0, 0, 8000, 8000

Actual, 0, 0, 6000, 0

Chapter 7

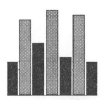

Charting

Objectives

After completing this chapter you will

1. Be able to define the different types of business graphs.

2. Understand the uses of bar graphs, stacked-bar graphs, multiple-bar graphs, pie charts, and line graphs.

3. Be able to define and explain charting terminology, including titles, legends, x-axis, y-axis, series, and variables.

4. Be able to create and print graphs using data generated by the spreadsheet tool in Microsoft Works.

5. Be able to modify graphs.

What Are Business Graphics?

Graphics capability allows a user to convey a message that is sometimes lost when it is buried in large amounts of numerical information. Personal computers have the capability to store and manipulate data in order to generate information. However, personal computer users sometimes have difficulty conveying this information to others in a meaningful way. Business charts provide a solution to this problem by representing data in a visual and easily understood format.

Many forms of charts are created from data generated by spreadsheets. The most common types of business charts are the bar graph, stacked-bar graph, multiple-bar graph, pie chart, and line graph. (The terms *chart* and *graph* are used interchangeably.)

Bar Chart

As an example, consider the sample spreadsheet in Fig. 7.1. Assume that we need to know which month has the most sales. One solution is to look at the totals and scan for the largest number. Another is to create a chart that compares the total sales for each month, as in Fig. 7.2. From Fig. 7.2 it is easy to see that February and March had the most sales. The bar chart allows you to compare quantities (sales) relating to descriptive parameters (months).

	Jan	Feb	Mar	Total
Smally Department Store **First Quarter Sales**				
Clothing	1,400	1,600	1,800	4,800
Toys	800	700	800	2,300
Housewares	1,200	1,600	1,700	4,500
Jewelry	900	1,100	700	2,700
Total	4,300	5,000	5,000	14,300

Fig. 7.1 Sample spreadsheet to be used for charting

When comparing total sales for the three months, you may also want to see the relative portion of sales of each category (e.g., clothing) attributable to the total. You could use a stacked-bar graph to do this. Fig. 7.3 shows a stacked-bar graph with each bar representing total sales for the month. The bars are shaded in four parts, with each part representing one of the sales categories.

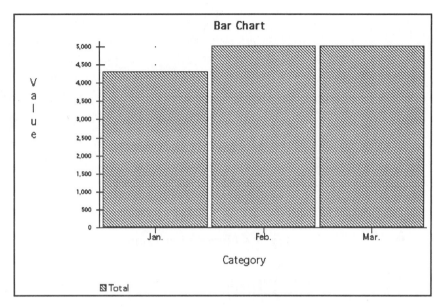

Fig. 7.2 Bar chart of Total Sales by month

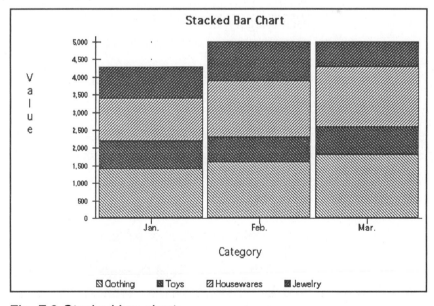

Fig. 7.3 Stacked-bar chart

Notice that, although the sales figures for each item are represented, it is difficult to see the actual quantity of sales for each item. You can use a multiple-bar graph, as shown in Fig. 7.4, to show the sales of each category for each of the three months. This has limited utility in showing the total sales for each month, but it allows you to compare the quantity of sales for each item.

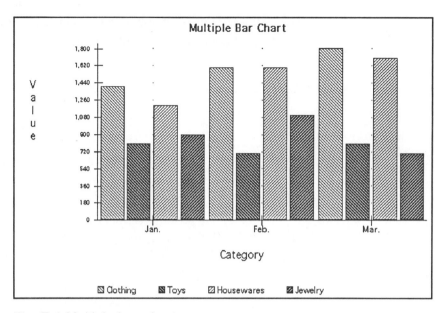

Fig. 7.4 Multiple-bar chart

Pie Chart

Pie charts represent values for a single variable (series) displayed in proportional relationships. Fig. 7.5 shows a pie chart of total sales for the three months. The individual segments are drawn in proportion to the total sales for each category, and the addition of all proportions totals 100 percent.

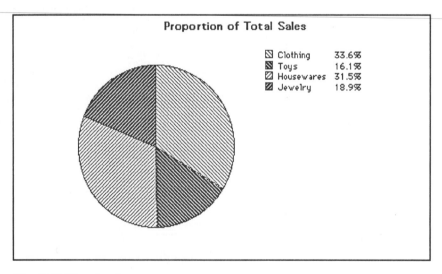

Fig. 7.5 Pie chart

Only one variable can be displayed in a pie chart. Notice that the pie chart in Fig. 7.5 has percentages shown for each wedge of the pie. To develop the pie chart, the graphics program calculated the total sales, then calculated the percentage contributed by each item, and finally drew each slice of the pie in proportion to the calculated percentage.

Line Chart

Line graphs plot a variable along the vertical axis (y) against a descriptive variable along the horizontal axis (x). Each data item is represented by a point on the graph. The points may be plotted in a sequence, a line may be graphed from point to point, or the graph may contain both a symbol at each point and a line connecting the symbols. Fig. 7.6 depicts a line graph of housewares and jewelry sales over the three-month period. It shows that, while jewelry sales showed an increase and then a decline, housewares sales continued to increase over the three-month period.

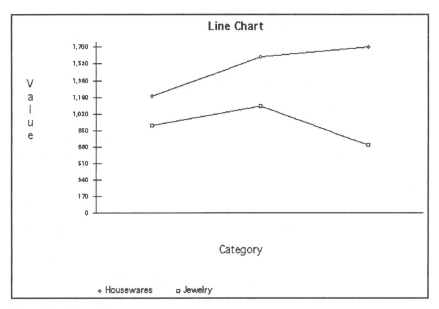

Fig. 7.6 Line chart

Generally a line graph is used to depict a trend over time. It works best when there are many data points to produce the graph. It can also be used to compare trends of two sets of data, such as current year sales compared to previous year sales.

Features of Charting

When creating charts, it is important to understand some of the terminology involved in graphs. There are many options available in charting programs, but only a handful of them are required to get started. The words that you need to understand in order to complete this chapter are

1. *Type*. The nature of the graph being plotted. Some standard types are bar, stacked-bar, multiple-bar, pie, and line.

2. *X-axis*. The horizontal axis, where descriptive variables (e.g., months) are displayed.

3. *Y-axis*. The vertical axis, where quantitative variables (e.g., sales amount) are displayed.

4. *Series*. The data items that correspond to one variable (e.g., sales for each of 12 months).

5. *Legends*. Labels that are attached to a series or a group of series in order to identify them on the graph.

6. *Titles*. The title is normally displayed on top of the graph.

Chart Development with Works

Creating a Chart

Before a chart can be created in Microsoft Works, a spreadsheet with the appropriate data must be created using the spreadsheet tool. To understand how to create a spreadsheet, you should refer to Chapters 5 and 6 in this book. Refer to the spreadsheet in Fig. 7.7 to see specific examples of source data.

	A	B	C	D	E
1		Smally Department Store			
2		First Quarter Sales			
3					
4		Jan	Feb	Mar	Total
5					
6	Clothing	1,400	1,600	1,800	4,800
7	Toys	800	700	800	2,300
8	Housewares	1,200	1,600	1,700	4,500
9	Jewelry	900	1,100	700	2,700
10					
11	Total	4,300	5,000	5,000	14,300

Fig. 7.7 Sample spreadsheet

To create a chart, select the New Chart option from the Chart pull-down menu (see Fig. 7.8). Following this selection, a dialog box will be displayed that shows the options available (see Fig. 7.9).

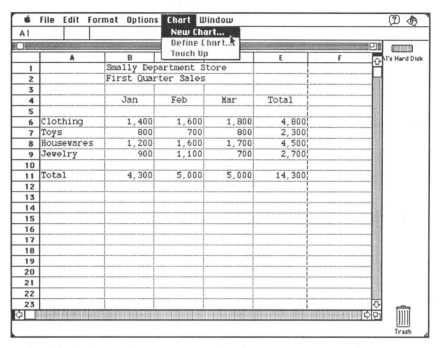

Fig. 7.8 Chart pull-down menu showing New Chart option

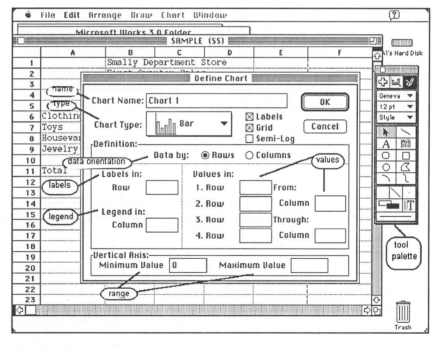

Fig. 7.9 Define Chart dialog box

The "Chart Type:" list box on the upper left of the dialog box is defaulted to "bar." If you want a stacked-bar, a line, a combination of line and bar, or a pie chart, select the corresponding option from the drop-down list box, and it will become active, making the bar option inactive. With different types of charts, some of the available options in the dialog box may change.

The "Data by:" (rows or columns) option is used to indicate whether the data values are stored in rows or columns in the spreadsheet. The default selection is Rows. If the Columns button is selected, the Labels, Legend, and Values entry boxes in the lower part of the dialog box will change accordingly. The following explanation of entries will assume that Rows is the option selected in the "Data by:" box.

The "Values in:" options are used to select the row or rows to be charted. The vertical boxes labeled "Row" will allow you to enter up to four rows of data to plot. For example, to chart the Total Sales for the three months shown in Fig. 7.7, you would enter an 11 (the row number) in the first "Row" box. The "From:" and "Through:" boxes allow you to enter the range of columns to chart. To chart the three-month range in Fig. 7.7, you would enter B and D in the boxes. (Note that if the data is being charted by columns, you select values in columns from one row through another row.)

The values to be charted can be entered quickly by highlighting the data series prior to selecting the New Chart option, thus causing a chart to be drawn when the option is selected. Then you can use the Define Chart option on the Chart pull-down menu (refer to Fig. 7.8) to add features to the chart.

The "Labels in:" box allows you to specify the row containing the labels to identify the descriptive categories in the chart (Jan, Feb, and Mar in the example). To label the three months, you would enter 4 in the box. The "Legend in:" box allows you to specify the column containing the names to be used to identify the series of data being plotted in the chart (Total in the example). To include a legend for "Total," you would enter A in the box.

The tool palette shown in Fig. 7.9 (on the right side of the desktop) can be used to enhance various aspects of the chart. When a chart is drawn or selected, the tool palette appears. It is closed by selecting the close box on its title bar.

Once all values are entered into the Define Chart dialog box, review them to see that they correlate to the spreadsheet and to each other. Then select the OK button to create the chart.

Viewing a Chart

The chart is stored in the spreadsheet and can be positioned within the spreadsheet work area as desired. It is displayed by opening the spreadsheet and then moving the spreadsheet as necessary until the chart is displayed in the window.

A chart can be made active by selecting the chart name from the Chart pull-down menu. This will cause handle boxes to appear on the edges of the chart, and the tool palette will be displayed for reference. Closing the tool palette will return reference to the spreadsheet cells.

Saving a Chart

Once you have defined the specifications of the chart and plotted it on the spreadsheet, you can save the chart by saving the spreadsheet. The chart can be displayed later if the spreadsheet is active.

To save the chart specifications on disk, first be sure the spreadsheet that is referenced is in the active window. Then select the Save option from the File pull-down menu to save the spreadsheet and all corresponding chart specifications onto disk. You can continue to use the spreadsheet or close the window once the spreadsheet is saved.

Printing a Chart

To print a chart, print the spreadsheet containing it. The chart will be printed with the spreadsheet as part of the spreadsheet. It is important to position the chart as necessary to have it print where you want it in conjunction with the spreadsheet data.

You can print the chart without the spreadsheet by first positioning it and then selecting the print area to include only the chart area. Position the chart within a range of cells. If you don't want cell grid lines displayed, select the Show Grid item from the Options pull-down menu to remove the display of grid lines. Highlight the range of cells in which the chart is displayed. Select the Print option from the File pull-down menu to print the range of cells displaying the chart.

Enhancing a Chart

The appearance of charts can be changed by adding or modifying features. Titles can be added to any of the charts produced in Works. Features such as grids and legends are optional in series charts. The range of values to include in the chart can be specified. The size or location of the chart can be changed.

Titles

All charts should have a title that identifies the graph. The default title given to each chart is Title "n," where n is 1, then 2, and so on, depending on the number of charts produced in the spreadsheet. You can change the title to something more meaningful by entering a different title in the Define Chart dialog box (refer to Fig. 7.9). The new title entered will be displayed on the chart.

Labels and Grids

The Labels check box in the Define Chart dialog box initially contains an X, meaning that category labels are included in the chart. Clicking on the box will remove the X, and category labels will not be displayed in the chart. The option can be selected again to have the labels displayed.

The Grid check box just below the Labels check box causes grid indicators to be displayed with the data. Clicking on that box to turn it off will remove the grid indicators from within the chart data displayed. The markers remain along the left edge of the chart but are removed from the data values displayed. Selecting the box again will reactivate the grid indicators.

Chart Range

The range of values to be included in the chart can be specified in the Define Chart dialog box (refer to Fig. 7.9). The "Vertical Axis:" box contains an entry box for minimum and maximum values to be included in the chart range.

The minimum value is defaulted to zero. If you want to specify a minimum value to be charted, enter it in the box. This will cause the display to start at the value rather than at zero.

The maximum value entry can be used to specify a larger value than the largest value in the data, causing the display to project the range to the value entered. Specifying a value that is smaller than the largest value to be displayed will cause the chart to extend to the largest data value rather than truncating it to the maximum value entered (i.e., this entry should be as large or larger than the largest data value to be displayed).

Chart Location

A chart can be moved within the spreadsheet to position it in relation to the spreadsheet data and in relation to other charts. Select the chart name from the Chart pull-down menu to make it active. Then point to the chart and drag the chart to its new location.

Chart Size

A chart can be resized as necessary to fit into the desired location in the spreadsheet. First, select the chart name from the Chart pull-down menu. With the chart active, use the handle boxes at the corners and along each side to drag the border of the chart and change its size. Point to the handle on any side of the chart, and drag the side border to make the chart larger or smaller, as necessary. Point to a handle box on any corner to drag the two adjacent borders of the chart diagonally to increase or decrease the size of the chart.

Using the Tool Palette

While a detailed discussion of the tool palette is beyond the scope of this book, it deserves mention and possibly further consideration by the user. The tool palette provides a means to incorporate several additional enhancements to charts. You can change the font, size, and style of text used in the chart. You can change background and foreground color. You can add text in any place in the chart. You can introduce drawings into the chart to support the presentation. Prior to adding the features, the chart should be positioned where you want it in the spreadsheet, since the features will become a part of the spreadsheet.

The tool palette can be used in conjunction with the Touch Up option on the Chart pull-down menu to modify existing text in the chart. Select the Touch Up item to activate it. Then click on the item in the chart to be modified and use the tool palette to implement the change (see Appendix A).

Managing Charts

To modify a chart definition, you can select the appropriate chart from the list of names provided in the Chart pull-down menu (see Fig. 7.10). Then select the Define Chart option from the Chart pull-down menu. Changes can then be entered in the Define Chart dialog box. The new specifications will be stored with the chart.

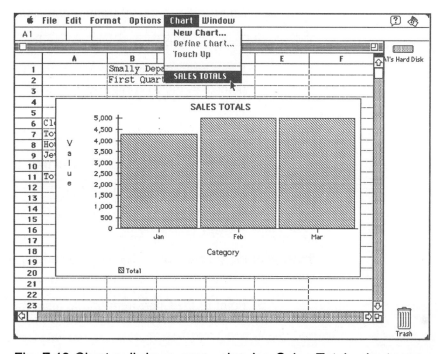

Fig. 7.10 Chart pull-down menu showing Sales Totals chart name

You may want to modify a specification, but keep the original one as well. This can be done by first selecting the chart to be copied from the Chart pull-down menu (refer to Fig. 7.10). Then select the Duplicate option from the Edit pull-down menu. The duplicate chart will have the same name as the original but with the word "copy" added to it. You can modify the chart specifications, as necessary, using the Define Chart option on the Chart pull-down menu.

Over time, you may choose to remove one or more of the chart definitions recorded with a spreadsheet. This can be done by selecting the chart name from the Chart pull-down menu. Then select the Cut or Clear option from the Edit pull-down menu. It will be removed from the list and removed from the spreadsheet. The spreadsheet must be saved to disk with the updated specifications.

Hands-on Charting

PART I

Creating a Series Chart

Using the sample spreadsheet in Fig. 7.11, you will create a bar chart depicting the toy sales for each of the three months in order to compare the sales volume. As seen in the figure, the total Toys sales for the quarter is $2,300.

First, create the spreadsheet.

1. From the Opening System Disk window, move the pointer to the Microsoft Works 3.0 Folder icon, and double click the ⬚.

This should open the Works Application window.

2. From a reference to the Microsoft Works 3.0 Folder, move the pointer to the icon representing Microsoft Works 3.0, and double click the ⬚.

You should now see the Works Opening dialog box.

3. Double click on the spreadsheet icon to create a new spreadsheet.

4. Enter the data depicted in Fig. 7.11 (using formulas or functions where appropriate), and save the spreadsheet with the name SAMPLE.

Now, with the spreadsheet in the active window, select the option to create a chart.

5. Point to the Chart item on the main menu.

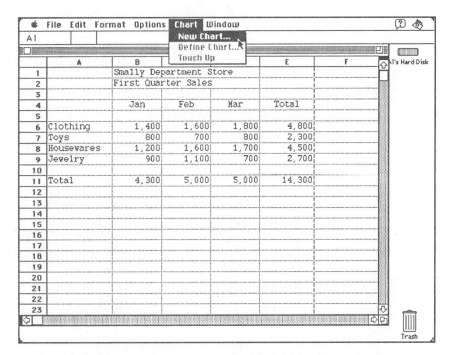

File Edit Format Options Chart Window

A1

SAMPLE (SS)

	A	B	C	D	E	
1		Smally Department Store				
2		First Quarter Sales				
3						
4		Jan	Feb	Mar	Total	
5						
6	Clothing	1,400	1,600	1,800	4,800	
7	Toys	800	700	800	2,300	
8	Housewares	1,200	1,600	1,700	4,500	
9	Jewelry	900	1,100	700	2,700	
10						
11	Total	4,300	5,000	5,000	14,300	
12						
13						
14						
15						
16						
17						
18						

Fig. 7.11 Sample data

6. Press and hold the 🖱.

7. Drag the pointer to the New Chart option (see Fig. 7.12).

8. Release the 🖱.

Fig. 7.12 Chart pull-down menu showing New Chart option

You should now have a dialog box in which to define the bar chart specifications (see Fig. 7.13).

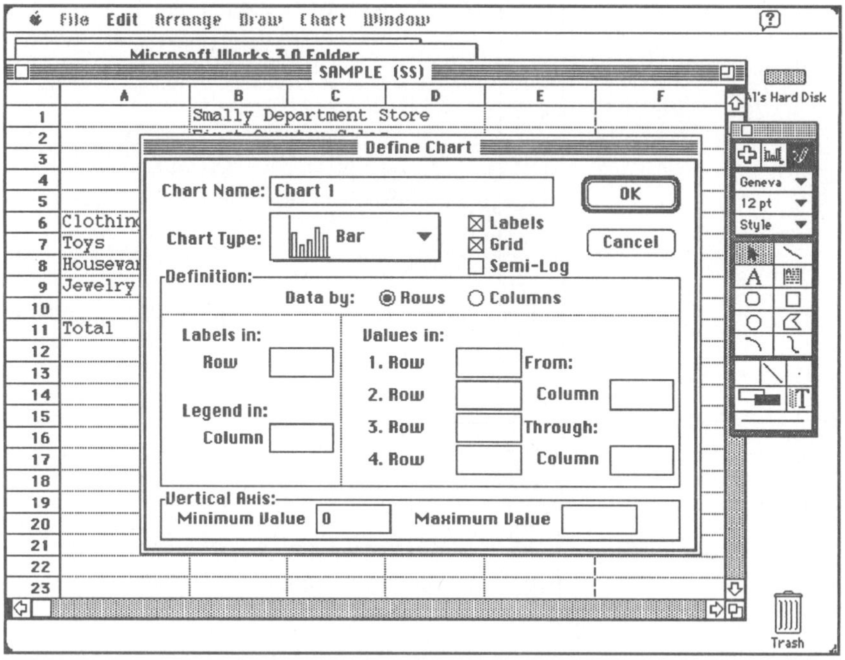

Fig. 7.13 Define Chart dialog box

Since Bar chart is the default, you don't need to change the chart type.

9. With the "Chart Name:" box highlighted, type **Toy Sales for the Three Months**.

10. Press [tab] to move the pointer to the "Labels in:" box.

11. Type **4** to enter the row number containing the labels.

12. Press [tab] to move the pointer to the "Legend in:" box.

13. Type **A** to indicate that the legend is in column A.

14. Press [tab] to move the pointer to the first "Values in:" box.

15. Type **7** to define the row containing the data.

16. Press [tab] four times to highlight the "From:" box.

17. Type **B** to enter the column containing the first data value.

18. Press [tab] to move the pointer to the "Through:" box.

19. Type **D** to enter the column containing the last data value.

20. Move the pointer to [OK].

21. Click the ⬜ to record the entries and create the chart.

Sizing and Moving the Chart

Use the handle boxes on the chart to size it within the page width and move it below the spreadsheet data.

1. Move the pointer to the handle box midway down the right border of the chart.

2. Drag this border to the left until it is to the left of the page break boundary, or within column E of the spreadsheet.

3. Move the pointer within the chart near the title area.

4. Drag the chart down in the spreadsheet until the top border of the chart is in row 13.

The spreadsheet should look similar to Fig. 7.14.

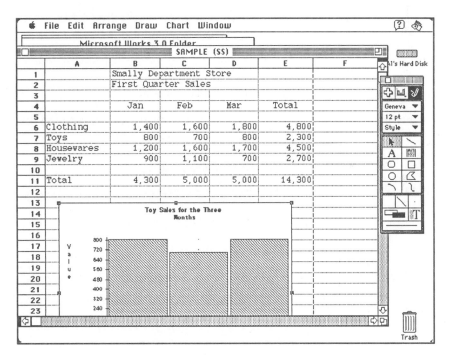

Fig. 7.14 Spreadsheet with chart

Saving the Chart

To save the chart on disk with the spreadsheet, save the spreadsheet.

1. Point to the File item on the main menu.

2. Press and hold the ⌫.

3. Drag the pointer to the Save option.

4. Release the ⌫.

The spreadsheet, including the chart, is now saved on disk.

Printing the Chart

You can print the chart by printing the spreadsheet.

First you must close the tool palette.

1. Move the pointer to the close box on the top left corner of the tool palette.

2. Click the ⌧ to close the tool palette.

3. Move the pointer to the File item on the main menu.

4. Press and hold the ⌧.

5. Drag the pointer to the Print option and release the ⌧.

6. Select ⌈ OK ⌋ on the print dialog box.

To print only the chart, highlight the portion of the spreadsheet containing the chart, then select the print option.

7. Move the pointer to just outside the upper left corner of the chart.

8. Press and hold the ⌧.

9. Drag the pointer to just outside the lower right corner of the chart, and release the ⌧.

10. Select the Print option from the File pull-down menu.

11. Select ⌈ OK ⌋ from the warning message.

12. Select ⌈ OK ⌋ from the print dialog box.

This should print the chart.

13. Click the ⌧ anywhere in the spreadsheet to remove the highlighting from the area.

Closing the File

You are now ready to close the file.

You can use the Close option on the File pull-down menu, or move the pointer to the close box on the left end of the title bar and click the ⌧.

1. Move the pointer to the close box.

2. Click the ⌧.

The spreadsheet should be gone from the desktop.

Exiting Works

To continue working on files once the file is closed, you would create a new file or open an existing one. Once you have completed the work session and are ready to leave Works, select the Quit option from the File pull-down menu. (If this option is not available, reopen SAMPLE by double clicking on the SAMPLE file icon, and close it again.)

1. Point to the File item on the main menu.

2. Press and hold the ⌖.

3. Drag the pointer to the Quit option.

4. Release the ⌖.

This should close the Works application.

To close the Works folder, select the Close Window option from the File pull-down menu, or point to the close box on the left end of the title bar, and click the mouse button.

5. Point to the File item on the main menu.

6. Press and hold the ⌖.

7. Drag the pointer to the Close Window option.

8. Release the ⌖.

This should return you to the Opening System Disk window.

If you have completed the work session, use the shut down procedure to terminate the machine operation.

PART II

Creating a Pie Chart

Using the sample spreadsheet in Fig. 7.11, you will create a pie chart depicting the percentage of January sales attributable to each of the four categories of sales. As seen in the figure, the total January sales were $4,300, which will represent 100% of the pie.

First, place the spreadsheet named SAMPLE into an active window.

1. From the Opening System Disk window, move the pointer to the Microsoft Works 3.0 Folder icon, and double click the ⌖.

This should open the Works Application window.

2. From a reference to the Microsoft Works 3.0 Folder, move the pointer to the icon representing Microsoft Works 3.0, and double click the ⌖.

You should now see the Works Opening dialog box. Retrieve the file named SAMPLE. (If you did not create the file in PART I of the Hands-on exercises, do it now.)

3. Click on the spreadsheet icon in the "Choose Type:" box to display the spreadsheet files.

4. Scroll through the list box of file names as necessary, and double click on the file named SAMPLE.

Now, with the spreadsheet in an active window, select the option to create a chart.

5. Point to the Chart item on the main menu.

6. Press and hold the ⬛.

7. Drag the pointer to the New Chart option (refer to Fig. 7.12).

8. Release the ⬛.

You should now have a dialog box in which to define the chart specifications (refer to Fig. 7.13).

Change chart type from Bar to Pie.

9. Move the pointer to the down arrow on the right side of the "Chart Type:" box.

10. Press and hold the ⬛ to display the chart types.

11. Drag the pointer to the Pie option, and release the ⬛.

You should see Pie displayed in the chart type box, and several options in the Define Chart box are changed.

12. With the "Chart Name:" box highlighted, type **January Sales by Department**.

13. Move the pointer to Columns in the "Data by:" box, and click the ⬛.

This will reverse the references in the labels and values boxes from row to column and from column to row.

14. Press ⬛tab⬛ until the insertion point is in the "Labels in: Column" box.

15. Type **A** to enter the column containing the labels.

16. Press ⬛tab⬛ until the insertion point is in the "Values in: Column" box.

17. Type **B** to enter the column containing the data values.

18. Press ⬛tab⬛ until the insertion point is in the "From: Row" box.

19. Type **6** to enter the row containing the first data value.

20. Press [tab] until the insertion point is in the "Through: Row" box.

21. Type **9** to enter the row containing the last data value.

The entries in the Define Chart box should appear similar to Fig. 7.15.

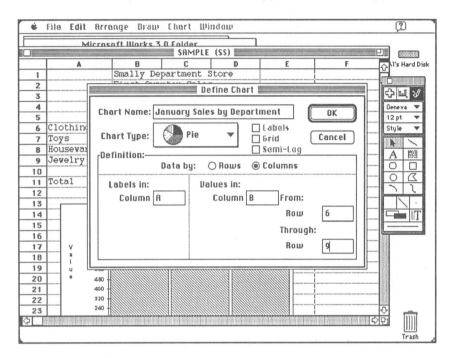

Fig. 7.15 Define Chart dialog box with pie chart entries

22. Select [OK] to create the chart.

The chart should appear similar to Fig. 7.16.

Narrow the chart until it is less than the width of the page boundaries.

23. Move the pointer to the handle box on the middle of the right border of the chart.

24. Drag the border to the left until the right border of the chart is to the left of the page boundary indicator (the dashed line).

Now drag the chart to the right of the spreadsheet data and to the right of the page boundary line.

25. Move the pointer to the left side of the chart, just inside the left border.

26. Drag the chart to the right until the left border is to the right of all data and to the right of the first page break boundary indicator.

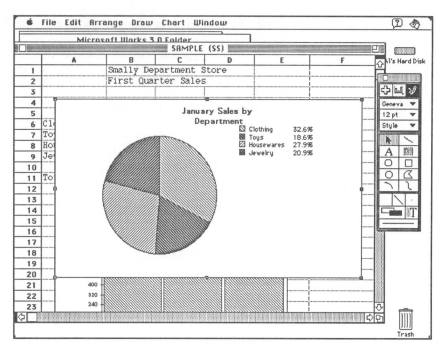

Fig. 7.16 Pie chart of January sales by department

Saving the Chart

To save the chart on disk with the spreadsheet, save the spreadsheet.

1. Point to the File item on the main menu.

2. Press and hold the ⌒.

3. Drag the pointer to the Save option.

4. Release the ⌒.

The spreadsheet, including the bar chart and the pie chart , is now saved on disk.

Printing the Chart

You can print the charts now in the spreadsheet by printing the spreadsheet.

First you must close the tool palette.

1. Move the pointer to the close box on the top left corner of the tool palette.

2. Click the ⌒ to close the tool palette.

3. Move the pointer to the File item on the main menu.

4. Press and hold the ⌒.

5. Drag the pointer to the Print option and release the ⌒.

6. Select ⟨OK⟩ on the print dialog box.

To print only the pie chart and exclude any grid lines, highlight the portion of the spreadsheet containing the pie chart. Then remove the grid lines and select the print option.

7. Move the pointer to just outside the upper left corner of the pie chart.

8. Press and hold the ⟨⟩.

9. Drag the pointer to just outside the lower right corner of the pie chart, and release the ⟨⟩.

10. Select the Show Grid option from the Options pull-down menu to remove the grid lines from the spreadsheet.

11. Select the Print option from the File pull-down menu.

12. Select ⟨OK⟩ from the warning message.

13. Select ⟨OK⟩ from the print dialog box.

This should print the chart.

14. Select the Show Grid option from the Options pull-down menu to display grid lines on the spreadsheet

15. Click the ⟨⟩ anywhere in the spreadsheet to remove the highlighting from the area.

Closing the File

You are now ready to close the file.

You can use the Close option on the File pull-down menu, or move the pointer to the close box on the left end of the title bar and click the the mouse button.

1. Move the pointer to the close box.

2. Click the ⟨⟩.

The spreadsheet should be gone from the desktop.

Exiting Works

To continue working on other files once the file is closed, you would create a new file or open an existing one. Once you have completed the work session and are ready to leave Works, select the Quit option from the File pull-down menu. (If this option is not available, reopen SAMPLE by double clicking on the SAMPLE file icon, and close it again.)

1. Point to the File item on the main menu.

2. Press and hold the ⌒.

3. Drag the pointer to the Quit option.

4. Release the ⌒.

This should close the Works application.

To close the Works folder, select the Close Window option from the File pull-down menu, or point to the close box on the left end of the title bar, and click the mouse button.

5. Point to the File item on the main menu.

6. Press and hold the ⌒.

7. Drag the pointer to the Close Window option.

8. Release the ⌒.

This should return you to the Opening System Disk window.

If you have completed the work session, use the shut down procedure to terminate the machine operation.

PART III

Duplicating the Chart

You will duplicate the series chart created in PART I of the Hands-on exercises, then modify it to create a second series chart.

First, place the spreadsheet named SAMPLE into an active window. (If you did not complete PART I above, do it now.)

1. From the Opening System Disk window, move the pointer to the Microsoft Works 3.0 Folder icon, and double click the ⌒.

This should open the Works Application window.

2. From a reference to the Works Application window, move the pointer to the icon representing Microsoft Works 3.0, and double click the ⌒.

You should now see the Works Opening dialog box. Retrieve the file named SAMPLE.

3. Click on the spreadsheet icon in the "Choose Type:" box to display the spreadsheet files.

4. Scroll through the list box of file names as necessary, and double click on the file named SAMPLE.

Now, with the spreadsheet in an active window, select the chart that you want to duplicate.

5. Point to the Chart item on the main menu.

6. Press and hold the .

7. Drag the pointer to the chart name "Toy Sales for the Three Months".

8. Release the .

The chart should now be active.

9. Point to the Edit item on the main menu.

10. Press and hold the .

11. Drag the pointer to the Duplicate option (see Fig. 7.17).

12. Release the .

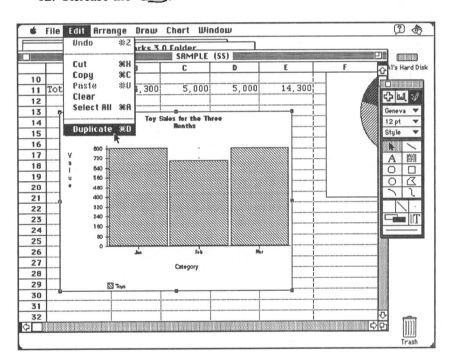

Fig. 7.17 Edit pull-down menu showing Duplicate option

You should now see a second chart for toy sales in the window, and it is now active.

Notice that it is named "Toy Sales for the Three Mo copy." The word "copy" is added to the name.

Modifying the Chart Definition

You will make this a multiple-bar graph, comparing Toys sales to Housewares sales.

1. With the chart copy active, point to Chart on the main menu.

2. Press and hold the ⌒.

3. Drag the pointer to the Define Chart option.

4. Release the ⌒.

You should now see a Define Chart window for the copy of the bar chart.

Change the title to Toys and Housewares Sales.

5. With the Chart Name box highlighted, type **Toys and Housewares Sales**.

6. Press [tab] until the pointer is in the "Values in: 2. Row" box.

7. Type **8** to include the housewares data in the chart.

8. Select [OK] to modify the chart.

You should now see a multiple-bar chart depicting toy and housewares sales for the three months.

Move the chart to another location in the spreadsheet.

9. With the multiple-bar chart active, move the pointer just inside the upper left corner of the chart.

10. Press and hold the ⌒.

11. Drag the chart to a position to the right of the page boundary and below the pie chart, and release the ⌒.

12. Move the window to view the chart, and be sure it is positioned above the lower page boundary. If it is not, move the chart up and, if necessary, move the pie chart up, until both charts are within the page boundaries.

You now have three charts in the spreadsheet.

Saving and Printing the Chart

You will save the spreadsheet containing the three charts, then print the multiple-bar chart just created.

To save the chart on disk with the spreadsheet, save the spreadsheet.

1. Point to the File item on the main menu.

2. Press and hold the ⌒.

3. Drag the pointer to the Save option.

4. Release the .

The spreadsheet, including the bar chart, the pie chart, and the multiple-bar chart, is now saved on disk.

To print only the multiple-bar chart and exclude any grid lines, close the tool palette, and then highlight the portion of the spreadsheet containing the multiple-bar chart. Then remove the grid lines, and select the print option.

5. Move the pointer to the close box on the left end of the tool palette, and click the .

6. Move the pointer to just outside the upper left corner of the multiple-bar chart.

7. Press and hold the .

8. Drag the pointer to just outside the lower right corner of the multiple-bar chart, and release the .

9. Select the Show Grid option from the Options pull-down menu to remove the grid lines from the spreadsheet.

10. Select the Print option from the File pull-down menu.

11. Select ⎡OK⎤ from the warning message.

12. Select ⎡OK⎤ from the print dialog box.

This should print the chart.

13. Select the Show Grid option from the Options pull-down menu to display grid lines on the spreadsheet

14. Click the anywhere in the spreadsheet to remove the high-lighting from the area.

Closing the File and Exiting Works

You are now ready to close the file.

You can use the Close option on the File pull-down menu, or move the pointer to the close box on the left end of the title bar and click the mouse button.

1. Move the pointer to the close box.

2. Click the .

The spreadsheet should be gone from the desktop.

Once you have completed the work session and are ready to leave Works, select the Quit option from the File pull-down menu. (If this option is not available, reopen SAMPLE by double clicking on the SAMPLE file icon, and close it again.)

3. Point to the File item on the main menu.

4. Press and hold the ⌖.

5. Drag the pointer to the Quit option.

6. Release the ⌖.

This should close the Works application.

To close the Works folder, select the Close Window option from the File pull-down menu, or point to the close box on the left end of the title bar, and click the mouse button.

7. Point to the File item on the main menu.

8. Press and hold the ⌖.

9. Drag the pointer to the Close Window option.

10. Release the ⌖.

This should return you to the Opening System Disk window.

If you have completed the work session, use the shut down procedure to terminate the machine operation.

Summary

Graphics capability allows a user to convey a message that is sometimes lost when using large amounts of information represented by numbers. Personal computers have the capability to store and manipulate data, and the data can be used to generate charts.

Charts have the capability to display large amounts of data in a pictorial format that is easy to understand. There are several commonly used types of charts.

1. Bar graphs plot the value of a numeric quantity relating to a descriptive category.

2. Multiple-bar graphs display several quantities in each category in a graph.

3. Stacked-bar graphs display values of a category in a cumulative fashion, with the bar representing the total for the category.

4. Pie charts represent a single series of data, with the individual values displayed in proportional relationships.

5. Line graphs plot one or more series of values on the vertical axis (y) against a descriptive variable along the horizontal axis (x).

To create a chart with Microsoft Works, data is first entered in the spreadsheet tool. A series chart is created by charting one or more data series relating to a descriptive variable. A pie chart is drawn using a single series of data.

Questions

1. What are labels that are attached to a series or a group of series called?

2. What type of graph is a chart that draws bars on top of one another?

3. What percentage must all the individual segments in a pie chart total?

4. Why is it important to use business graphics?

5. What is a bar graph?

6. When is it appropriate to use a bar graph?

7. When is it appropriate to use a line graph?

8. What are the advantages of using a line graph over a bar graph?

9. How many series can be plotted in a pie chart? Why?

10. What is a stacked-bar graph?

Exercises

Exercise 1

Using the data below, create a spreadsheet.

Person	John	Judy	Mark	Peter	Susan
Sales	44,823	51,088	36,721	32,903	34,332

1. Enter Sales Person in row 1 and Total Sales in row 2.

2. Create a bar graph that displays the Sales Person on the x-axis and the Total Sales on the y-axis.

3. Save the spreadsheet as GDATA1.

Exercise 2

Create a spreadsheet using the data below.

	Pants	Shirts	Shoes	Hats
Store 1	25,000	35,000	12,000	17,000
Store 2	26,000	43,000	10,000	19,000
Store 3	30,000	27,000	15,000	21,000

1. Create a multiple-bar graph that displays the items sold on the x-axis and the sales totals on the y-axis.

2. Add the following title to the graph: "Total Sales"

3. Save the spreadsheet and graph as GDATA2, and print the graph.

Problems

Problem 1

Create the following spreadsheet.

Total Sales for 1994

	Store 1	Store 2	Store 3	Total
Pants	25,000	26,000	30,000	81,000
Shirts	35,000	43,000	27,000	105,000
Shoes	12,000	10,000	15,000	37,000
Underwear	11,000	12,000	11,500	34,500
Ties	7,000	6,000	5,000	18,000
Accessories	17,000	19,000	21,000	57,000
Total	107,000	116,000	109,500	332,500

1. Create a stacked-bar graph showing total dollars for each store, displayed by clothing category.

2. Create a multiple-bar graph with each store displayed by clothing category.

3. Save the graphs and spreadsheet as GDATA3.

4. Print the graphs.

Problem 2

Retrieve the spreadsheet and graphs created in Problem 1.

     1. Add the title "Total Sales" to each graph.

     2. Save the spreadsheet and graphs.

     3. Print the graphs.

Problem 3

Use the spreadsheet created in Problem 1.

     1. Create a pie chart showing the percentage of total sales attributed to each type of clothing.

     2. Save the spreadsheet and chart.

     3. Print the pie chart.

Chapter 8

Database Management

Objectives

After completing this chapter you will

1. Understand the common uses of a database.

2. Be familiar with the characteristics of a database.

3. Be able to define and explain database terms, including *field*, *record*, *file*, *text field*, and *numeric field*.

4. Be able to distinguish between form and list modes in data management.

5. Be able to manage pointer movement effectively in the design and data views of Works.

6. Be able to modify a database form using the design view of Works.

7. Be able to maintain a database using the data view of Works.

8. Be able to manage pointer movement effectively in the list view of Works.

9. Be able to create, save, and print a database using the list view of Works.

10. Be able to maintain a database in the list view of Works.

The Database Tool

What Is a Database?

A database consists of a series of data with similar characteristics. An example of a commonly used database is a telephone book. It contains a series of names, addresses, and telephone numbers stored in the same type of sequence. There is inherent consistency in that for each name there is a corresponding address and telephone number, and for each telephone number there is a corresponding name and address. In database terminology, name, address, and telephone number are called *fields*. The combination of name, address, and telephone number for any one person is called a *record*, and the telephone book is called a *file* or *database*.

Other examples of commonly used business database applications include personnel, customer, and inventory management. A personnel database includes such fields as name, address, employee number, job grade, salary, employment date, and many other fields of data. The data for any one employee is called a record. A customer database includes one record for each customer, and fields might include name, address, rating code, last purchase date, year-to-date purchases, and many other items. An inventory database includes a record for each item of inventory. Each inventory item will have a field for inventory numbers, quantity on hand, reorder point, price, and various other data. We normally refer to the database fields as the data and the extracted results as the information.

Whether the above databases are stored in books, manila folders, or shoe boxes, they share the common characteristics described. The size of the database will generally determine the degree of sophistication involved in storing and processing the data. Also, there is a method by which the data is maintained and accessed. Think for a moment how impractical a telephone book would be if the names were not stored in alphabetical order.

Using a database typically includes the planning of what data will be stored and how it will be maintained. It also involves defining how data will be retrieved from the database. The telephone book is intended to store all persons with telephones in a given area and provide easy reference "by name" to each person's address and telephone number. Therefore the name is listed first in each record, and the records are listed in alphabetical order.

Planning a Database

When developing a database, it is important to look at what uses will be made of the data. The intended use of the database will dictate which fields are needed, which fields will be used with each other, and how often fields will be used. This in turn will dictate the fields to be included in the database and how they are to be maintained.

While it is difficult to define all possible uses of the database in the planning stage, it is possible to clarify its primary purpose. All potential users should be asked to identify their intended uses of the data, including such things as which reports are expected, how often they are needed, and what data will be included in them. By reviewing the proposed uses, the specific fields needed can be listed. Then the importance of each field can be weighed against the overhead of storing and maintaining it. It is good to know, for example, an employee's previous address, but if it is used only in rare cases when accessing personnel information, its utility may be questioned. Fields that are accessed more often than others may need to be updated more often to keep them current.

Creating and Maintaining a Database

It is important to clarify how the data will be stored in a database. Consistency is vital in providing easy access and maintainability. In such areas as personnel, for example, a form is typically used to store all relevant fields of data, thus providing consistency of format and ensuring that all data is collected. Each employee's records may be kept in a separate folder, but the data in each folder should be in a common format.

Maintenance procedures should be well defined. How and when updates are made to the data will ultimately determine the integrity of the data. As new records are introduced (e.g., a new employee is hired), a record must be created containing all the required fields. When a record is no longer needed (e.g., a part is deleted from inventory), the record should be removed from the database. Any changes in a field of data (e.g., salary increases) must be entered in a timely manner, or the database will become useless.

Automating the Database

None of the procedures above requires a computer. However, in today's environment, it is unlikely that they will be performed without one. Generally, an automated database requires the same planning and implementation as a manual one. Depending on the sophistication of the database program, more rigid rules may be followed in defining the user requirements, listing all the required fields to be maintained (referred to as a data dictionary), and in creating and maintaining the database. The rules associated with an automated database are intended to help ensure the integrity of the data.

As with other applications, the typical reasons for automating a database are the speed with which the user can extract information from it, the accuracy of the data, and the flexibility of usage. Database applications have been common on large computers since the early 1970s, and they became common on the microcomputer in the early 1980s. A major attraction to the user is the ability to interactively query the database and extract information in various forms, without extensive programming and without waiting several days or weeks for the results. The database concept has extended far beyond the mainstay applications of payroll and inventory into such things as mailing lists, maintenance logs, and monitoring of activity. Any application that involves a series of similar data and periodic extraction and usage of information from the data is a candidate for an automated database.

Creating a Database File with Works

The Database Window

As seen in Chapter 2, Works is started the same way, regardless of which application is being used. When the Works Application is selected from the Opening System Disk window, the Microsoft Works 3.0 Folder window will display the folders and files pertaining to the Works program (see Fig. 8.1). To use the Works Application program, move the pointer to the icon containing the small pictures, and double click the mouse button. The desktop will then display the Works Opening dialog box (see Fig. 8.2).

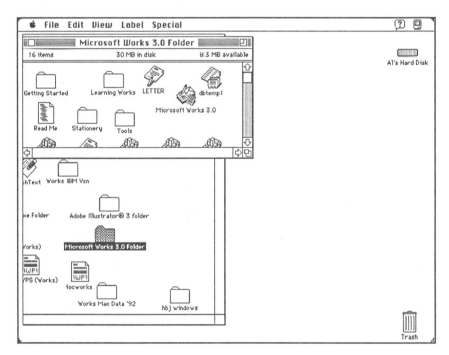

Fig. 8.1 Microsoft Works 3.0 Folder window

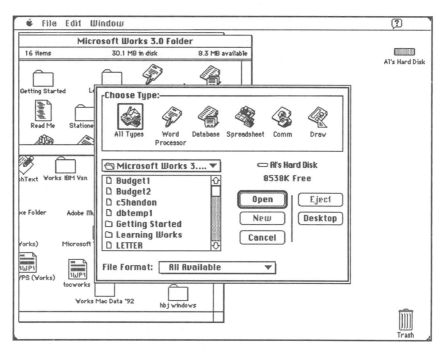

Fig. 8.2 Works Opening dialog box

The boxed icon at the top of the window indicates the currently active application type and the list box on the lower left shows the folders and files in the active application. Remember that a folder is simply a compartment that can contain more files and folders. To open an existing folder or file, move the pointer to the desired name and double click the mouse button, or highlight the name by clicking the mouse button, and then select the Open button by clicking on it. The lower right portion of the dialog box includes options to open a highlighted folder or file or to cancel an operation. If a desired folder or file is on another disk, it can be referenced by selecting the Desktop button and then the appropriate disk name. To open a new file, move the pointer to the icon representing the type of new file desired (e.g., Database), and double click the mouse button (or click on the type and then click on the New button).

Whether you are using an existing database file or creating a new one, the database window will appear and allow for entering and editing text. There are two form views used to display only one record, called design view and data view. A third view, called list view, displays the data as a list of records, showing as many records as possible in the window. The database is initially created in data view, then modified using data, design, or list view. The window display will differ depending on which view is in use.

The data view of the database is displayed similar to the design view (see Fig. 8.3). It is used to enter and modify data. Records can be searched and sorted in this view. One record is displayed at a time. Enhancements can be made to the data view by using the draw feature.

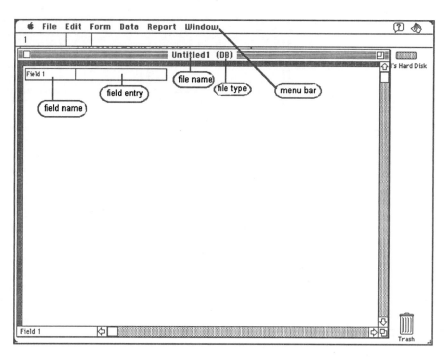

Fig. 8.3 Data view of database

The design view of the database is used to add and delete fields to and from the database. It is also used to resize, rename, and format fields on a form. Fig. 8.4 shows the items available in design view. Notice that handle boxes are visible on the field name and the field entry area. When multiple fields are on the form, only one of them will be actively referenced and will have the handle boxes displayed. Enhancements can be made to the design view by using the draw feature.

Changes made in design view will be displayed in data view. Fields added in the design view will be added to the database and to list view if not already there. Fields deleted in design view will not be deleted from list view. It is not necessary to have all the fields in the database included in a design or data view, since form views are used to maintain the database and several forms may be used simultaneously with a single database.

The list view of the database displays multiple records in the window. It can be used to add and delete records and fields. It can be used to enter and modify data. You can also search and sort data when in list view. Fig. 8.5 shows the display format of list view.

The method of entering and maintaining data will be explained using data view as a reference. The process of designing a database form will be explained using design view as the reference. Finally, the method of modifying the database and maintaining data will be explained using list view. It is recommended that you maintain data primarily from either data or list view exclusively, until you become familiar with, and relatively proficient in, the use of both.

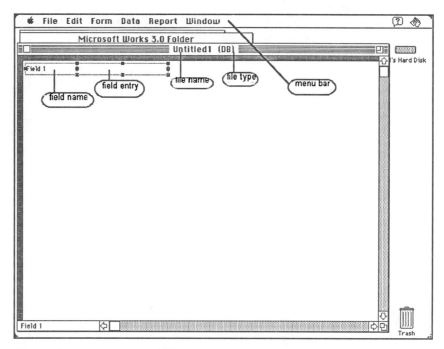

Fig. 8.4 Design view of database

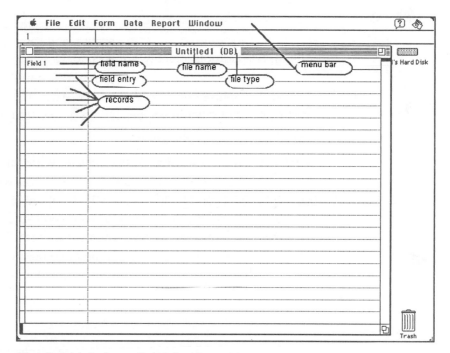

Fig. 8.5 List view of database

Data View

Characteristics of Data View

Data view provides the capability of simply listing the field names down the left side of the window. The fields can be structured to match the appearance of the document. Fig. 8.6 shows an example of a data view display, containing field names and a data record.

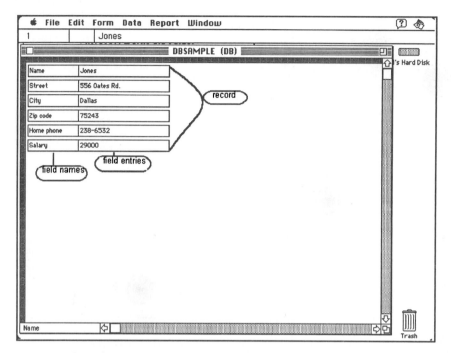

Fig. 8.6 Sample display showing data view

Data view displays one record at a time. The fields contained in a record can be in one or more windows, depending on the size of the record, but no more than one record will appear in any window.

When a database is created, Works will provide an opportunity to define the fields to be used. The first window shown to you will be a New Field dialog box that allows you to add fields to the database (see Fig. 8.7). By entering a field name, then selecting the OK button, you can define as many field names as desired. Each one will be placed in the database. If you do not want the field name displayed, select the Show Name Field box to turn off the display. Once you have defined all the fields, select the Done button. Other fields can be added later by using the design view and selecting the Place Field option on the Form pull-down menu.

Formatting Fields

Each field is assigned a format "type" as it is created. The types of field formats available in Works include Text, Number, Date, and Time. Text treats the data as a string of characters. Number treats the data as a number. Date format displays the entry as a date, and Time format displays it as time. The default assignment is Text format. The format type can be changed when the field is created by selecting the Format button from the New Field dialog box (refer to

Fig. 8.7), then assigning the format in the Format Field dialog box (see Fig. 8.8).

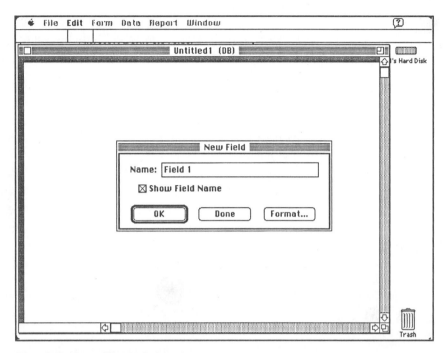

Fig. 8.7 New Field dialog box

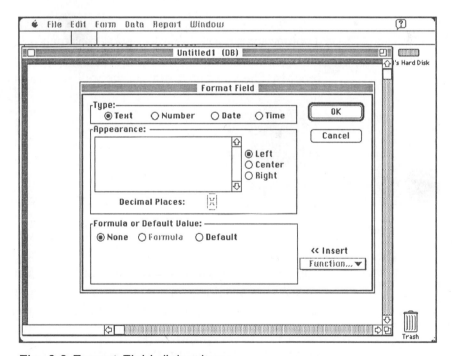

Fig. 8.8 Format Field dialog box

You can assign the format to be text, number, date, or time by selecting the corresponding button. With number, date, or time format, you can select the specific format characteristics from the Appearance list box. For number format, you can also specify options that include fixed, comma, currency, percentage, and scientific notation, and the number of decimal places can also be assigned. You can choose the Left, Center, or Right button to specify the placement of the data in the field. The default location for data is left justified.

Entering Records

Once the field names are entered, you are ready to enter data into the file. Use the pointer to refer to the appropriate field, and click the mouse button to make the field active. Use the TAB key to move down a field in the current record and the SHIFT/TAB keys to move up a field in the current record. You can also use the arrow keys to move from one entry to the next. The TAB key will stay within the current record by rolling from the last to the first field or from the first to last field, depending on the direction. The arrow keys will move to the next consecutive record after reaching the last field in the current record.

To move quickly from record to record, use the COMMAND key and the HOME or END key. Use COMMAND/= to move to the next consecutive record, and use COMMAND/- to move to the previous consecutive record. The HOME key will display the first record in the file. The END key will display the last record that contains data.

You can also use the tool palette to navigate through records. Select the Show Tools option from the Window pull-down menu. Then use the arrows to move through the records and the slide arrow to drag the reference point through the records. The numbered box on the tool palette indicates the current record number. To remove the tool palette, select Hide Tools from the Window pull-down menu.

Saving a Database

Any database that is created should be saved from memory onto disk periodically to prevent loss or damage to it if an error or system failure occurs during processing. Two options exist on the File pull-down menu that allow for saving the database and continuing to work with it without needing to retrieve it again. The Save option allows for saving it under its currently assigned name. The Save As option allows for changing or assigning the name of the database to be saved. With either option, the database remains in memory for continued processing.

When a database is created, the name area indicates "Untitled1" (or Untitled "n"). When the database is saved, a name must be assigned to it. The name must be unique from other files stored in the folder. Any previous file saved under that name would be destroyed and any future file saved under that name will destroy the current one. To assign a name to a file, use the Save As option. When that option is used, a dialog box will allow for entering a name. Once the name is typed, move the pointer to the Save button and click the mouse button to save the file and return to the database.

If a document has already been assigned a name and you don't want to change it, the Save As option is not needed. Selecting the Save option will save the file under its current name and return you to the database. Saving the memory copy of a database causes it to replace any version previously saved under the same name. If a backup or duplicate copy is desired, it should be saved under a separate name with the Save As option or stored in a separate folder.

Printing Records in Data View

To print all the records in the file at this point, you can select the Print option from the File pull-down menu. This will print one record per page in the format of the data view. To get a printout of a form view without data, refer to the topic of printing design view. If you want to print selected records, study the record selection feature covered in Chapter 9, and select the records prior to printing. If you want to print in a different format, study the report option in Chapter 9 and create a report format prior to printing.

Updating a Database

Retrieving a Database

To retrieve an existing database from the disk into memory, select the document icon from the window, or select the folder icon of the folder containing the file, or select the file from a list of file names in the Works Opening dialog box. If you are in the Opening System Disk window, first select the Microsoft Works 3.0 Folder from the folders on your disk. Then select the Works icon indicating Microsoft Works 3.0 to access the Works Opening dialog box. To retrieve the database from the disk into memory, select the name of the file from the names in the list box or select the folder containing the file. If the file is not in data view, select Data View from the Form pull-down menu. One record will be displayed in the window. The current record number will be displayed in the box on the left side of the desktop on the second line from the top.

Updating a Field

The COMMAND/= and COMMAND/- keys can be used to locate the record that is to be updated. Once the appropriate record is in the window, use the TAB or arrow keys to move to the appropriate field entry, or use the pointer to highlight the appropriate field. To edit the field entry, point to the field contents on the edit line, and click the mouse button to create an insertion point. Then use the arrow keys and other keys as necessary to correct the entry. This is often more practical than retyping the entire entry. Pressing the RETURN or ENTER key completes the edit process. Use the paging and pointer control as necessary to update other fields.

If a field entry is to be removed, you can highlight the field contents with the pointer and press the DELETE key. Then press ENTER to complete the deletion process and keep that cell active. The contents of the field can then be left blank or replaced by typing in a new entry.

Adding or Deleting a Record

A record can be added by moving the pointer to the record immediately following the last record containing data. You can enter one field at a time and use the TAB, RETURN, or arrow keys to move from field to field. This is referred to as appending a record to the end of the database. More records can be added by continuing to move into new record areas and entering data.

A record can be added within existing records by using the Insert Record option on the Data pull-down menu (see Fig. 8.9). Move the cell pointer to the record number where you want the record inserted and select the option. A blank record will be inserted at the current record location. The record previously there and all subsequent records will be moved down one record number, creating one more record number in the database. The data for the new record can then be entered using the procedure defined above.

A record can be deleted by using the Delete Record option on the Data pull-down menu (refer to Fig. 8.9). Move the pointer anywhere in the record to be deleted and select the option. The record will be deleted, and all subsequent records will be moved up one record location in the database.

Restructuring the Database in Design View

Once a database is defined, it is common to position and size the fields in a way that is meaningful to the user. You will typically want to have them in a preferred sequence. You may want them to appear similar to a form that the data is coming from. The field size should also be correlated to the size of the data being stored in the field. It is common to add fields to the database, and therefore to the form referencing it. Fields may also be removed from the data view, since they may be deleted from the database or not needed in a particular form reference.

The Design View option on the Form pull-down menu (see Fig. 8.10) is used to modify the format of the form display and to add and delete fields from the form. A check beside it indicates that it is the currently active view. When the design view is active, you can move and size fields using the handle boxes to reference any field and make the necessary changes.

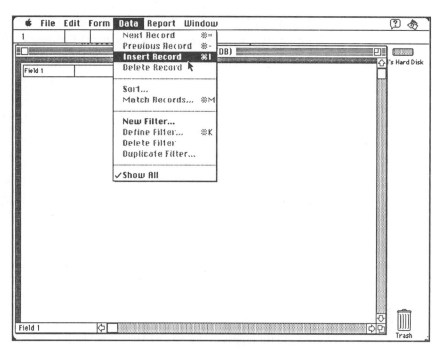

Fig. 8.9 Data pull-down menu showing Insert Record option

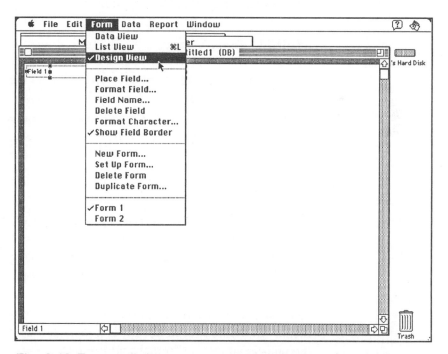

Fig. 8.10 Form pull-down menu showing Design View option

Clicking on a field will make it active and display the handle boxes. You can move the field with the handle boxes by positioning the pointer in the field area and dragging it to the desired location. You can size the name area by pointing to the handle box on the left end of the name area and dragging it to the desired position. You can make a field longer or shorter by dragging the middle handle box on the right border of the entry area of the field. You can make a field taller or shorter by dragging on the middle upper or lower border handle box on the entry area. You can use the corner handle boxes to drag the entry box diagonally to make it larger or smaller. You can modify the format of an existing field by using the Format Field option on the Form pull-down menu (refer to Fig. 8.10). This will allow you to change such things as the field type and the position of data in the field (refer to Fig. 8.8). You can also change the name of a field by selecting the Field Name option from the Form pull-down menu.

To delete a field from the form, first click on the field to make it active. Then select the Delete Field option from the Form pull-down menu (refer to Fig. 8.10). The field will be removed from the form, but will remain in the database, since it could be included in other forms. Any number of fields can be deleted from a form in this manner.

To add a field to a form, select the Place Field option from the Form pull-down menu (refer to Fig. 8.10). A Place Field dialog box will be displayed that allows you to choose fields that are currently in the database, but not on the form. There is also a New button in the Place Field dialog box, and selecting it will allow you to create a new field on the form. A New Field dialog box will be displayed to allow you to create and format a new field (refer to Fig. 8.7). New fields created will automatically be added to the database.

Multiple Data Views

Works provides the ability to have up to 16 data views for a database. Each one can include all or part of the fields in the database. When a database is created, a database and a data view are defined, including all the fields specified. This provides initial reference to all the fields in a database. As new data views are created, some or all of the original fields may be included, and new ones may be added, thus providing multiple ways of viewing fields and maintaining data in a database.

A new data view can be created by selecting the New Form option from the Form pull-down menu (refer to Fig. 8.10). A New/Set Up Form dialog box will allow for naming the form and including existing fields and/or creating new fields to be included in it. The Set Up Form option on the Form pull-down menu can be used to change the name of any form currently in use. An existing form can be referenced by choosing the form name from the Form pull-down menu. All defined forms for the active database will be listed at the bottom of the pull-down menu (Form 1 and Form 2 in Fig. 8.10).

A form may no longer be needed because of changes in the database or in the maintenance of it. A data view can be deleted by making it active, then choosing the Delete Form option from the Form pull-down menu.

A form can be duplicated by making it active and selecting the Duplicate Form option from the Form pull-down menu. This is helpful when wanting two data

240

views that are similar. You can make a duplicate, then modify it, rather than having to create the data view from nothing.

List View

Entering List View Mode

List view provides an alternative way of viewing and maintaining the database. Rather than displaying one record at a time in the window, the fields are stored in columns across the window and each line (row) represents a record. List view is intended to provide easy access to many fields and records simultaneously. Although you can use data and list views interchangeably with the same database to provide flexibility, it is recommended that you avoid unnecessary changing of modes until you are comfortable with both. The recommended approach is to use data view(s) to enter and modify records, and use list view to review data and extract information.

List view is entered from the Form pull-down menu by selecting the List View option (see Fig. 8.11). Many of the operations in list view will be similar to those used in spreadsheets, and the data has the appearance of a spreadsheet.

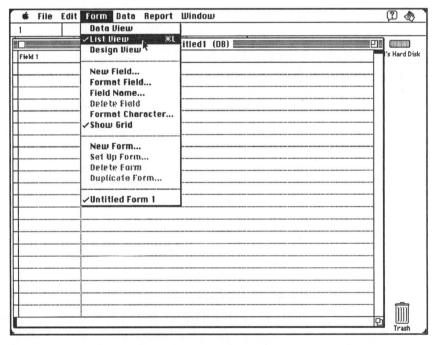

Fig. 8.11 Form pull-down menu showing List View option

Cell Pointer Control

In list view, use the pointer to refer to the appropriate field, and click the mouse button to make the field active. Use the TAB key to move one field to the right in the current record and the SHIFT/TAB keys to move one field to the left in the current record. The TAB key will wrap from one record to the next after reaching the last field in the current record. You can also use the arrow keys to move from one entry cell to the next in any direction. The arrow keys will also move to the next consecutive record after reaching the last field in the current record.

To move from record to record, you can also use the COMMAND key. Use COMMAND/= to move to the next consecutive record, and use COMMAND/- to move to the previous consecutive record.

Changing Field Width

Field width is changed in list view the same way it is changed in data view. Move the pointer to the right side border of the heading box of the field to be resized. You should see the pointer symbol change its shape to a cross. Press and hold the mouse button. Drag the pointer to the right or left to make the field width larger or smaller. When you are at the appropriate size, release the mouse button.

Naming Fields

If the fields were created in data view, they will already be named. A field name can be changed in list view by first selecting the field by pointing to the field name (you should see the hand symbol) and clicking the mouse button to highlight the field. Then select the Field Name option from the Form pull-down menu (refer to Fig. 8.11). Entering a new field name in the dialog box will change the name in both list view and data view.

Formatting a Field

A field can be formatted at the time it is created, or formatting can be added later. The Format option in the New Field dialog box provides the formatting option when a field is created. After a field is in a database, it can be formatted or the format can be modified. First, make the field active by moving the pointer to a cell in the field and clicking the mouse button to make it active. Then select the Format Field option on the Form pull-down menu. This will display the Format Field dialog box and allow you to set the formatting characteristics.

Each field is assigned a format "type" as it is created. The types of field formats available in Works include Text, Number, Date, and Time. Text treats the data as a string of characters. Number treats the data as a number. Date format displays the entry as a date, and Time format displays it as time. The default assignment is Text format. You can assign the format to be text, number, date, or time by selecting the corresponding button. With number, date, or time format, you can select the specific format characteristics from the Appearance list box. For number format, you can also specify options that include fixed, comma, currency, percentage, and scientific notation, and the number of decimal places can also be assigned. You can choose the Left, Center, or Right button to specify the placement of the data in the field. The default location for data is left justified.

Adding a Field

A new field can be added by selecting the New Field option on the Form pull-down menu (refer to Fig. 8.11). Before selecting the option, place the pointer in the column where you want the field inserted, and click the mouse button. The active field will move to the right, and the new field will be inserted to its immediate left. A New Field dialog box will allow you to name the field (refer to Fig. 8.7). The name must be different than the name of any existing field in the database. You can also format the field at the time it is created by selecting the Format option in the New Field dialog box.

Deleting a Field

To delete a field from the database, point to the field name (you should see the hand symbol) and click the mouse button to highlight the field. Then select the Delete Field option from the Form pull-down menu (refer to Fig. 8.11). When the warning box is displayed, select the OK button to delete the field. If you want to delete only the data and not the field, rather than using the Delete Field option, select the Cut or Clear option from the Edit pull-down menu after highlighting the field (see Fig. 8.12). The Cut option will put the data on the clipboard. The Clear option will not put it in the clipboard.

Moving a Field

To move a field, first place the pointer on the field name (you should see the hand symbol). Then press and hold the mouse button. Drag the pointer to the left or right until the field is in the appropriate position. Then release the mouse button. As you drag the pointer, you will notice that field names are being highlighted as you cross them. The field being moved will be placed following the current one highlighted, in the direction you are moving. The move process will close the cell space being vacated and create space for the field in the new location.

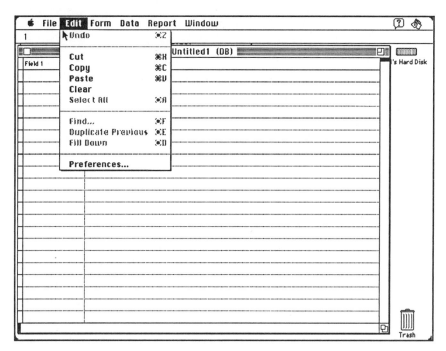

Fig. 8.12 Edit pull-down menu

Updating a Record

To change the contents of a field entry in a record, first make the cell containing the current entry active by pointing to it and clicking the mouse button. You will then see its contents on the edit line (just below the menu bar). Move the pointer to the edit line and to the portion of the data to be changed, and click the mouse button to create an insertion point. Make the change to the data. Press the RETURN or ENTER key (RETURN moves the pointer down a record, ENTER keeps the pointer at the same record), or click on the check box to record the change.

It is sometimes more practical to enter the new contents of an entry rather than modify the existing contents. First make the cell active. Then select the Cut or Clear option from the Edit pull-down menu (refer to Fig. 8.12). The Cut option will store the contents of the field in the clipboard. The Clear option will not. Then enter the correct data, and press the RETURN or ENTER key, or click on the check box to record the entry.

Deleting a Record

A record can be deleted by moving the pointer to the small box at the left end of the record and clicking the mouse button to highlight the record. Then select the Clear option from the Edit pull-down menu (refer to Fig. 8.12) to delete the record. This does not, however, remove the record from the database. To remove the data and the record from the database, select the Cut option from the Edit pull-down menu, rather than the Clear option.

Adding a Record

To append a new record, move the pointer to the row of cells below the last record and enter the data. To insert a record within existing records, make a cell active in the record that will be the first record to follow the record being inserted. Then select the Insert Record option from the Data pull-down menu (refer to Fig. 8.9). This will create a blank record and move all records at and below the active cell down one record. The data can be entered into the newly created blank area.

Moving a Record

Moving a record requires a two-step process. First cut the record from the file, then paste it in the new position. Move the pointer to the small box at the left end of the record to be moved. Click the mouse button to highlight the record. Then select the Cut option from the Edit pull-down menu (refer to Fig. 8.12). The record and its entry cells should disappear. Move the pointer to the box at the left of the record location where you want the record to be placed, and click the mouse button to highlight the record. (The highlighted record will be moved down.) Select the Paste option from the Edit pull-down menu. A new record position will be created with the active and all subsequent records being moved down, and the record will be inserted in the new location.

Printing in List View

It is not intended that you print from list view. However, you can create a report view to print a small database by selecting New Report from the Report pull-down menu. Once the report view is created, select Print from the File pull-down menu to print the records. This has inherent limitations and is not considered a practical solution to printing data. You should refer to Chapter 9 for information on printing reports.

Hands-on with Database

PART I
Managing a Database in Data View

Creating the Database

To create a database using the data illustrated in Fig. 8.13, first enter Works and create a database file. Works should be properly installed and should access the appropriate disk drive. Refer to Chapter 2, as necessary, for instructions on accessing software on your disk.

First Name	Last Name	Street	City	State	Zip
Fred	Brown	426 Cliff Drive	Garland	TX	75042
Sally	Carter	1434 Saturn Road	Dallas	TX	75238
Tom	Saunders	1082 Vickers #408	Dallas	TX	75218
Jim	Thompson	1115 Birchwood	Garland	TX	75043

Fig. 8.13 Sample data

1. From the Opening System Disk window, move the pointer to a folder icon labeled Microsoft Works 3.0 Folder (or something indicating the Works program), and double click ⌐⟍.

A Works Application window containing Microsoft Works programs and possibly other Works related software should appear (see Fig. 8.14). If it doesn't, refer to Chapter 2 and check the system.

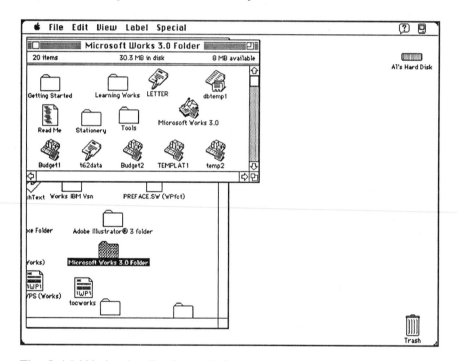

Fig. 8.14 Works Application window

The icon containing small pictures is used to access Works files created by the user.

2. Move the pointer to the Works icon containing the small pictures, and double click the ⌐⟍.

The dialog box shown in Fig. 8.15 should now appear. If it doesn't, try the selection process again or get help.

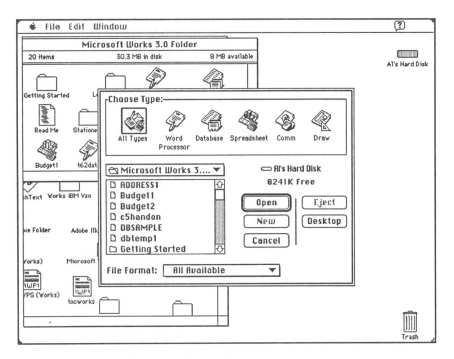

Fig. 8.15 Works Opening dialog box

You want to create a new database file.

     3. Point to the icon labeled Database at the top of the dialog box.

     4. Click the ⌫.

The icon should now be boxed.

     5. Move the pointer to [New].

     6. Click the ⌫.

You should now see the window displayed in Fig. 8.16, with Untitled1 (or Untitled"n") (DB) displayed on the title bar and a New Field dialog box displayed. If not, you may have selected the wrong type of file to create.

You are now ready to enter the data displayed in Fig. 8.13.

Creating the Fields

You will create six fields in the database, which will be used to enter first name, last name, street address, city, state, and zip code for each record. With the New Field dialog box displayed, enter the field names specified in Fig. 8.13.

     1. Type **First Name** in the "Name:" box, and press ‖ **return** ▌.

You should see the First Name field appear in the database window, and the entry in the dialog box will then be Field2, rather than Field1.

     2. Type **Last Name** in the "Name:" box, and press ‖ **return** ▌.

3. Type **Street** in the box, and press [return].

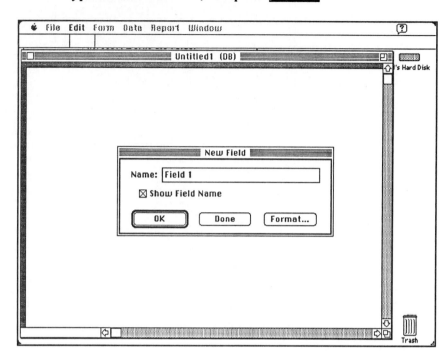

Fig. 8.16 Opened new database file with fields not yet defined

4. Type **City**, and press [return].

5. Type **State**, and press [return].

6. Type **Zip**, and press [return].

You should now see all six fields identified along the left side of the database window.

7. Point to [Done], and click the 🖰.

You will change the view from data to design and size the fields to fit the data being entered.

8. Point to Form on the main menu.

9. Press and hold the 🖰.

10. Drag the pointer to the Design View option (see Fig. 8.17).

11. Release the 🖰.

The First Name field should now have handle boxes on it.

Using the data in Fig. 8.13 as a gauge, resize the field entry areas to more appropriately reflect the size of the data. They can be resized again later if necessary.

12. Move the pointer to the middle box on the right side border of the entry area for First Name.

13. Press and hold the 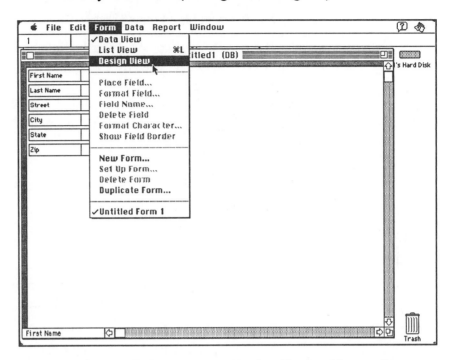 ⌕.

14. Drag the pointer slowly to the left until the area has decreased in size by about 30% (use Fig. 8.18 as a guide).

Fig. 8.17 Form pull-down menu showing Design View option

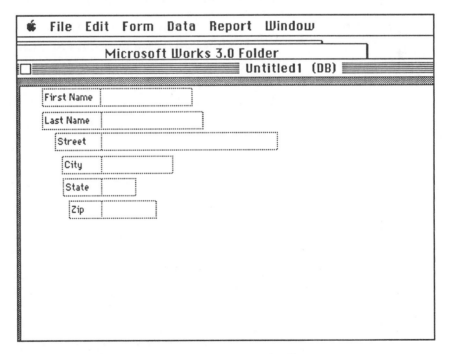

Fig. 8.18 Database form showing resized fields

15. Release the ⌁.

16. Move the pointer to the box on the left border of the First Name box (to the left of the First Name label).

17. Press and hold the ⌁.

18. Drag the pointer slowly to the right until the area for the first name label has decreased by about 25% (use Fig. 8.18 as a guide).

19. Release the ⌁.

20. Move the pointer to the Last Name field entry area.

21. Click the ⌁ to make it active.

The last name field should now have handle boxes.

22. Move the pointer to the middle box on the right side border of the entry area for Last Name.

23. Press and hold the ⌁.

24. Drag the pointer slowly to the left until the area has decreased in size by about 25%. (Use Fig. 8.18 as a guide.)

25. Move the pointer to the box on the left border of the Last Name box (to the left of the Last Name label).

26. Press and hold the ⌁.

27. Drag the pointer slowly to the right until the area for the last name label has decreased by about 25% (use Fig. 8.18 as a guide).

28. Release the ⌁.

29. Repeat the process above for the remaining fields, approximating the sizes shown in Fig. 8.18.

Change the view from design view to data view.

30. Move the pointer to the Form item on the main menu.

31. Press and hold the ⌁.

32. Drag the pointer to the Data View option (refer to Fig. 8.17).

33. Release the ⌁.

The fields are now ready to be used to enter records. The entry form should look like Fig. 8.18.

Entering Records

You will now enter the four records shown in Fig. 8.13.

1. Point to the entry area for First Name, and click the ⌐⌐ to highlight the box.

2. Type **Fred**, and press `return` to record the entry and move to the next field.

3. Type **Brown**, and press `return` to record the entry and move to the next field.

4. Using the data in Fig. 8.13, enter the street address, city, state, and zip for the first record in the same manner.

Notice that upon entering the zip code and pressing the RETURN key the field entries are blank, but the record number, displayed on the left end of the edit line, indicates record 2. You have moved from record 1, which now has data in it, to record 2. You can use the record indicator to monitor which record you are in and to change records as necessary.

5. Using the data in Fig. 8.13 and the RETURN key, continue entering fields until all of the fields in the four records have been entered.

Saving the Database

You now have a database containing four records. To protect it from possible loss, it is necessary to save it on the disk. However, you want to keep the file in memory so that you can keep using it. Therefore, you want to use the Save As option, and you want to assign a name to the file. Since this is an address file, you can name it ADDRESS1. The Save As option is found on the File pull-down menu (see Fig. 8.19).

1. Point to the File item on the main menu.

2. Press and hold the ⌐⌐.

3. Drag the pointer to the Save As option, and release the ⌐⌐.

A dialog box should now be on the desktop, with "Untitled1" (or Untitled"n") (DB) highlighted in the name box.

4. Type the name **ADDRESS1**.

5. Press `return` to save the database file and return you to the database. (If you already have a file by that name, the program will ask whether you want to replace it with this one.)

You should be returned to the database once the save operation is completed. If you encounter problems here, check your disk drive.

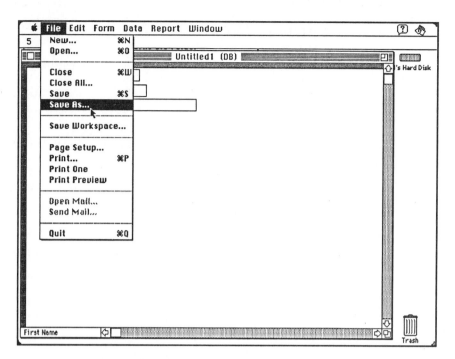

Fig. 8.19 File pull-down menu showing Save As option

The database remains in memory for reference and editing, but a copy is now saved on disk as a permanent copy.

Browsing the Records

You may want to review the data in the database. You can use control commands to move up and down through the records to review data.

1. If you have not changed your reference point, your pointer should be at the First Name entry box of record 5, where it moved after entering the zip code in record 4. If it is not there, use ⌘ = (hold down the command key and press the "=" key) and arrow keys to move up or down through the records and fields to that location.

2. From the first field entry area of record 5, press ⌘ − (hold down the command key and press the "-" key) to move to record 4.

You should see record 4 in the window.

3. Press ⌘ − to move to record 3.

You should see record 3 in the window.

4. Press ⌘ − twice to move to record 1.

You should see record 1 displayed in the window.

252

You can use the COMMAND/= keys as needed to move forward through the records.

You can use the TAB, SHIFT/TAB, and arrow keys to move forward and backward through fields within any particular record and from the last field of one record to the first field of the next.

5. With the First Name entry field of record 1 highlighted (containing Fred), press `tab` to move to the Last Name entry field (you could have pressed DOWN ARROW).

6. Press `tab` again to move to the street address of record 1 (you could have pressed DOWN ARROW).

7. Press `⌂ ⌘` `=` to move to the street address of record 2.

8. Press `shift` `tab` twice to move to the First Name field (you could press UP ARROW twice).

9. Press `⌂ ⌘` `=` as necessary to move to the First Name field of record 5.

Adding a Record

You will now position the pointer at the First Name field in record 5, which immediately follows the last record containing data. (It should be there now.)

1. Use control keys, as necessary, to make the First Name entry box of record 5 the active cell.

2. Type **Joan** in the First Name field, and press `return`.

3. Type **Jeffcoat** in the Last Name field, and press `return`.

4. Type **1802 Walnut** in the Street field, and press `return`.

5. Type **Garland** in the City field, and press `return`.

6. Type **TX** in the State field, and press `return`.

7. Type **75042** in the Zip field, and press `enter`.

You now have five records in the database.

Modifying a Record

Sally Carter, in record 2, has moved from the Saturn Road address to 2214 Jupiter, which is in the same city and has a 75214 zip code.

The Zip entry box of record 5 should be highlighted.

1. With the Zip entry box of record 5 highlighted, press `⌂ ⌘` `-` three times to move to record 2.

2. Press ⬆ key three times to move to the Street field.

3. Type **2214 Jupiter**, and press ⎰ return ⎱.

4. With the City entry box highlighted, press ⬇ two times to move the pointer to the Zip code entry.

5. Move the pointer to the right of the 8 on the edit line.

6. Click the ⬯ to create an insertion point.

7. Press ⎰ delete ⎱ twice to remove the 38 from the zip code.

8. Type **14** to change the zip code to 75214.

9. Move the pointer to the box on the edit line containing the check symbol, and click the ⬯ to record the entry.

You discover that Joan Jeffcoat in record 5 actually lives at 1832 Walnut, rather than 1802.

10. Press ⎰⌘⎱ ⎰=⎱ three times to move to record 5.

11. With the zip code highlighted, press ⬆ three times to highlight the street address.

12. Move the pointer to the right of the 0 in 1802 on the edit line.

13. Click the ⬯ to create an insertion point.

14. Press ⎰ delete ⎱ to remove the 0.

15. Type **3** to make the address 1832.

16. Move the pointer to the check box on the edit line, and click the ⬯ to record the entry.

With the changes made, you will save the file again, as a precaution. You can use the mouse to select the Save option from the File pull-down menu, or use the Command and S keys to enter the Save command (refer to Appendix E).

17. Press ⎰⌘⎱ ⎰s⎱ to save the updated database file.

Adding a Field

It is sometimes necessary to add a field to the database after it is developed and in use. You will add a field to store the salary of the persons. Use the Place Field option on the Form pull-down menu to add the field. The field will be located directly below the Zip code field.

To add a field, you must be in design view, so change the view to the design view prior to adding the field.

1. Point to the Form item on the main menu.

2. Press and hold the ⬯.

3. Drag the pointer to the Design View option (refer to Fig. 8.20).

4. Release the 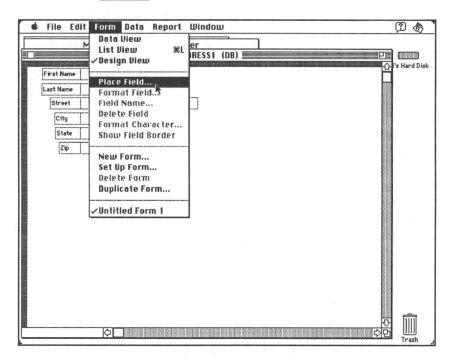.

You should now be in design view.

5. If you see handle boxes on a field, click the ⬜ anywhere in the work area outside of the fields to remove the handle boxes.

You will add a salary field.

6. Point to the Form item on the main menu.

7. Press and hold the ⬜.

8. Drag the pointer to the Place Field option (see Fig. 8.20).

9. Release the ⬜.

10. In the Place Field box, select New to create a new field.

11. In the New Field box, type the name **Salary**.

12. Press return to add the field.

Fig. 8.20 Form pull-down menu showing Place Field option

You have now added a Salary field to each record in the database. Notice that it is positioned over the First Name field. You need to position it and size it as necessary.

Moving a Field

With the database in design view, you will move the Salary field to the right portion of the form and size it appropriately.

1. Point to the Salary field entry box.

2. Click the 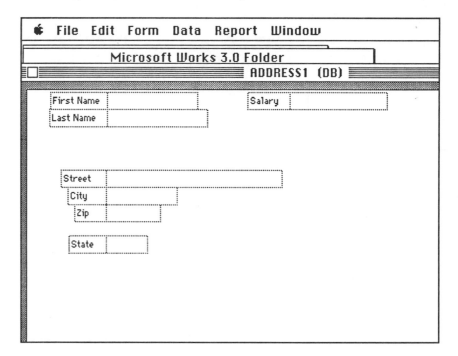 to create handle boxes on the field.

3. With the pointer on the field, press and hold the ⬭.

4. Drag the field to the right until it is past the First Name field and directly to its right (see Fig. 8.21).

5. Point to the middle handle box on the right border of the entry area.

6. Drag the pointer to the left to reduce the size of the entry area by about a third.

7. Point to the handle box on the left border of the name (to the left of the Salary label).

8. Drag the border to the right until the label box is approximately the right size for the word "Salary."

Fig. 8.21 Design view of database form with fields positioned

Position the other fields for easy reference.

9. Point to the Last Name field.

10. Drag it up until the upper border coincides with the lower border of the First Name field (refer to Fig. 8.21).

256

11. Point to the State field.

12. Drag it down until it is below the Zip field (refer to Fig. 8.21).

13. Point to the City field.

14. Drag it down until the bottom border coincides with the top border of the Zip field.

15. Point to the Street field.

16. Drag it down until the bottom border coincides with the top border of the City field.

The form should now look like Fig. 8.21.

Deleting a Field

The State field is not vital, since all addresses are in Texas and since a state can be derived from the zip code if necessary. You will remove the State field from the form. To remove a field from the form, select the Delete Field option from the Form pull-down menu.

1. Move the pointer to the State field entry area.

2. Click the 🖱 to make the field active.

The State field should now have handle boxes.

3. Move the pointer to the Form item on the main menu.

4. Press and hold the 🖱.

5. Drag the pointer to the Delete Field option.

6. Release the 🖱.

The field should now be gone from the form, but it will remain in the database.

Formatting a Field

You will now format the salary field, using the Format Field option on the Form pull-down menu. You must be in design view with the appropriate field referenced.

1. With the form in design view, point to the Salary field.

2. Click the 🖱 to make the field active.

You should see handle boxes on the field entry box.

3. Point to Form on the main menu.

4. Press and hold the 🖱.

5. Drag the pointer to the Format Field option.

6. Release the 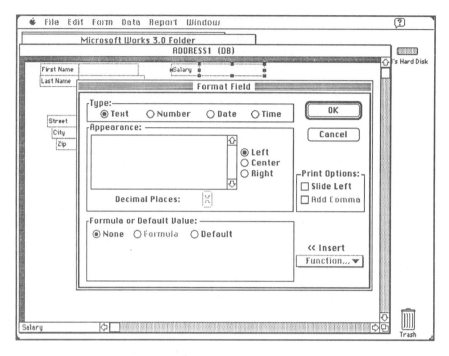.

You should see a Format Field dialog box (see Fig. 8.22).

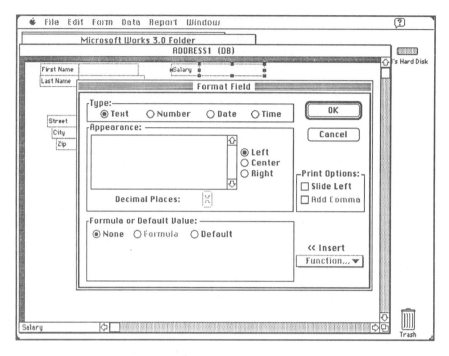

Fig. 8.22 Format Field dialog box

7. Point to the Number ○.

8. Click the ⬭ to select numeric format.

In the list box of numeric format options, select the one with commas, and assign zero decimal places.

9. Point to the numeric option that has a comma and fixed decimal place (1,234.56).

10. Click the ⬭ to highlight it.

11. With the Decimal Places box highlighted, type **0** (zero) to assign zero decimal places to the numbers.

12. Point to the Right ○ that indicates placement of the numbers right justified in the cells.

13. Click the ⬭ to select the option.

14. To assign the format options to the field, point to ⌷ OK ⌷ and click the ⬭.

You have now completed the design of the form, and you can return to data view to enter data and maintain the database.

15. Point to the Form item on the main menu

16. Press and hold the ⬫.

17. Drag the pointer to the Data View option.

18. Release the ⬫.

You should now see the fields containing data for the five records.

Adding Data

You will enter data into the Salary field in each of the five records.

1. Use ⬚⌘ ⬚− and the arrow keys as necessary to move the pointer to the Salary field entry area for record 1.

2. Type **22000** and press ⬚enter to record Fred Brown's salary. (If you pressed RETURN rather than ENTER , record 2 is now displayed because the next consecutive field is the first field of record 2.)

Notice in record 1 that the salary entry is right justified and has a comma included because of the formatting.

3. From the salary field of record 1, press ⬚⌘ ⬚= to move the pointer to the salary field of record 2. (If you are already in record 2, use the arrow keys as necessary to move the pointer to the salary field.)

4. Type **36000**, and press ⬚enter to record Sally Carter's salary.

5. From the salary field of record 2, press ⬚⌘ ⬚= to move the pointer to the salary field of record 3.

6. Type **32000**, and press ⬚enter to record Tom Saunders' salary.

7. Press ⬚⌘ ⬚= to move the pointer to the salary field of record 4

8. Type **31000**, and press ⬚enter to record Jim Thompson's salary.

9. Press ⬚⌘ ⬚= to move the pointer to the salary field of record 5

10. Type **23000**, and press ⬚enter to record Joan Jeffcoat's salary.

The database now contains salary information for all five records.

As a precaution, save the revised database.

11. Press ⬚⌘ ⬚s to save the database.

Printing the Records

You now have a database that has been entered and has correct information. It has been saved on disk for later reference. Information can now be drawn from the database and printed in report form. The process for creating and producing reports is covered in Chapter 9.

You can, however, print records from the data view using the Print option on the File pull-down menu.

Be sure the printer is on line and paper is loaded.

1. Point to the File item on the main menu.

3. Press and hold the 🖰.

4. Drag the pointer to the Print option (see Fig. 8.23).

5. Release the 🖰.

6. Select ⌈ OK ⌋ from the print dialog box.

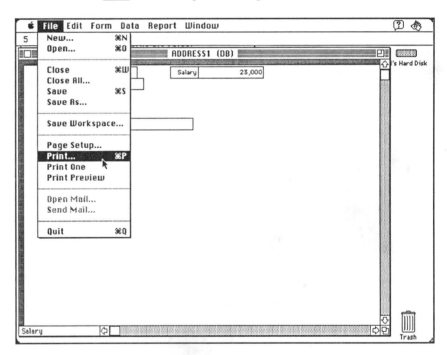

Fig. 8.23 File pull-down menu showing Print option

The five records should be printed.

Printing the Form

The design view of the form can also be printed for later reference. Change the reference to design view, and then select the Print option from the File pull-down menu.

1. Point to the Form item on the main menu.

2. Press and hold the ⌒.

3. Drag the pointer to the Design View option.

4. Release the ⌒.

You should see the design view of the form, without any data included.

5. Point to the File item on the main menu.

6. Press and hold the ⌒.

7. Drag the pointer to the Print option.

8. Release the ⌒.

9. Select [OK] from the print dialog box.

This should print the design view with no data in it.

Change the reference back to data view for maintenance purposes.

10. Point to Form on the main menu.

11. Press and hold the ⌒.

12. Drag the pointer to the Data View item.

13. Release the ⌒.

You should see the data view, with data included in the field areas.

Closing the File

Once you have completed the document, you are ready to close the file, which removes it from memory but leaves the saved copy on disk for later use. If you have made changes since the last time you saved it, the program will ask you if you want to save the changes prior to closing the file.

The Close option is on the File pull-down menu (refer to Fig. 8.23). The file can be closed by selecting the File option from the main menu, then selecting the Close option. It can also be closed by selecting the close box on the left end of the title bar.

1. Point to the File item on the main menu.

2. Press and hold the ⌒.

3. Drag the pointer to the Close option.

4. Release the ⌒.

5. If you are prompted to save changes, select [Yes].

Exiting Works

To continue working on files once the file is closed, you would create a new file or open an existing one. Once you have completed the work session and are ready to leave Works, with the Microsoft Works 3.0 Folder active, select the Quit option from the File pull-down menu. (If this option is not available, reopen ADDRESS1 by double clicking on the ADDRESS1 file icon, and close it again.)

1. Point to the File item on the main menu.

2. Press and hold the ⌂.

3. Drag the pointer to the Quit option.

4. Release the ⌂.

This should close the Works application, thus changing the icon to a picture rather than a shaded image.

To close the Works folder, select the Close Window option from the File pull-down menu, or point to the close box on the left end of the title bar, and click the the mouse button.

5. Point to the File item on the main menu.

6. Press and hold the ⌂.

7. Drag the pointer to the Close Window option.

8. Release the ⌂.

This should return you to the Opening System Disk window.

PART II
Managing a Database in List View

Creating the Database

To create a database using the data illustrated in Fig. 8.13, first enter Works and create a database file. (Works should be properly installed and should access the appropriate disk drive. Refer to Chapter 2, as necessary, for instructions on accessing software on your disk.)

1. From the Opening System Disk window, move the pointer to a folder icon labeled Microsoft Works 3.0 Folder (or something indicating the Works program), and double click the ⌂.

A Works Application window containing Microsoft Works programs and possibly other Works related software should appear (refer to Fig. 8.14). If it doesn't, refer to Chapter 2 and check the system.

The icon containing small pictures is used to access Works files created by the user.

>   2. Move the pointer to the Works icon containing the small pictures, and double click the ⌧.

The dialog box shown in Fig. 8.15 should now appear. If it doesn't, try the selection process again or get help.

You want to create a new database file.

>   3. Point to the icon labeled Database at the top of the dialog box.

>   4. Click the ⌧.

The icon should now be boxed.

>   5. Move the pointer to New .

>   6. Click the ⌧.

You should now see the window displayed in Fig. 8.16, with "Untitled1" (or Untitled"n") (DB) displayed on the title bar and a New Field dialog box displayed. If not, you may have selected the wrong type of file to create.

You are now ready to enter the data displayed in Fig. 8.13.

Creating the Fields

You will create six fields in the database, which will be used to enter first name, last name, street address, city, state, and zip code for each record. With the New Field dialog box displayed, enter the field names specified in Fig. 8.13.

>   1. Type **First Name** in the "Name:" box, and press return .

You should see the First Name field appear in the database window, and the entry in the dialog box will then be Field2, rather than Field1.

>   2. Type **Last Name** in the "Name:" box, and press return .

>   3. Type **Street** in the box, and press return .

>   4. Type **City**, and press return .

>   5. Type **State**, and press return .

>   6. Type **Zip**, and press return .

You should now see all six fields identified along the left side of the database window.

>   7. Point to Done , and click the ⌧.

You will change the view from data to design and size the fields to fit the data being entered.

8. Point to Form on the main menu.

9. Press and hold the ⬛.

10. Drag the pointer to the Design View option (refer to Fig. 8.17).

11. Release the ⬛.

The First Name field should now have handle boxes on it.

Using the data in Fig. 8.13 as a gauge, resize the field entry areas to more appropriately reflect the size of the data. They can be resized again later if necessary.

12. Move the pointer to the middle box on the right side border of the entry area for First Name.

13. Press and hold the ⬛.

14. Drag the pointer slowly to the left until the area has decreased in size by about 30% (use Fig. 8.18 as a guide).

15. Release the ⬛.

16. Move the pointer to the box on the left border of the First Name box (to the left of the First Name label).

17. Press and hold the ⬛.

18. Drag the pointer slowly to the right until the area for the first name label has decreased by about 25% (use Fig. 8.18 as a guide).

19. Release the ⬛.

20. Move the pointer to the Last Name field entry area.

21. Click the ⬛ to make it active.

The last name field should now have handle boxes.

22. Move the pointer to the middle box on the right side border of the entry area for Last Name.

23. Press and hold the ⬛.

24. Drag the pointer slowly to the left until the area has decreased in size by about 25%. (Use Fig. 8.18 as a guide.)

25. Move the pointer to the box on the left border of the Last Name box (to the left of the Last Name label).

26. Press and hold the ⬛.

27. Drag the pointer slowly to the right until the area for the last name label has decreased by about 25% (use Fig. 8.18 as a guide).

28. Release the ⬛.

29. Repeat the process above for the remaining fields, approximating the sizes shown in Fig. 8.18.

Change the view from design view to data view.

30. Move the pointer to the Form item on the main menu.

31. Press and hold the ⬭.

32. Drag the pointer to the Data View option (refer to Fig. 8.17).

33. Release the ⬭.

The fields are now ready to be used to enter records. The entry form should look like Fig. 8.18.

Entering Records

You will now enter the four records shown in Fig. 8.13.

1. Point to the entry area for First Name, and click the ⬭ to highlight the box.

2. Type **Fred**, and press ‖ return ‖ to record the entry and move to the next field.

3. Type **Brown**, and press ‖ return ‖ to record the entry and move to the next field.

4. Using the data in Fig. 8.13, enter the street address, city, state, and zip for the first record in the same manner.

Notice that upon entering the zip code and pressing ‖ return ‖, the field entries are blank, but the record number, displayed on the left end of the edit line, indicates record 2. You have moved from record 1, which now has data in it, to record 2. You can use the record indicator to monitor which record you are in and to change records as necessary.

5. Using the data above and ‖ return ‖, continue entering fields until all of the fields in the four records have been entered.

Saving the Database

You now have a database containing four records. To protect it from possible loss, it is necessary to save it on the disk. But you don't want to close the file; you want to keep using it. Therefore, you want to use the Save As option, and you want to assign a name to the file. Since this is a second address file, you can name it ADDRESS2. The Save As option is found on the File pull-down menu (refer to Fig. 8.19).

1. Point to the File item on the main menu.

2. Press and hold the ⬭.

3. Drag the pointer to the Save As option, and release the 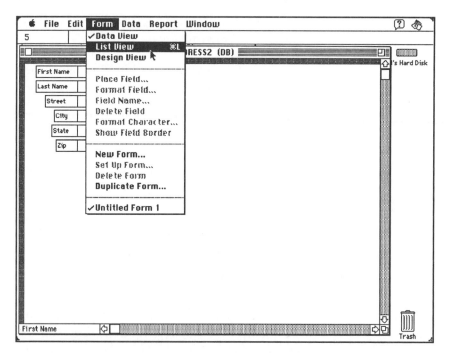.

A dialog box should now be on the desktop, with "Untitled1" (or Untitled"n") (DB) highlighted in the name box.

4. Type the name **ADDRESS2**.

5. Press ⏎ return ⏎ to save the database file and return you to the database. (If you already have a file by that name, the program will ask whether you want to replace it with this one.)

You should be returned to the database once the save operation is completed. If you encounter problems here, check your disk drive.

The database remains in memory for reference and editing, but a copy is now saved on disk as a permanent copy.

Changing to List View

In list view, you will be viewing the database in a format similar to a spreadsheet, although all the rules associated with the database will apply. To change to list view mode, you will select the List View option from the Form pull-down menu (see Fig. 8.24).

Fig. 8.24 Form pull-down menu showing List View option

1. Point to the Form item on the main menu.

2. Press and hold the ⟨▱⟩.

3. Drag the pointer to the List View option.

4. Release the ⟨▱⟩.

The database should now be in list view.

Changing the Field Width

You need to modify the field width to correspond to the data entered. In list view, the field widths will also need to include space for the field name. The right side of the field name box is used to control the field width. Using Fig. 8.25 as a guide, change the field widths as follows

1. Move the pointer to the right side border of the box containing First Name (you should see a cross symbol).

2. Press and hold the ⟨▱⟩.

3. Drag the border to the left and stop just prior to reaching the "e" in "Name" (refer to Fig. 8.25).

4. Release the ⟨▱⟩.

5. Move the pointer to the right side border of the Last Name box (you should see a cross symbol).

6. Press and hold the ⟨▱⟩.

7. Drag the border to the left until it is near the "e" in "Name."

8. Release the ⟨▱⟩.

9. Move the pointer to the right side border of the Street field name.

10. Press and hold the ⟨▱⟩.

11. Drag the border to the right to increase the width of the Street field slightly.

12. Release the ⟨▱⟩.

13. Using the same procedure as above, narrow the City, State, and Zip fields.

Your database structure should now be similar to Fig. 8.25. You can adjust the widths later as needed. Changing the field widths in list view has no effect on the widths shown in design or data view.

	File	Edit	Form	Data	Report	Window	

5

ADDRESS2 (DB)

First Name	Last Name	Street	City	State	Zip	
Fred	Brown	426 Cliff Drive	Garland	TX	75042	
Sally	Carter	1434 Saturn Road	Dallas	TX	75238	
Tom	Saunders	1082 Vickers #408	Dallas	TX	75218	
Jim	Thompson	1115 Birchwood	Garland	TX	75043	

Fig. 8.25 List view with modified field widths

14. Press ⌘ s to save the database with the modified field widths.

Adding a Record

You will add a record into the fifth record position (following Jim Thompson).

1. Point to the First Name field in record 5 (first row following the last data record).

2. Click the 🖱 to activate the cell.

3. Type **Joan**, and press tab.

4. Type **Jeffcoat**, and press tab.

5. Type **1802 Walnut**, and press tab.

6. Type **Garland**, and press tab.

7. Type **TX**, and press tab.

8. Type **75042**, and press tab.

This is referred to as appending a record. Note that a record can be inserted between existing records by using the Insert Record option of the Data pull-down menu.

With the changes made, as a precaution, you will now save the database again. You can use the mouse to select the Save option from the File pull-down menu,

268

or use the Command and S keys to enter the Save command (refer to Appendix D).

9. Press [⌘] [S] to save the updated database file.

Modifying a Record

Sally Carter, in record 2, has moved from the Saturn Road address to 2214 Jupiter, which is in the same city and has a 75214 zip code.

1. Point to the Street address field of record 2 (Sally Carter).
2. Click the to make it the active cell.
3. Type **2214 Jupiter**, and press [return].
4. Point to the Zip code field of record 2.
5. Click the to make it the active cell.
6. Move the pointer to the right of the 8 on the edit line.
7. Click the to create an insertion point.
8. Press [delete] twice to remove the 38 from the zip code.
9. Type **14** to change the zip code to 75214.
10. Move the pointer to the box on the edit line containing the check symbol, and click the to record the entry.

You discover that Joan Jeffcoat in record 5 actually lives at 1832 Walnut, rather than 1802.

11. Point to the Street address of record 5.
12. Click the to make it the active cell.
13. Move the pointer to the right of the 0 in 1802 on the edit line.
14. Click the to create an insertion point.
15. Press [delete] to remove the 0.
16. Type **3** to make the address 1832.
17. Move the pointer to the check box on the edit line, and click the to record the entry.

Deleting a Record

You will delete the third record (Tom Saunders) from the database.

1. Move the pointer to the small box at the left end of the record.
2. Click the to highlight the record.

3. Point to the Edit item on the main menu.

4. Press and hold the 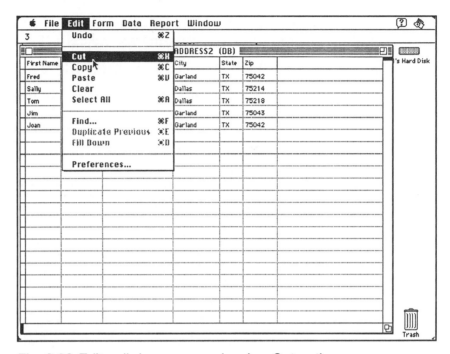.

5. Drag the pointer to the Cut option (see Fig. 8.26).

6. Release the .

Fig. 8.26 Edit pull-down menu showing Cut option

The record containing Tom Saunders is now gone, and Jim Thompson's data has moved to record 3.

Adding a Field

It is sometimes necessary to add a field to the database after it is developed and in use. Add a field to store the salary of the persons. Use the New Field option on the Form pull-down menu (see Fig. 8.27). The field will be added at the location of the active cell. You will make the salary field the third field in the database (following last name).

1. Point to the Street name at the top of the street field (the pointer should be a hand symbol).

2. Click the to highlight the field.

3. Point to the Form item on the main menu.

4. Press and hold the .

5. Drag the pointer to the New Field option.

270

6. Release the ⌒.

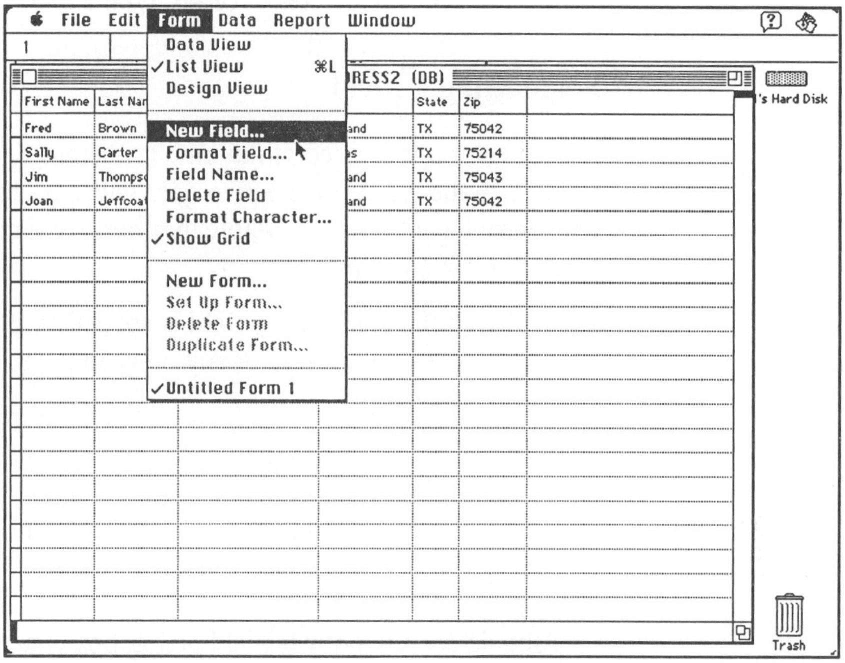

Fig. 8.27 Form pull-down menu showing New Field option

You should see a dialog box with the field name Field 7 highlighted.

7. Type **Salary** to name the new field and press | return | to create the field.

You should now have the new field in the database window.

Reduce the field width by about a third of the current width.

8. Move the pointer to the right side border of the Salary field name box (you should see the cross symbol).

9. Press and hold the ⌒.

10. Drag the pointer to the left approximately a third of the current field width.

11. Release the ⌒.

You can adjust the field width later as necessary.

12. Move the pointer to the Salary field of record 1 (Fred Brown).

13. Click the ⌒ to make it the active cell.

14. Type **22000**, and press | return |.

The Salary field of record 2 (Sally Carter) should now be active.

15. Type **36000**, and press | return |.

271

16. In Jim Thompson's record, type **31000**, and press `return`.

17. In Joan Jeffcoat's record, type **23000**, and press `enter`.

Formatting a Field

A field can be formatted at the time it is created, or formatting can be added later. With the salary field active, you will now format it to be fixed numeric with zero decimal places (whole numbers) and commas. You will also right justify the data in the cells.

1. If the Salary entry field is not active, point to it and click the ⌂. (The entire field or any entry in it can be active.)

2. Point to the Form item on the main menu.

3. Press and hold the ⌂.

4. Drag the pointer to the Format Field option (refer to Fig. 8.27).

5. Release the ⌂.

You should see the Format Field dialog box (see Fig. 8.28).

6. Point to the Number ○.

7. Click the ⌂ to select numeric format.

In the list box of numeric format options, select the one with commas and assign zero decimal places.

8. Point to the numeric option that has a comma and fixed decimal place (1,234.56).

9. Click the ⌂ to highlight it.

10. With the Decimal Places box highlighted, type **0** (zero) to assign zero decimal places to the numbers.

11. Point to the Right ○ that indicates placement of the numbers right justified in the cells.

12. Click the ⌂ to select the option.

13. To assign the format options to the field, point to `OK` and click the ⌂.

Deleting a Field

You conclude that you don't need the state field, because it can be derived from the zip code field if necessary. You will remove the state field from the file by using the Delete Field option on the Form pull-down menu (refer to Fig. 8.27).

1. Point to the State field name (you should see the hand symbol).

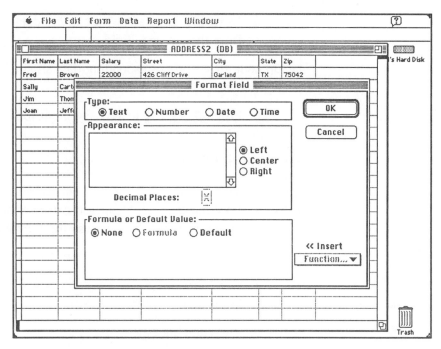

Fig. 8.28 Format Field dialog box

2. Click the to highlight the field.

3. Point to the Form item on the main menu.

4. Press and hold the ⌒.

5. Drag the pointer to the Delete Field option.

6. Release the ⌒.

You will get a warning box in which to verify that you want to delete the field.

7. Click on ⌐OK⌐ to delete the field.

The state field column is now gone, and the zip code field has moved next to the city field.

8. As a precaution, press ⌐⌘⌐ ⌐s⌐ to save the modified database.

Moving a Field

You will move the zip code field between the salary and street fields.

1. Point to the Zip field name (you should see the hand symbol).

2. Press and hold the ⌒.

3. Drag the field to the left until the Street field is highlighted.

4. Release the ⌒.

5. Click the 🖱 anywhere in the data to remove the highlighting from the zip code field.

The zip code field and corresponding data should now be between the salary field and the street field.

6. Press ⌘ S to save the modified database.

Printing the Records

You now have a database that has been entered and corrected. It has been saved on disk for later reference. Information can now be drawn from the database and printed in report form. The process for creating and producing reports is covered in Chapter 9.

You can, however, print records from list view by creating a report form.

1. Point to the Report item on the main menu.

2. Press and hold the 🖱.

3. Drag the pointer to the New Report option.

4. Release the 🖱.

You will see a dialog box to name the report.

5. Type **Address Listing** in the name entry box.

6. Click on Create to create the report.

The report view is now available and is active.

Be sure the printer is on line and paper is loaded.

7. Point to the File item on the main menu.

8. Press and hold the 🖱.

9. Drag the pointer to the Print option.

10. Release the 🖱.

11. Select OK from the print dialog box.

The five records should be printed. This is simply a quick way to print the data to paper and is not intended as a solution to your output needs. Refer to Chapter 9 for report creation and use.

12. Press ⌘ S to save the database with the report format included.

Closing the File

Once you have completed the document, you are ready to close the file, which removes it from memory but leaves the saved copy on disk for later use. If you have made changes since the last time you saved it, the program will ask you if you want to save the changes prior to closing the file.

The file can be closed by selecting the File option from the main menu, then selecting the Close option or by selecting the close box on the left end of the title bar.

1. Point to the File item on the main menu.

2. Press and hold the ⌐.

3. Drag the pointer to the Close option.

4. Release the ⌐.

5. If you are prompted to save changes, select Yes .

Exiting Works

To continue working on files once the file is closed, you would create a new file or open an existing one. Once you have completed the work session and are ready to leave Works, with the Microsoft Works 3.0 Folder active, select the Quit option from the File pull-down menu. (If this option is not available, reopen ADDRESS2 by double clicking on the ADDRESS2 file icon, and close it again.)

1. Point to the File item on the main menu.

2. Press and hold the ⌐.

3. Drag the pointer to the Quit option.

4. Release the ⌐.

This should close the Works application, thus changing the icon to a picture rather than a shaded image.

To close the Works folder, select the Close Window option from the File pull-down menu, or point to the close box on the left end of the title bar, and click the mouse button.

5. Point to the File item on the main menu.

6. Press and hold the ⌐.

7. Drag the pointer to the Close Window option.

8. Release the ⌐.

This should return you to the Opening System Disk window.

Summary

A database can be developed and maintained using data view, design view, and list view. Data view displays one record at a time. Design view is used to position the fields for easy entry and correlate them to an entry form. List view uses a table format, much like a spreadsheet, and places each record in one line and each field in one column. Field entries can be modified or deleted in either data or list view.

The database can be restructured by moving a field from one position to another in either design or list view. Field names can be changed as necessary. Records can be added or deleted in either data or list view, and fields can be added or deleted in design or list view.

Printing the window in data view prints one record at a time. Printing in design view prints the active form with no data. Data seen in list view can be printed by creating a report view.

Questions

1. Describe the general characteristics of a database.

2. What is a field? What is a record? What is a file?

3. What is the difference between a text field and a number field?

4. What are the general differences between using data view and list view in maintaining a database?

5. Define the function of the following keys in data view.

   ARROW

   TAB

   SHIFT/TAB

   COMMAND with =

   COMMAND with -

   RETURN

   ENTER

6. Define the function of the following keys in list view.

   ARROW

   TAB

SHIFT/TAB

RETURN

ENTER

7. How do you name a field in design view?

8. How do you add a record in data view?

9. Explain how to add a field in list view.

10. Explain how to delete a record in list view.

11. Describe how to modify a record in data view.

12. Describe how to modify a record in list view.

Exercises

Exercise 1

Using data view and design view, create a database, including the data below.

Name	Status	Dept	Hire Date	Salary
Brown	PT	R&D	6/8/89	22000
Carter	FT	R&D	3/12/87	38000
Jeffcoat	FT	ADMIN	6/20/90	44000
Saunders	PT	R&D	4/18/89	26000
Thompson	FT	MKT	7/2/86	34000

1. Create a form containing the five fields, with appropriate corresponding sizes to hold the data.

2. Enter records 1 through 5.

3. Store Salary in numeric format with commas.

4. Save the database as EMPLOYEE.

5. Print record 3 of the database.

Exercise 2

Using list view, create a database, including the data below.

Description	Inv Code	Qty on Hand	Unit Price
Bun	108	68	0.62
Lettuce	112	46	0.24
Tomato	117	47	0.12
Pickle	123	22	1.04
Onion	125	64	0.13
Beef	172	480	0.42

1. Use data view to create the fields needed.

2. Create a list view, including appropriate field width for the data identified.

3. Enter records 1 through 6.

4. Store Quantity and Unit Price in numeric format.

5. Save the database as MOREBUNS.

6. Print the database.

Problems

Problem 1

Using the data below, create a phone list for the persons. Plan the database for easy reference. Create it using data and design view. Enter the data in alphabetical order by last name, and put first name in a separate field. Also put area code in a separate field from the phone number. Save the database.

Name	Phone
Fred Smith	(287)423-6971
Tom Cramer	(118)323-2244
Jane Carter	(817)913-8614
Sally Rodgers	(921)672-4991
Bill Zimmer	(238)412-8704
Gary Abbott	(617)218-2792
Mindy Taylor	(817)933-1707

Problem 2

Using the data below, create a customer database. Plan the database for easy reference. Use list view to enter the data. Organize it for easy access. Enter the records in alphabetical order by city. Save the database.

Acct	CustomerName	Street	City	State	Zip
2246	Plains Petro	P.O. Box 420	Tulsa	OK	74102
4532	U. S. Oil	P.O. Box 13326	Philly	PA	19101
1590	Bradford Gas	8675 Mill St.	Chicago	IL	60648
7609	Pretro Magic	4432 Embry Rd.	Englewood	NJ	07632
3534	Oxi-Oil Inc.	7760 Josey Ln.	Boston	MA	02116

Problem 3

Starting with the database created in Exercise 1, make the following changes.

1. Convert the database to a list view and adjust field widths as appropriate.

2. Change Brown's salary from 22000 to 24000.

3. Change Saunders' status from PT to FT.

4. Move Carter from R&D to MKT.

5. Add a field for the first name, following the last name field, and enter the following first names in this order: Fred, Sally, Joan, Tom, and Jim.

Save the database.

Problem 4

Starting with the database created in Exercise 2, make the following changes.

1. Change the database to a design view and adjust field widths as appropriate.

2. Change the unit price of tomatoes from 0.12 to 0.14.

3. Change the quantity of pickles on hand to 38.

4. Save the database.

Chapter 9

Applying the Database

Objectives

After completing this chapter you will

1. Be able to define and explain the concepts of selecting, sorting, and summarizing data.

2. Be able to list commonly used relational, logical, and mathematical operators and define the order in which they are applied.

3. Be able to distinguish between the ascending and descending sort, and explain the use of multiple sort keys.

4. Be able to explain the benefit of a report generation feature.

5. Be able to find a record in a Works database using one or more criteria of identification.

6. Be able to select multiple records meeting one or more criteria from a Works database.

7. Be able to sort records in a Works database using one or more sort keys.

8. Be able to create a report format in Works based on output specifications.

9. Be able to produce summary information from a Works database through use of the report generator.

Using the Database Tool

How the Data Is Used

Generally, the database is developed and the data stored in it is updated as necessary to keep the information current and accurate. How and when the data is used can vary considerably. Uses include the selection of one or more fields or records from the database, the reordering of data into different sequences, and providing a variety of summary information, including totals, averages, and other aggregate information. The data may be used daily, weekly, monthly, or on an as needed basis to review the current situation, analyze the past, or forecast the future.

Selecting Data

It is common to need only some of the records in a database. In a database of employees, you may want to review those with a specific job code. In a database of customers, you may want to extract those whose business has been above a certain amount to offer them a preferred customer status, or you may want those below a certain amount in order to target them for potential sales growth. In a database of sales data, you may want to select employees with sales above a specified amount, in order to give them a bonus. In an inventory database, you may want to select those records where inventory level is below a specified volume, because that indicates it is time to reorder inventory for those items. There are countless ways in which portions of the database can be extracted for specific purposes.

The process of selecting data usually involves stating criteria that fields must meet in order to be selected or excluded from selection. The fields used to select records may not necessarily be the fields that are needed. For example, the Purchase Volume field used to select preferred customers identifies the records, but the Priority Code field is used to designate them as preferred, and the Name and Address fields are used to correspond with them. Other fields in the selected records may be totally ignored in a particular situation.

Relational operators are used to compare both numeric and text field entries to select desired records. The most commonly used relational operators are found in Table 9.1. They include equal (=), greater than (>), less than (<), not equal (<>), greater than or equal (>=), and less than or equal (<=). To identify customers above a specific sales volume, select records in which the Total Sales field contains a value greater than the specific amount (e.g., >20000). Any record containing a Total Sales field entry of more than 20000 will be selected; all others (including any with exactly 20000) will not be selected. (To get records with 20000 or more, you would use >=20000 as the selection criteria.)

Generally, we say that if the selection criteria are TRUE, the record is selected, and if the criteria are FALSE, it is not selected.

Category	Operator
Algebraic	^
	* /
	+ -
Relational	= < > >= <= <>
Logical	AND
	OR

Parentheses "()" supercede natural order, in that anything in parentheses is done first.

Left-to-right precedence means that at the same level of priority, operations are done left to right.

Table 9.1 Order in which operations are performed

Sometimes the selection criteria involve tests on more than one field or more than one test on the same field. In these situations, logical operators are used to make the selection. The most common logical operators (found in Table 9.1) are AND and OR. AND operates on the two values it sits between and has a result of TRUE if both operands are true; otherwise it is FALSE. OR operates on the two values it sits between and has a result of TRUE if either or both operands are true; otherwise it is FALSE. An example of a logical operation is AGE > 17 AND AGE < 26 to select all persons who range in age from 18 through 25 years. The relational operators are processed before the logical operator.

Expressions used to select records can also include algebraic formulas (involving mathematical operators). These were presented in Chapter 5. If you have not studied Chapter 5, refer to it now. Table 9.1 shows the order of processing of expressions that include algebraic, relational, and logical operators. For example, the expression .075 * SALARY + YTDHOLD > 38000 would multiply .075 by the SALARY entry, add the YTDHOLD entry, and then compare the result to 38000. If the result is greater than 38000, the record will be selected.

Sorting Data

The records are stored in the database in what is called physical order. When you want a listing of the records or fields in a specific order, such as alphabetical by name, that is referred to as the logical order. From time to time the data may be needed in order by different field values, such as name, salary, employee number, and the like. To accommodate the varying needs at various times, the data is sorted into the sequence specified. The field on which the data is being sorted is referred to as the sort key.

Data can be sorted in ascending or descending order, whether numeric or text. An ascending numeric sort goes from small numbers to large. A descending numeric sort goes from large numbers to small. Text sorts use the ASCII equivalent of the character when sorting. In the ASCII coding sequence, B is larger than A, C is larger than B, and so on. Thus, to place name field in alphabetic order, an ascending sort is used.

Sorts can involve more than one field. A two-level sort has a primary and a secondary field, sometimes referred to as high level sort key and low level sort key. A printout that requires that a database be sorted by city and have names listed alphabetically within each city is using city as the primary field and name as the secondary field.

It is possible to have a sort use several levels, involving several fields. The sequence of sort fields is defined to be from high level to low level or major to minor level. A sort of an employee database by store, then department, then employee, would group the people in each store together, then group the people in each department number within a store together, and then list employees alphabetically within each department within each store. Store number is the major key, department number is the intermediate key, and name is the minor key.

Summarizing Data

It is common to want summary information regarding a field or fields in the database. You may want to know the total amount of payroll in the salary field. You may want the total quantity of all inventory items on hand. You may also want subtotals of a field, such as the salary subtotals for employees living in different cities or working in different departments. You may want subtotal quantities of inventory items in different departments. Field totals are obtained by totaling field entries for all records printed on the report. Subtotals are obtained by creating a subtotal each time a key field changes (sometimes called a control break) in the records being printed. To obtain subtotals, the records need to be sorted on the key field prior to printing.

Sometimes you want to compute information from fields in a record, forming a new field called a computed field. To project a salary increase and its effects, you might want to add a percentage of increase to the existing salary for each employee and put it in a new field, for temporary study. You may want to record hours worked for each week in a separate field, and then add them together into a monthly field. The technique of using computed fields allows you to have computed information from one or more fields in each record of the database stored in a separate field.

Reporting the Results

In many situations, a combination of selecting, sorting, and summarizing is applied to the data to achieve the desired results. For example, you may select the customers living in a particular city, sort them alphabetically by name, and print a list of their names and the amount of each customer's purchases. You may include in the report the average amount of purchases made in the city. This would require selecting, sorting, and then summarizing the results.

How results are presented can vary from program to program. Selected and sorted records may be listed as output, with all resulting records and all fields included. It may be desirable, however, to include only relevant fields in the output. Also, you may structure the printed fields in a particular format. In addition, heading information and column headers can be included, and you may provide summary information on the report. To facilitate all of these features, many programs include a report generation capability that allows you to structure the output in a desired fashion and include only relevant data.

Using the Database in Works

Sorting Records

Records can be sorted in data or list view, using the Sort option on the Data pull-down menu (see Fig. 9.1). When the Sort option is chosen, a dialog box is displayed (see Fig. 9.2) that indicates the field to be used to sort (the sort key). It also has a check box to signify ascending or descending order.

It is sometimes necessary to do a multilevel sort. This can be accomplished by sorting on the minor level field first and then the higher level fields in order from low to high, with the major sort key being the highest level. Using this technique, the data can be sorted on as many fields as desired. The end result will be the same as if multiple sort keys had been applied in a single operation.

Searching the Database

Finding a Field Entry

The Find option on the Edit pull-down menu is used to search for a specific data value. It can be used in data or list view. Once the Find option is selected, a dialog box will appear on the desktop (Fig. 9.3). The search data should be entered in the space provided. For example, if you are looking for someone named Smith, enter Smith. A check box is included that provides for searching only text fields or searching all fields. Selecting the Find Next button will begin the search.

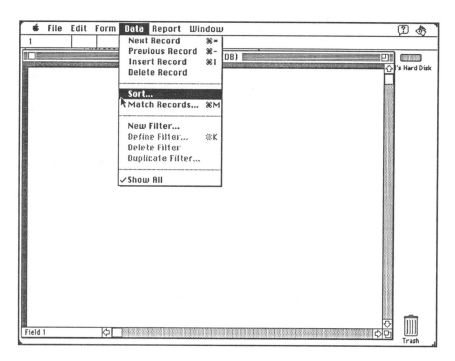

Fig. 9.1 Data pull-down menu showing Sort option

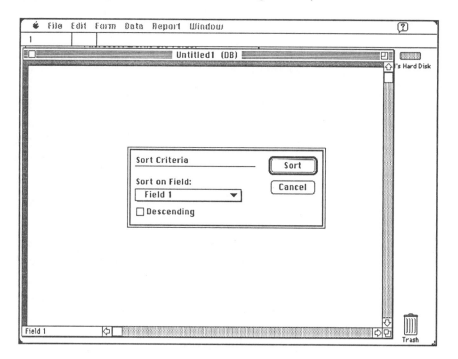

Fig. 9.2 Dialog box for specifying the sort field

The search begins at the active cell and proceeds record by record, searching each field of the record, looking for a matching character sequence. If the search reaches the end of the database, it will continue at the beginning of it and search until it reaches the first cell searched. If there is no active cell, the search will start at the beginning of the database and search the entire database. If the field is numeric, click on the Search Text Fields Only box to turn it off prior to selecting the Find Next button. If no match is found, a dialog box will indicate to you that the data was not found.

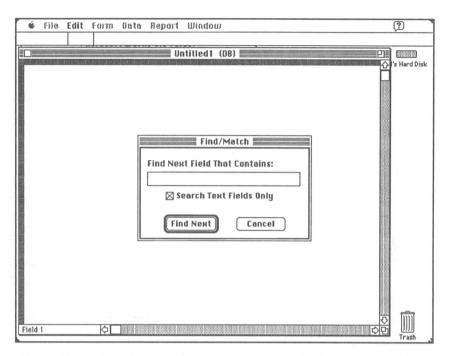

Fig. 9.3 Dialog box for searching for a specific field

Matching Multiple Field Entries

You can extract multiple records containing a specific entry. The data to be matched can be in any field in a record. All records containing the data will be extracted. The command used is the Match Records option on the Data pull-down menu (refer to Fig. 9.1). You can use the match records feature in data view or list view.

When the Match Records option is selected, a dialog box will be displayed in which to enter the data to search for. You can also specify whether to search all fields or only text fields using the check box provided. Selecting the Match button causes the search to take place. Only records containing the data searched for will now be visible. To return all records to view, select Show All from the Data pull-down menu (refer to Fig. 9.1).

Selecting a Group of Records

In Works, using criteria to identify and extract records from the database is done through the filter options on the Data pull-down menu (refer to Fig. 9.1). When the New Filter option is selected, a dialog box will appear that includes a series of conditions (see Fig. 9.4). The dialog box is used to identify the criteria used in extracting records from the database. The record selection criteria can consist of one or several selection rules. Each rule will be listed in the dialog box, and the "And" and "Or" buttons will indicate how many of the rules must be met when selecting records. The filter can be given a name in the Filter Name box, and several filters can be created and stored with the database.

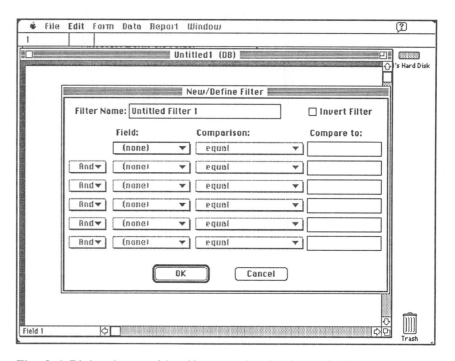

Fig. 9.4 Dialog box to identify record selection criteria

The record selection criteria are entered by highlighting a field name on the drop-down list box, highlighting a comparison criterion on the drop-down list box, and entering the comparison information in the "Compare to:" box. Then enter a name into the "Filter Name:" box. The field box includes all fields in the database. The comparison box includes relational operators such as greater than and equals and other more literal criteria such as begins with. The comparison information includes the actual data to compare such as "30000" for a salary or "Dallas" for a city. When multiple criteria are applied, the logic operators AND and OR are used to designate whether one or more of the criteria must be met. Once all the query information has been entered, use the OK button to implement the record selection. Records matching the filter criteria will be displayed. The "Invert Filter" check box can be used to select all records not meeting the specified criteria, rather than those meeting the criteria.

Once you have seen and used the records and wish to return to the display of all the records, select the Show All Records option from the Data pull-down menu (refer to Fig. 9.1). This will display the entire database.

Once a query filter has been created, it will be stored with the database, and its name will be displayed on the Data pull-down menu. It can be applied at any time by selecting the name from the pull-down menu. A filter can be modified by selecting the Define Filter option on the Data pull-down menu. There are also options to duplicate or delete the filter on the Data pull-down menu.

Using the Report Writer

Creating a Report

To create a report format, select New Report from the Report pull-down menu (see Fig. 9.5). Once this option is selected, a window will appear that allows you to create a format for a report. Unless otherwise specified, reports will benamed Untitled Report 1, Untitled Report 2, and so on. A name can be assigned at the time a report format is created. Names can be modified using the Report Name option on the Report pull-down menu (refer to Fig. 9.5). The names of all reports stored with the database will be displayed on the Report pull-down menu.

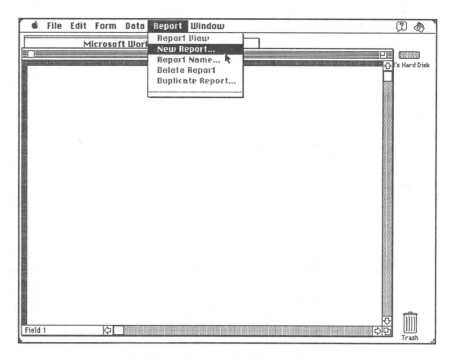

Fig. 9.5 Report pull-down menu showing New Report option

The two arrows pointing inward on the ruler line indicate the report margins. The report width can be changed by using the Page Setup option on the File pull-down menu or by using the pointer to move the right margin arrow to the left or right. Margins are restricted to the size of paper defined. Each report format maintains its own margin settings. Only the fields included within the margin settings will be printed on the report. For a wide report, you might choose horizontal orientation from the Page Setup dialog box to provide increased width.

289

A heading can be placed in the report by selecting the Show Header option on the Window pull-down menu and entering a title in the Header box (see Fig. 9.6). A footer can be added by selecting the Show Footer option on the Window pull-down menu. The header and footer can be left off the first page by selecting the Title Page check box in the Document dialog box under the Page Setup option. For more information on the creation of header and footer information (e.g., numbering pages), refer to the corresponding section in Chapter 4.

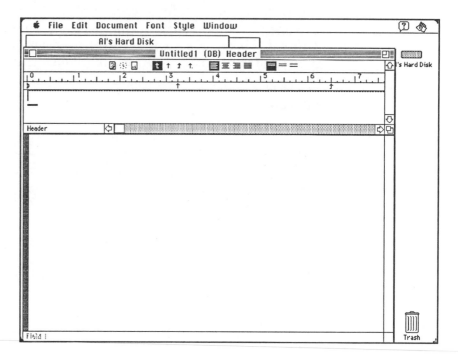

Fig. 9.6 Header dialog box

Fields are included on the report by positioning them between the margin arrows in the New Report window. The order can be rearranged by selecting field names and moving them to the right or left of other fields. Fields can be resized by selecting the right border of the field name box and adjusting the field size.

All records are included in the report, unless a filter is applied in the report format. The filter options on the Data pull-down menu can be used to access the dialog box from which to select only records meeting specific criteria (refer to Fig. 9.4). The procedure for entering rules is the same as described above in the section on selecting records.

Records are printed in the order that they are stored in the database. To have records printed in a desired order, sort the database, as described in the sort section above, prior to printing the report.

Once the page is formatted and the fields and records are specified in the report format, it can be printed and/or stored for later use. The report format can be applied to the database at any time by selecting the report name from the Report pull-down menu (refer to Fig. 9.5). Multiple reports can be created by using the New Report option repeatedly. Each report format created will be given a new name and added to the list of report formats stored with the database.

The default when printing reports is to display the grid lines. If you want the report to print without grid lines, select the Show Grid option from the Form pull-down menu when viewing the report format. The grid lines will no longer be displayed and will not print on the report. Selecting the option again will display the grid lines. You can have each report set independently and the setting will remain with the report format until changed.

Printing a Report

Once a report format is created, it is given a name and stored with the database for later reference. The default names are Untitled Report 1, Untitled Report 2, etc., but other names can be assigned to the reports. Any report formats currently stored with the database can be seen by selecting the Report name from the Report pull-down menu. The names of the reports are listed at the bottom of the pull-down menu. A report format can be viewed by selecting the name of the report.

At this point the report can be printed by selecting the Print option on the File pull-down menu. Whether or not the report is printed, you can select another report view by selecting the report name from the Report pull-down menu. You can return to the database at any time by selecting Data View, Design View, or List View from the Form pull-down menu.

Modifying a Report

Once a report view is created and named, it can be modified as necessary. This is done by first selecting the report name from the Report pull-down menu (see Fig. 9.7). The report format will display in the window. Then make changes to the report, as necessary, using the same features you used to create the format, as explained above.

Managing Report Formats

You can create many report formats and store them with the database. It will become practical at some point to copy report formats or delete report formats from the database. Copying a format can help when creating a similar report to one that you have by making minor changes to the existing format. When a format is no longer needed, it should be removed from the list of formats to make room for other report formats.

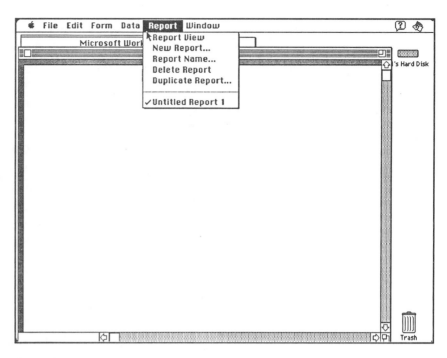

Fig. 9.7 Report pull-down menu

To copy a format, use the Report pull-down menu (refer to Fig. 9.7). The list of report names will appear at the bottom of the pull-down menu. Select the name of the report format to be duplicated, to make it active. Then select Duplicate Report from the Report pull-down menu. The current report name and the duplicate report name will appear in a dialog box (see Fig. 9.8). The default name will be assigned, or you can enter a name to assign to the duplicate report. Select the OK button to complete the process. Modify the report to include the desired characteristics. You now have an additional report format in the list of reports available.

To delete a report format, select the report name from the Report pull-down menu (refer to Fig. 9.7). Then select the Delete Report option from the Report pull-down menu. A dialog box will ask you to confirm the deletion. Select the OK button. The name will be removed from the list, and the format will no longer be stored in memory. This option is particularly important once you have stored many report formats with the database and need space for a new one. You should be careful, however, not to delete a format that may be needed later.

Summarizing Data

Summary information pertaining to fields and records in the database can be included in the report. Field totals and subtotals can be included by selecting options from the Totals pull-down menu (see Fig. 9.9) when creating a report format. The Sum this Field option causes a total of the contents of the highlighted field to be printed on the report. The Subtotal when Contents

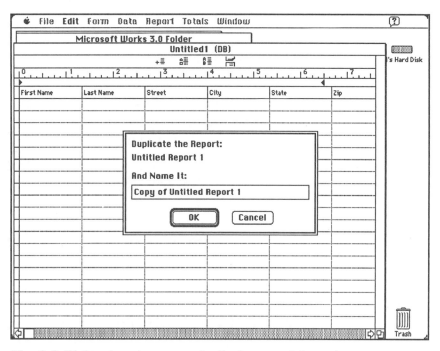

Fig. 9.8 Dialog box to name duplicate report format

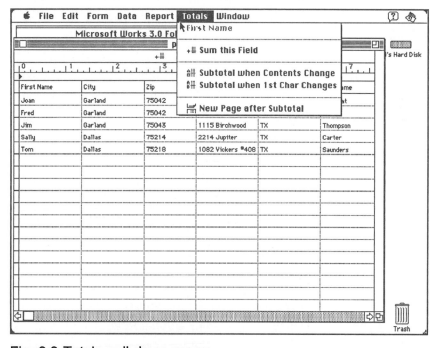

Fig. 9.9 Totals pull-down menu

Change option (selected with the Sum this Field option) causes a subtotal to print on summed fields each time the value in the field to be summed changes. The Subtotal when 1st Char Changes option (selected with the Sum this Field option) causes a subtotal to print on summed fields each time the first character of the value in the field to be summed changes. In large reports, you may also use the New Page After Subtotal option to have each subgroup of records and

293

subtotal for that group on a separate page. Buttons for each of the options are available on the ruler line. Refer to the Totals pull-down menu to see the symbol that corresponds to each option.

A computed field can be created in design view by selecting the Format Field option from the Form pull-down menu. Designate the field as Number, Data, or Time, and then select the Formula option in the "Formula or Default Value:" box. You can then enter a formula or select a function from the Function box. A formula can include many of the functions available in Works, and it can include field names and numeric values.

Hands-on with Database

PART I
Creating the Database

Using the data depicted in Fig. 9.10, create a database using data view, with field names of First Name, Last Name, Address, City, Zip, and Salary. Size the fields using design view, and then change to list view.

Jacob	Carroll	1310 Pembrook	Garland	75040	18000
Daisy	Cavenaugh	4317 Mill River	Garland	75043	34000
Julie	Chiles	1205 Castle Drive	Garland	75040	16000
Paula	Dabney	6614 Briarwood Dr.	Rowlett	75087	27000
Terri	Danielson	2885 Keller Springs	Dallas	75006	41000
Michael	Fogle	1922 Ripplewood Dr.	Garland	75044	36000
Mary	Graham	2802 Homestead	Garland	75044	17000
Laura	Hammontree	3905 Linda Lane	Richardson	75081	28000
William	Harris	2335 Fairfield	Plano	75074	31000
Victor	Manuel	5132 Clearwood	Richardson	75081	47000
Leonard	McGee	P.O. Box 118302	Carrollton	75011	32000
Bill	Milkey	2105 S. Bernice	Garland	75042	23000
Craig	Morley	4413 Abrams Road	Dallas	75081	27000
Michael	Self	7406 Lisa Drive	Rowlett	75088	28000
Tommy	Valle	3410 Longleaf Drive	Garland	75042	24000

Fig. 9.10 Sample database

Works should be properly installed and should access the appropriate disk drive. Refer to Chapter 2, as necessary, for instructions on accessing software on your disk.

1. From the Opening System Disk window, move the pointer to a folder icon labeled Microsoft Works 3.0 Folder (or something indicating the Works program), and double click the ⌒.

A Works Application window containing Microsoft Works programs and possibly other Works related software should appear. If it doesn't, refer to Chapter 2 and check the system.

The icon containing small pictures is used to access Works files created by the user.

2. Move the pointer to the Works icon containing the small pictures, and double click the ⌒.

The Works Opening dialog box should now appear. If it doesn't, try the selection process again or get help.

You want to create a new database file.

3. Point to the icon labeled Database at the top of the dialog box.

4. Click the ⌒.

The icon should now be boxed.

5. Move the pointer to (New).

6. Click the ⌒.

You should now see a window with Untitled1 (or Untitled"n") (DB) displayed on the title bar and a New Field dialog box displayed. If not, you may have selected the wrong type of file to create.

You are now ready to enter the data displayed in Fig. 9.10.

Creating the Fields

You will create the six fields needed to build the database.

1. Type **First Name** in the "Name:" box, and press ⟦ return ⟧.

You should see the First Name field appear in the database window, and the entry in the dialog box will then be Field2, rather than Field1.

2. Type **Last Name** in the "Name:" box, and press ⟦ return ⟧.

3. Type **Address** in the box, and press ⟦ return ⟧.

4. Type **City**, and press ⟦ return ⟧.

5. Type **Zip**, and press ⟦ return ⟧.

6. Type **Salary**, and press │ return ▌.

You should now see all six fields identified along the left side of the database window.

7. Point to ⌐Done⌐, and click the ⟨⟩.

You will change the view from data to design and size the fields to fit the data being entered.

8. Point to Form on the main menu.

9. Press and hold the ⟨⟩.

10. Drag the pointer to the Design View option.

11. Release the ⟨⟩.

The First Name field should now have handle boxes on it.

Using Fig. 9.11 as a gauge, resize the field entry areas.

12. Using the pointer and the handle boxes, resize each of the fields to appear similar to those in Fig. 9.11.

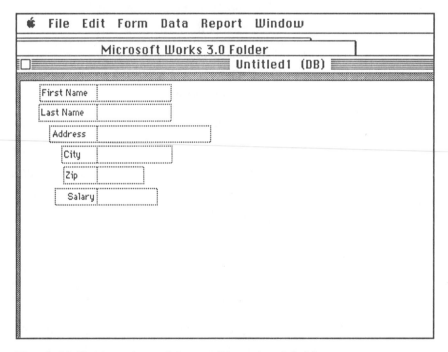

Fig. 9.11 Design view of form with resized fields

Change the format of the Salary field to number format with commas and zero decimal places, and right justify the entry.

13. Point to the Salary field, and click the ⟨⟩, if necessary, to make it active.

14. Select Format Field from the Form pull-down menu.

15. Select the Number ○.

16. Select the appearance option containing a comma and decimal places (1,234.56).

17. Type **0** (zero) in the decimal places box.

18. Select the Right ○.

19. Select ⌈**OK**⌉ to record the format.

Change the view from design view to data view.

20. Select Data View from the Form pull-down menu.

The fields are now ready to be used to enter records.

21. Point to the entry box for the First Name field in Record 1, and click the ⟨⟩ to make it active.

22. Referring to Fig. 9.10, enter the data for the 15 records identified.

You now have a database that can be used to extract information. You will change the display to list view in order to see more records and more easily view the processing results.

23. Select the List View item from the Form pull-down menu.

24. Moving the pointer to the right side border of the Address field name box, drag the field border to adjust the Address field to be about one and one-half inches wide.

25. Adjust the First Name, Last Name, and City fields to be about one-inch wide.

26. Adjust the Zip and Salary fields to be about three-quarters of an inch wide.

You should now have all the fields displayed in the window. If not, adjust the size of the fields further as necessary.

The database should now look like Fig. 9.12, with the name Untitled"n" (DB).

27. Using the Save As option, save the database under the name PERSONL1.

You can continue the session now or later. You have a database that is formatted to be used in data or list view, as appropriate.

First Name	Last Name	Address	City	Zip	Salary	
Jacob	Carroll	1310 Pembrook	Garland	75040	18,000	
Daisy	Cavenaugh	4317 Mill River	Garland	75043	34,000	
Julie	Chiles	1205 Castle Drive	Garland	75040	16,000	
Paula	Dabney	6614 Briarwood Dr.	Rowlett	75087	27,000	
Terri	Danielson	2885 Keller Springs	Dallas	75006	41,000	
Michael	Fogle	1922 Ripplewood Dr.	Garland	75044	36,000	
Mary	Graham	2802 Homestead	Garland	75044	17,000	
Laura	Hammontree	3905 Linda Lane	Richardson	75081	28,000	
William	Harris	2335 Fairfield	Plano	75074	31,000	
Victor	Manuel	5132 Clearwood	Richardson	75081	47,000	
Leonard	McGee	P.O. Box 118302	Carrollton	75011	32,000	
Bill	Milkey	2105 S. Bernice	Garland	75042	23,000	
Craig	Morley	4413 Abrams Road	Dallas	75081	27,000	
Michael	Self	7406 Lisa Drive	Rowlett	75088	28,000	
Tommy	Valle	3410 Longleaf Drive	Garland	75042	24,000	

Fig. 9.12 Personnel file displayed in list view

Sorting Records

With the database in list view, you will sort the records using first the City field, then the Salary code field, and print the results of each. The Sort option is found on the Data pull-down menu.

1. Point to the City field name (you should see a hand symbol).

2. Click the ⌖ to highlight the field.

3. Point to the Data item on the main menu.

4. Press and hold the ⌖.

5. Drag the pointer to the Sort option.

6. Release the ⌖.

You should see the sort dialog box. Since you want to sort in ascending order, you don't need to change the button selection.

7. With the City field listed in the "Sort on Field:" box, point to ⌜ Sort ⌟, and click the ⌖.

The database is now sorted alphabetically by city name.

8. Click the ⌖ with the pointer anywhere in the data to remove the highlighting.

You will print a listing of the records sorted by city. Be sure the printer is on and ready for printing.

9. Point to the Report item on the main menu.

10. Press and hold the ⟨⟩.

11. Drag the pointer to the New Report option.

12. Release the ⟨⟩.

13. Point to [Create], and click the ⟨⟩.

14. Point to the File item on the main menu.

15. Press and hold the ⟨⟩.

16. Drag the pointer to the Print option.

17. Release the ⟨⟩.

18. Select [OK].

The records should print. If you did not get all the fields, check the margins on the ruler line and modify the ruler line and page setup as necessary.

Now you will sort the database by Salary, with the higher-numbered salaries first (descending order). Rather than select the field first, you will select it from the drop-down list box in the sort dialog box.

19. Point to the Data item on the main menu.

20. Press and hold the ⟨⟩.

21. Drag the pointer to the Sort option.

22. Release the ⟨⟩.

You should see the sort dialog box. Use the list box to select Salary as the sort field. Since you want the numeric data in descending order, select the Descending check box.

23. Point to the down arrow on the right side of the "Sort on Field:" box.

24. Press and hold the ⟨⟩.

25. Drag the pointer to the Salary field name (see Fig. 9.13).

26. Release the ⟨⟩.

Salary should now be listed in the box.

27. Point to the Descending □.

28. Click the ⟨⟩ to select the option.

29. Point to [Sort], and click the ⟨⟩.

The records are now in descending order from highest salary to lowest salary.

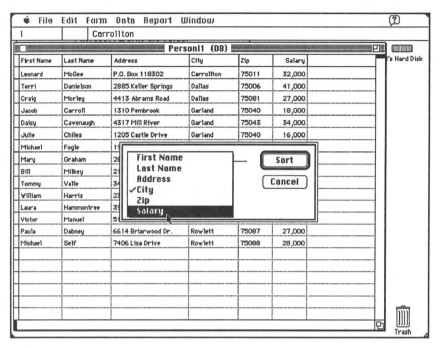

Fig. 9.13 Sort dialog box showing Sort on Field: drop-down list
box

30. Click the 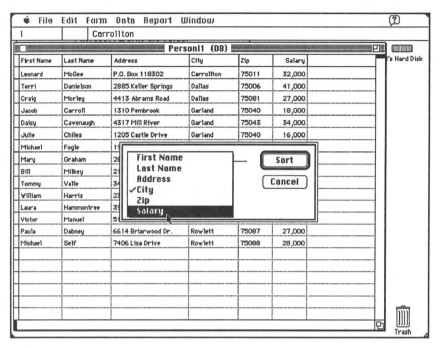 with the pointer anywhere in the data to remove the
highlighting.

You will now print the records sorted in descending order by salary. You
should still be in report view.

31. If you are not still in report view, select "Untitled Report 1" from
the Report pull-down menu.

32. Point to the File item on the main menu.

33. Press and hold the ◁▷.

34. Drag the pointer to the Print option.

35. Release the ◁▷.

36. Select OK.

The records should print.

You can implement a sort using more than one sort field by conducting first the
minor level sort and then the major level. You will sort the records
alphabetically by city and have the persons in each city sorted alphabetically by
last name.

Last Name is the minor level sort key.

1. Point to the Last Name field name.

2. Click the ⟨⟩ to highlight the field.

3. Point to the Data item on the main menu.

4. Press and hold the ⟨⟩.

5. Drag the pointer to the Sort option.

6. Release the ⟨⟩.

In the sort dialog box, "Last Name" should be listed in the "Sort on Field:" box.

7. If the Descending ☐ is checked (and it should be from the previous sort), point to the box and click the ⟨⟩ to turn the option off. (You want the sort to be ascending.)

8. Point to ⟨ Sort ⟩, and click the ⟨⟩.

The database records are now in order by Last Name.

City is the major level sort key.

9. Point to the City field name.

10. Click the ⟨⟩ to highlight the field.

11. Point to the Data item on the main menu.

12. Press and hold the ⟨⟩.

13. Drag the pointer to the Sort option.

14. Release the ⟨⟩.

15. In the sort dialog box, with the City field name listed, move the pointer to ⟨ Sort ⟩, and click the ⟨⟩.

The records are now in order by City. Notice that the records for any city (e.g., Garland) are in order by last name. You have completed the two-level sort.

You should still be in report view from the previous sort and print operation.

16. If you are not in report view, select "Untitled Report 1" from the Report pull-down menu.

17. To print the data, select the Print item from the File pull-down menu.

18. Select ⟨ OK ⟩ from the print dialog box. The records should print.

It is important to be aware of which view you are in. You are currently in report view. For the sake of continuity, change to list view.

19. Point to Form on the main menu.

20. Press and hold the 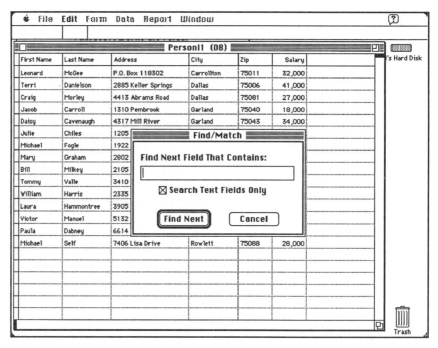.

21. Drag the pointer to the List View item.

22. Release the ⌐⇩.

This should place the window in list view.

Searching the Database

Finding a Field

With the database still in list view, you will search for a specific field entry. You want to know if anyone in the file lives in Plano. You can use the Find option on the Edit pull-down menu.

To begin the operation at the beginning of the database, make the first field of the first record active, and then conduct the search.

1. Point to the first record entry of the First Name field (containing Leonard).

2. Click the ⌐⇩ to make the cell active.

3. Point to the Edit item on the main menu.

4. Press and hold the ⌐⇩.

5. Drag the pointer to the Find option.

6. Release the ⌐⇩.

You should see a dialog box similar to the one in Fig. 9.14.

Fig. 9.14 Dialog box to identify search data

7. Type **Plano** in the "Find Next Field That Contains:" box.

8. Point to [Find Next], and click the ⌐⌐⌐.

The field containing Plano should now be highlighted.

To search for other occurrences of Plano, select the option again.

It is common to search for a field entry in order to review the contents of the entire record or of other fields in the record. This is often done in data view in order to display only the desired record in the window.

Change the window to data view and look for a record containing the name "Fogle."

9. Point to the Form item on the main menu.

10. Press and hold the ⌐⌐⌐.

11. Drag the pointer to the Data View option.

12. Release the ⌐⌐⌐.

You should now be in data view.

13. Point to the Edit item on the main menu.

14. Press and hold the ⌐⌐⌐.

15. Drag the pointer to the Find option.

16. Release the ⌐⌐⌐.

17. In the dialog box, type **Fogle**.

18. Point to [Find Next], and click the ⌐⌐⌐.

The field entry containing "Fogle" and the corresponding field entries in the record are displayed in the window.

19. After reviewing the record, select List View from the Form pull-down menu to return to list view.

Finding Multiple Records

You will select the records of all persons living in Dallas by using the Match Records option on the Data pull-down menu.

1. Point to the Data item on the main menu.

2. Press and hold the ⌐⌐⌐.

3. Drag the pointer to the Match Records option.

4. Release the ⌐⌐⌐.

5. Type **Dallas** in the dialog box.

6. Point to ⌈ **Match** ⌉, and click the 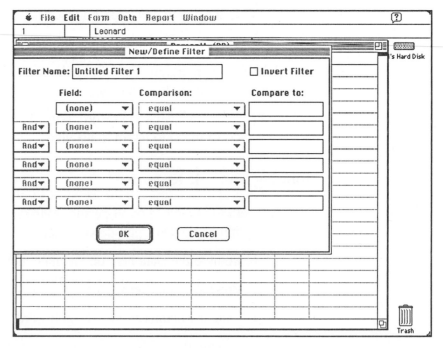.

You should see the two records displayed that contain the word Dallas. Note that if someone's name were Dallas, that record would also be displayed.

After you have reviewed the records, display all records in the database.

7. Point to Data on the main menu.

8. Drag the pointer to the Show All option.

9. Release the ⌐⌐.

You should now see all records displayed.

Selecting a Group of Records

You will select the records of all persons living in Richardson by using the New Filter option on the Data pull-down menu to create and apply a filter.

1. Point to the Data item on the main menu.

2. Press and hold the ⌐⌐.

3. Drag the pointer to the New Filter option.

4. Release the ⌐⌐.

In the filter dialog box (see Fig. 9.15), name the filter, and then define a rule that the City must be Richardson.

Fig. 9.15 New/Define Filter dialog box

5. With the "Filter Name:" box highlighted, type **City of Richardson** to name the filter.

6. In the first "Field:" box, point to the down arrow at the right side of the box.

7. Press and hold the ⌐◇ to display the drop-down list of field names.

8. Drag the pointer to the field name City.

9. Release the ⌐◇.

The name "City" should now be displayed in the box.

10. In the first "Comparison:" box, point to the arrow at the right side of the box.

11. Press and hold the ⌐◇ to display the drop-down list of field names.

12. With the pointer on "equal," release the ⌐◇. (It would have been the default selection.)

13. Point to the first "Compare to:" box.

14. Click the ⌐◇ to create an insertion point.

15. Type **Richardson** in the entry box.

16. Point to ⌐OK⌐, and click the ⌐◇.

You should now see only the records containing the city of Richardson.

Note that the filter will be stored with the database for later reference. If you want to print after applying the filter, you should create the filter from report view.

Once you have reviewed the records, display the entire database.

17. Point to the Data item on the main menu.

18. Press and hold the ⌐◇.

19. Drag the pointer to the Show All option. (Notice that the filter named "City of Richardson" is now stored as an option on the pull-down menu.)

20. Release the ⌐◇.

You should now have all records displayed.

Using Multiple Rules

You will now select records of persons who live in Garland AND have a salary of $20,000 or more.

1. Point to the Data item on the main menu.

2. Press and hold the ⟳.

3. Drag the pointer to the New Filter option. (Notice that the previous filter is still available for selection as needed.)

4. Release the ⟳.

5. With the "Filter Name:" box highlighted, type **City and Salary** to name the filter.

6. In the first "Field:" box, point to the arrow at the right side of the box.

7. Press and hold the ⟳ to display the drop-down list of field names.

8. Drag the pointer to the field name City.

9. Release the ⟳.

The name City should now be displayed in the box.

Since "equal" is the comparison that is wanted, you do not need to change the entry.

10. Point to the "Compare to:" box.

11. Click the ⟳ to create an insertion point.

12. Type **Garland** in the entry box.

13. Point to the arrow on the right side of the second "Field:" box.

14. Press and hold the ⟳ to display the drop-down list of field names.

15. Drag the pointer to the field name Salary.

16. Release the ⟳.

The name Salary should now be displayed in the second field box. The "And" to the left of the field name is now active.

17. Point to the arrow to the right of the "And."

18. Press and hold the ⟳.

19. With "And" highlighted, release the ⟳. (Notice that "And" is the default selection.)

20. Point to the arrow on the right side of the second "Comparison:" box (to the right of the Salary field box).

21. Press and hold the ⟳ to display the drop-down list of comparison rules.

22. Drag the pointer to "greater than or equal."

23. Release the 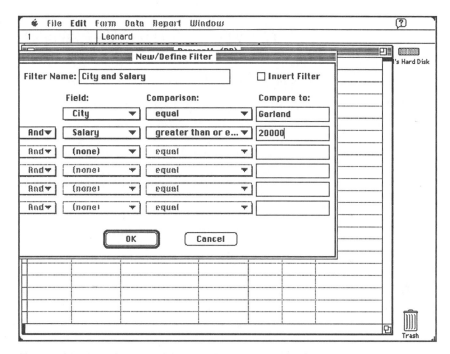.

The "greater than or e..." should be displayed in the second comparison box.

24. Point to the second "Compare to:" box.

25. Click the ⌂ to create an insertion point.

26. Type **20000** in the entry box.

The dialog box should now look similar to Fig. 9.16.

Fig. 9.16 New/Define Filter dialog box with city and salary entries

27. Point to [OK], and click the ⌂.

You should now have four records displayed, each of which represents a person living in Garland with a salary of $20,000 or more.

After you have reviewed the records, display the entire database.

28. Select Show All from the Data pull-down menu to display all records in the database.

(Notice on the Data pull-down menu that you now have the City and Salary filter available for reference as needed.)

All records should now be in view.

Saving the Database and Exiting

Since the filters have been added to the database, you should save the database before exiting.

1. Select the Save item from the File pull-down menu to save the database.

2. Select the close box on the left end of the title bar.

3. Select the Quit option from the File pull-down menu.

4. Select the close box on the Microsoft Works 3.0 Folder.

You should now be at the Opening System Disk window.

PART II
Retrieving the Database

You will retrieve the PERSONL1 database created in PART I.

1. From the Opening System Disk window, select the Microsoft Works 3.0 Folder.

2. From the Works Application window, select the Works program icon.

3. From the Works Opening dialog box, select the database named PERSONL1.

You should now have a database window displaying the PERSONL1 database.

Reports

Creating a Report Format

Select the New Report option from the Report pull-down menu. Then format a report containing Last Name, City, Zip code, and Salary.

1. Point to the Report item on the main menu.

2. Press and hold the ⟨⟩.

3. Move the pointer to the New Report option.

4. Release the ⟨⟩.

You should see a dialog box in which to name the report. Name the report Salary Report.

5. In the "Name the Report:" box, type **Salary Report**.

6. Point to [Create], and click the ⌒.

You should see the records with a ruler line at the top and the First Name field (or another field) highlighted.

Move the First Name and Address fields to the right end of the display, since they will not be included in the report.

7. Move the pointer to the First Name field name (you should see a hand symbol).

8. Press and hold the ⌒.

9. Drag the field to the right until the Salary field name is highlighted.

10. Release the ⌒.

The First Name field should be to the right of the Salary field.

11. Point to the Address field name.

12. Press and hold the ⌒.

13. Drag the field to the right until the First Name field name is high-lighted.

14. Release the ⌒.

The Address field should be to the right of the First Name field.

Move the right margin of the report to a position between the Salary and First Name fields.

15. Point to the small arrow on the right end of the ruler line (the arrow should be pointing to the left).

16. Press and hold the ⌒.

17. Drag the arrow to the border separating the Salary and First Name fields.

18. Release the ⌒.

The database should now appear similar to Fig. 9.17.

Place the title "Employee Salary Data by City" on the report.

19. Select the Show Header item from the Window pull-down menu.

20. Type **Employee Salary Data by City**.

21. Point to the close box on the header dialog box, and press the ⌒.

The report format is complete. It is now stored with the database under the name Salary Report.

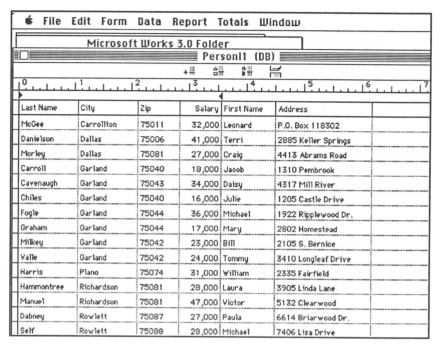

Fig. 9.17 Salary report format containing four fields

To view the database rather than the report format, display list view.

22. Select List View from the Form pull-down menu.

You should see the database in its actual sequence of fields, starting with first name.

Summarizing Data

The report format is now stored with the database under the name Salary Report.

Commands to add summary information could have been included at the time the report format was created, or you can add them later. You will add a salary total to the report format.

1. Point to the Report item on the main menu.

2. Press and hold the ⬭.

3. Drag the pointer to the Salary Report name.

4. Release the ⬭.

You should see the report format for the salary report.

Format the report to include a total of the Salary field data and subtotals for each city.

(Note that for the subtotals to be effective, the data must be sorted by city.)

5. Point to the Salary field name.

6. Click the 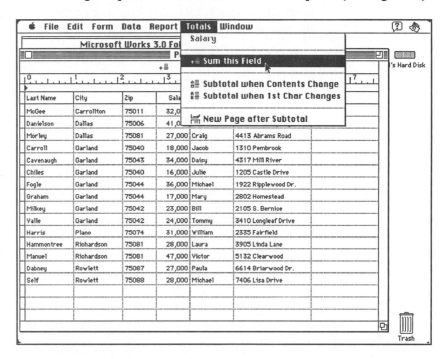 to highlight the field.

7. Point to the Totals item on the main menu.

8. Press and hold the .

9. Drag the pointer to the Sum This Field option (see Fig. 9.18).

Fig. 9.18 Totals pull-down menu showing Sum this Field option

10. Release the .

11. Point to the City field name.

12. Click the to highlight the field.

13. Point to the Totals item on the main menu.

14. Press and hold the .

15. Drag the pointer to the Subtotal when Contents Change option.

16. Release the .

Remove the grid lines from the report.

17. Point to the Form item on the main menu.

18. Press and hold the .

19. Drag the pointer to the Show Grid option.

20. Release the .

Preview the report format with the subtotals and total salaries in the report.

21. Select Print Preview from the File pull-down menu.

22. Select [Print] to produce a printed copy of the report.

23. Select [OK] in the print dialog box.

Using the printed copy as a guide, increase the top and left margin sizes to position the report more to the center of the page, and add spacing in front of the title to position it over the data.

24. Select Page Setup from the File pull-down menu.

25. Select [Document...] from the dialog box.

26. Increase the top margin by one inch beyond its current value.

27. Increase the left margin by one inch beyond its current value.

28. Decrease the right margin by one inch from its current value to maintain the proper data area size to include all fields.

29. Select [OK] in the Document dialog box to record the change.

30. Select [OK] in the Page Setup dialog box to record the change.

31. Select the Show Header item from the Window pull-down menu.

32. Using the space bar, add ten spaces before the heading to move it closer to the center of the report data.

33. Use the close box to close the Header dialog box.

Preview the report format.

34. Select Print Preview from the File pull-down menu.

If necessary, make minor changes to the margins before printing the report.

35. Select [Print] to produce a printed copy of the report.

36. Select [OK] in the print dialog box.

The report should be properly positioned on the page.

Change the view to list view.

37. Select List View from the Form pull-down menu.

Creating a Report with Rules

You will create a report format that will select and print the employees living in Dallas or Richardson.

1. Point to the Report item on the main menu.

2. Press and hold the ⌫.

3. Drag the pointer to the New Report option.

4. Release the ⌫.

5. In the "Name the Report:" box, type **DalRich Employees**.

6. Point to ⌷Create⌷, and click the ⌫.

You should see the records with a ruler line at the top and the First Name field (or another field) highlighted.

All fields will be included in the report. Position the right margin arrow at the right border of the Salary field (if it is not already there).

7. Move the pointer to the right margin arrow on the ruler line.

8. Press and hold the ⌫.

9. Drag the arrow to the right border line of the Salary field.

10. Release the ⌫.

Add the filter.

11. Point to the Data item on the main menu.

12. Press and hold the ⌫.

13. Drag the pointer to the New Filter option.

14. Release the ⌫.

You should have the New/Define Filter dialog box displayed.

15. With the "Filter Name:" box highlighted, type **DalRich** to name the filter.

16. In the first "Field:" box, point to the arrow at the right side of the box.

17. Press and hold the ⌫ to display the drop-down list of field names.

18. Drag the pointer to the field name City.

19. Release the ⌫.

The name City should now be displayed in the box.

Since "equal" is the comparison that is wanted, you do not need to change the "Comparison:" entry.

20. Point to the "Compare to:" box.

21. Click the ⌫ to create an insertion point.

22. Type **Dallas** in the entry box.

23. Point to the arrow on the right side of the second "Field:" box.

24. Press and hold the 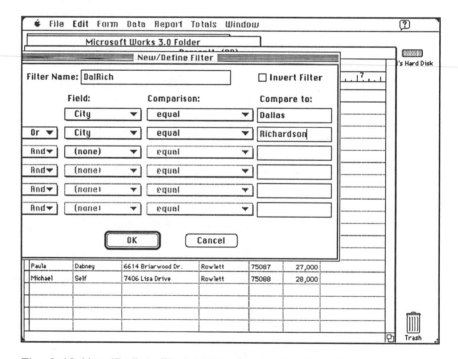 to display the drop-down list of field names.

25. Drag the pointer to the field name City.

26. Release the ⌐▷

The name City should now be displayed in the second field box. The "And" to the left of the field name is now active.

27. Point to the arrow to the right of the "And."

28. Press and hold the ⌐▷.

29. Drag the pointer to the "Or" option.

30. Release the ⌐▷.

Since "equal" is the comparison that is wanted, you do not need to change the "Comparison:" entry.

31. Point to the second "Compare to:" box.

32. Click the ⌐▷ to create an insertion point.

33. Type **Richardson** in the entry box.

The dialog box should now look similar to Fig. 9.19.

Fig. 9.19 New/Define Filter dialog box with city entries

314

34. Point to [OK], and click the <mouse>.

You should now have four records displayed, two representing persons who live in Dallas and two representing persons who live in Richardson.

Note that the filter will be used whenever this report format is selected. The filter is also stored as a filter that can be used apart from this report to view the database with the filter applied.

Change the display to list view.

35. After reviewing the report format, select List View from the Form pull-down menu to change the display to list view.

Display the entire database.

36. Select Show All from the Data pull-down menu to display all records in the database.

(Notice on the Data pull-down menu that you now have the DalRich filter available for reference as needed.)

Printing a Report

You now have three report formats specified for the database. You will print the salary report and the report containing Dallas and Richardson employees. Be sure the printer is on and has paper loaded.

Print the Salary Report. Prior to printing, use the Print Preview option to preview the output format.

1. Point to the Report item on the main menu.

2. Press and hold the <mouse>.

3. Drag the pointer to the Salary Report option.

4. Release the <mouse>.

You should see the Salary Report format displayed.

5. Point to File on the main menu.

6. Press and hold the <mouse>.

7. Drag the pointer to the Print item.

8. Release the <mouse>.

9. Select [OK] in the print dialog box.

The report should print.

You are returned to the Salary Report format.

10. Point to Report on the main menu.

11. Press and hold the ⟨mouse⟩.

12. Drag the pointer to the name DalRich Employees.

13. Release the ⟨mouse⟩.

You should see the report format and the four filtered records.

14. Point to File on the main menu.

15. Press and hold the ⟨mouse⟩.

16. Drag the pointer to the Print option.

17. Release the ⟨mouse⟩.

18. Select ⟨OK⟩ in the print dialog box.

The report should print.

You are returned to the DalRich report format.

Change the format to list view.

19. Select List View from the Form pull-down menu.

Display all the records in the database.

20. Select Show All from the Data pull-down menu.

Saving the Database and Exiting

To be sure that all new formats and filters have been added to the database, you should save the database before exiting. Then close the file and exit Works.

1. Select the Save item from the File pull-down menu to save the database.

2. Select the close box on the left end of the title bar.

3. Select the Quit option from the File pull-down menu.

4. Select the close box on the Microsoft Works 3.0 Folder.

You should now be at the Opening System Disk window.

Summary

The database, when developed and maintained properly, can provide you with much information. Selecting, sorting, and summarizing data can provide information at scheduled time intervals and on an as needed basis.

Sorting data refers to rearranging the records in ascending or descending order by using the entries in one or more fields as sort keys. Sort key fields can be alphanumeric or numeric. The sorted data is physically reordered in the database.

A find technique can be used to select a single field that contains a value matching a specific data value. A select technique can be used to identify all records containing a specific data value in a field. Selecting records using more complex criteria or using multiple fields is also done with the select technique.

Summary information can be derived from records and fields, providing statistical information about the database. Reports can be designed that include titles, column headings, data entries, filters, and summary information. The report formats can be named and stored for later reference.

Questions

1. Describe the process of finding or selecting records in a database, including an example.

2. Contrast the use of ascending and descending sort, giving an example of each.

3. Explain the use of multiple sort fields, distinguishing between major and minor sort keys.

4. List at least two examples of summary information that can be derived from a database.

5. What is the benefit of having the report facility when using a database?

6. Explain the purpose of relational operators, and list the six most commonly used ones.

7. Explain the purpose of logical operators, and list the two most commonly used ones.

8. List the commonly used mathematical operators, and define the hierarchy of processing.

9. Contrast the use of data view, design view, and list view in Works.

10. Briefly explain the process of producing a report using the report feature of Works.

Exercises

Exercise 1

Using data view and design view, create a database using the data below.

Name	Status	Dept.	Hire Date	Salary
Brown	PT	R&D	6/8/89	22000
Carter	FT	R&D	3/12/89	38000
Jeffcoat	FT	ADMIN	6/20/90	44000
Saunders	PT	R&D	4/18/90	26000
Thompson	FT	MKT	7/2/86	34000

1. Store the five records in five fields, with appropriate sizing. Name the database EMPLOYE2. (If you created the database in Chapter 8, simply change the name.)

2. Create a list view of the database and size fields as appropriate.

3. Select all FT employees, using the record selection option.

4. Create a report format, and print the FT employees, including all fields.

5. Save the database.

Exercise 2

1. Using the complete database in Exercise 1 above in list view, sort the records in ascending order by salary level.

2. Save the database.

3. Print the sorted database by first creating a report format, and then printing it.

4. Name the report format Employee Data.

5. Include a title on the report using the header option.

Exercise 3

Using the data depicted in Fig. 9.10, create a database in list view. Add the Employee Number field, Department field, and Phone field and corresponding data depicted below.

First Name	Last Name	Emp. No.	Dept.	Phone
Jacob	Carroll	217	B	530-2234
Daisy	Cavenaugh	266	D	279-1681
Julie	Chiles	221	B	840-0854
Paula	Dabney	291	E	412-7743
Terri	Danielson	206	A	418-0284
Michael	Fogle	271	D	495-9654
Mary	Graham	272	D	495-7633
Laura	Hammontree	284	E	437-1711
William	Harris	282	E	422-1580
Victor	Manuel	287	E	669-2597
Leonard	McGee	204	A	394-4346
Bill	Milkey	241	C	276-0955
Craig	Morley	213	A	680-9212
Michael	Self	293	E	475-4546
Tommy	Valle	245	C	272-2922

1. Change the name of the modified database to PERSONL2.

2. Sort the database in ascending order using department as the major key and in ascending order using salary as the minor key.

3. Save the database.

4. Print the database using a report format.

Problems

Problem 1

Starting with the data in Fig. 9.10 and the additional data depicted in Exercise 3, create a file named PERSONL3. Add the records below to the database.

Diane	Bitner	3214 Sprucewood Ln	Garland	75040	40000	229	B	414-8774
Ralph	Durdon	3215 Country Square	Carrollton	75006	30000	203	A	416-4266
Steven	Eisele	1457 Apollo #1004	Garland	75044	24000	274	D	530-5753
Karen	Estrada	2126 Highridge	Garland	75041	19000	236	C	270-9834
Chuck	Flanigen	1320 Highmesa	Garland	75041	27000	277	D	271-6443
Gerald	Haas	2518 Englecrest	Richardson	75081	19000	285	E	783-9233
Douglas	Hahn	4105 Lawler	Garland	75042	31000	248	C	272-0431
Freddie	Johnson	906 Garden Way	Garland	75040	32000	225	B	278-7832
Debra	Kemp, Jr.	2441 Thomas	Garland	75040	23000	223	B	276-8933
Stan	Kennedy	12990 Audelia Rd	Dallas	74243	24000	205	A	343-7312
Donetta	Lindsey	2317 Highridge	McKinney	75069	26000	280	E	542-9690

Daniel	Malesich	2210 Chesterwood Dr	Richardson	75080	24000	283	E	699-1211
Roberta	Montgomery	6134 Merrimac Trail	Garland	75043	31000	265	D	840-1341
Charles	Nelson	1605 BlueRidge	Garland	75042	20000	256	C	276-2905
Diane	Payne	1238 Jupiter #2203	Garland	75042	32000	263	D	276-7432
Jimmy	Strawn	314 Edgefield Circle	Garland	75041	27000	234	C	487-8221
John	Trott	3405 Clemson	Garland	75042	32000	247	C	276-2354
Thomas	Valdez	7714 Timbercreek	Garland	75042	22000	260	C	487-6732
Jackie	Walker	2433 Clearfield Cir.	Richardson	75081	43000	289	E	234-2856
Richard	Wilson	2325 Berrywood	Garland	75040	36000	226	B	495-8521

Select all employees in department E, then sort them in alphabetical order by city, and print the data.

Problem 2

Using the database created in Problem 1 above, sort the file by department and alphabetically by last name within each department. Print a report including only the department, last name, and salary fields, in that order. Include a report heading on the report.

Problem 3

Using the database created in the problems above do the following:

Select the persons living in Dallas, Garland, and Richardson who have a salary of more than $25,000.

Sort them alphabetically by city with the names alphabetical by last name within each city.

Print a report containing city, last name, first name, salary, and department, in that order. Include a report heading. Include the total salary of all persons listed.

Problem 4

Using the complete database from Problem 1 above, produce the following report. Sort the records using department as the major key, city as the intermediate key, and last name as the minor key. Print a report containing department, city, last name, employee number, and salary, in that order. Include the salary subtotal by department and the total salary for all employees at the end of the report.

Chapter 10

Integrating Works

Objectives

After completing this chapter you will

1. Understand integrated applications.

2. Be able to integrate a spreadsheet document with a text document.

3. Be able to integrate a chart into a text document.

4. Understand the concept of mail merge.

5. Be able to produce form letters.

Integrated Applications

The application tools included in Microsoft Works can be used independently of each other. There are times, however, when you may want to combine information from two or more of the applications. For example, you might want to include information from a spreadsheet or database in a word processing document. In stand-alone programs, the spreadsheet or database data might have to be reentered in the word processing document. This process is time consuming and creates redundancy that could result in introducing errors as the data is reentered. One of the strengths of Works is its ability to provide communication among the different tools that comprise the package.

Multiple Tools

Microsoft Works combines the spreadsheet, word processor, graphics, and database tools into a single easy-to-use application package. Because all tools reside inside an application, the tools share a common interface, or command structure. This has the advantage that once a user learns one of the application tools, learning the others becomes an easier task. For example, the process of saving a document is the same in the word processor as it is in the spreadsheet or database tool. The end result is less time learning the software and more time using it. In addition, moving among the different tools and transferring data among them is easier than with stand-alone programs. This reduces the time required to complete a project and improves the final product.

Windows

Moving among the different application tools and transferring data is accomplished by having multiple windows on the desktop (see Fig. 10.1). Each window displays output from a single application tool. Their size and position can be changed, and any one of the windows can be the active window (the one that the user is currently working with) at any moment.

Integrating the Microsoft Works Tools

This chapter of the book assumes that you have read the chapters on word processing, spreadsheets, graphics, and databases in this book. Without a working knowledge of these tools, this material will have little meaning to you. In addition, it is assumed that you know how to access the different windows and menus for the above-described application tools. If necessary, you should practice the Hands-on sections in the previous chapters of this book.

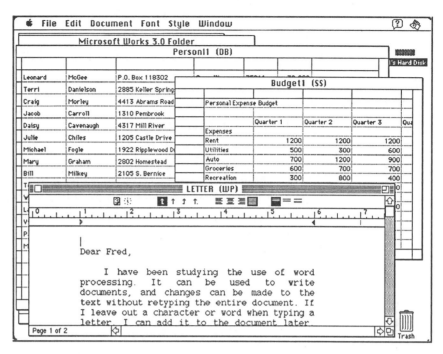

Fig. 10.1 Multiple windows

On most occasions, the word processor is used as the starting point for integrating information among the various tools. Information from a spreadsheet or database is often included as part of a text document. Additionally, the word processor can be used to create mailing labels and form letters.

Using Multiple Tools

If two or more documents are to be integrated, the documents must be present in memory. To integrate spreadsheet data with a text document, you must first create the spreadsheet and the letter. Then, with both of them in memory, you can place the spreadsheet data into the document.

The document illustrated in Fig. 10.2 contains a letter. The letter references data that can be stored in a spreadsheet, such as the one displayed in Fig. 10.3. After the documents have been created and placed into memory, you can produce the integrated document, containing both the letter and the spreadsheet.

Using Windows

Each document, when loaded into memory, is placed in a window. The size of the window determines how much data is displayed. Windows can be sized and moved. Fig. 10.4 displays two documents (as shown in Figures 10.2 and 10.3) at the same time on the desktop by resizing the original windows so both can be seen on the desktop.

May 4, 1994

Ms. Alice Hitech
2001 Chip Drive
Silicon Valley, CA 20304

Dear Ms. Hitech,

These are the figures you requested. I will be happy to discuss them with you. Please call me at your convenience.

Sincerely,

Howard Ross

Fig. 10. 2 Sample word processing document

	A	B	C	D	E
1		Smally Department Store			
2		First Quarter Sales			
3					
4		Jan	Feb	Mar	Total
5					
6	Clothing	1,400	1,600	1,800	4,800
7	Toys	800	700	800	2,300
8	Housewares	1,200	1,600	1,700	4,500
9	Jewelry	900	1,100	700	2,700
10					
11	Total	4,300	5,000	5,000	14,300

Fig. 10.3 Sample spreadsheet

Only one window can be active at any moment. The active window is the one that you are currently working with. To make a different window active, you can display the Window pull-down menu. At the bottom of the pull-down menu there is a list of all document windows that currently reside in memory. To move from one active window to another, drag the mouse pointer over the name of the window desired and release the mouse button. This will make the window containing that application active and move the window to the foreground on the desktop.

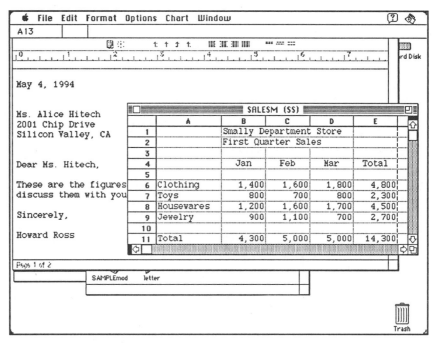

Fig. 10.4 Overlapping windows

Another way to activate a window is to click on any visible portion of the desired window. The active window can be resized by clicking the zoom box and dragging the size box until the desired window size is obtained. Works will respond by displaying the window in the new size (see Fig. 10.5).

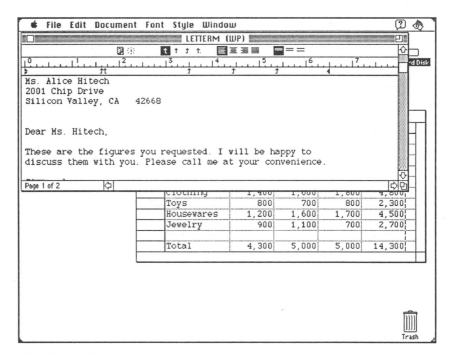

Fig. 10.5 Resized text document

The Clipboard

Data is transferred among the documents in memory by using a clipboard. First copy the data from an active document onto the clipboard. Then make the second document active and paste the contents of the clipboard into the document. This is the process by which integration is accomplished among all the tools in Microsoft Works. This same concept is used by many of the integrated tools on the market today.

Using the Clipboard to Integrate Documents

You will use the clipboard in Works to transfer data among two or more documents. For example, to transfer spreadsheet data into the text document discussed previously, you highlight the data in the spreadsheet document, then activate the Edit pull-down menu and select Copy (see Fig. 10.6). Next, make the text document the active document by displaying the Window pull-down menu and selecting the name of the document in which you want to insert the spreadsheet data. When the new document becomes active, move the pointer where you want the data copied to, then display the Edit pull-down menu and select Paste. The text document will then have a copy of the spreadsheet data in it (see Fig. 10.7).

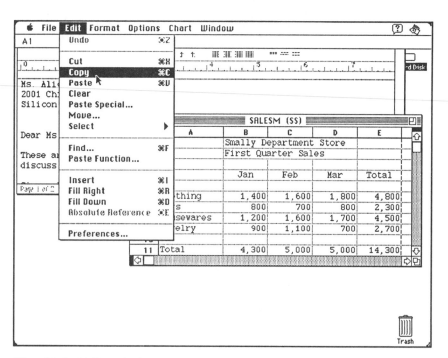

Fig. 10.6 Edit pull-down menu displaying Copy option

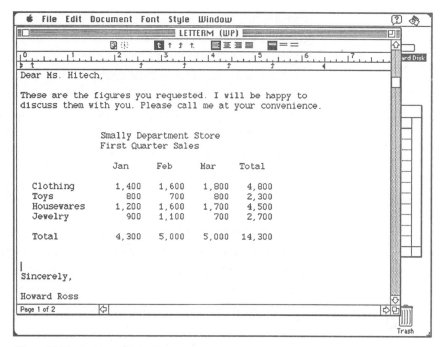

Fig. 10.7 Integrated document

To add a graph to a document, the process is the same. In the example above, assume that you want a graph of the spreadsheet data included in the text document. First create the graph from the spreadsheet data (see Fig. 10.8). Once the graph is created and is active (has handle boxes), display the Edit pull-down menu and select Copy. Activate the text document in which the graph is going to be placed by choosing the name of the document from the Window pull-down menu. Move the pointer to the location where the graph will be displayed. Then display the Edit pull-down menu and choose Paste.

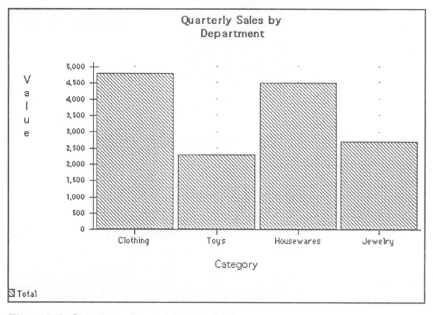

Fig. 10.8 Graph to be added to letter

The graph is superimposed on the text document. This is normal in Works since graphics can be anywhere in a document. The Draw tool palette will be displayed on the desktop and can be used to modify the chart. Click anywhere in the chart and drag it to its final destination in the document. The chart can also be resized by dragging any of the handle boxes that define the boundary of the chart. When the final size and position of the chart is found, display the Window pull-down menu and select Draw Off or click on the close box on the tool palette. Any text that is still covered by the chart may have to be moved. To do this the mouse pointer is moved to the paragraph to be moved and the RETURN key can be pressed several times to move the text down and create space for the chart.

To see the chart inside the document as it will show on the printer, display the File pull-down menu and select Print Preview. This will display a full page as it will be printed on the printer. In Fig. 10.9 you can see that the graph is included in the document following the text and the spreadsheet data. You can cancel the option or print a paper copy by selecting the appropriate button.

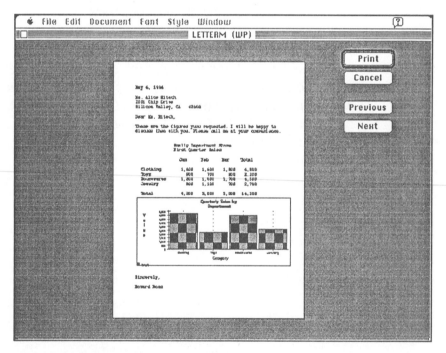

Fig. 10.9 Print preview of document including spreadsheet and chart

Form Letters

A word processing document and database can be used to create personalized letters, mass mailings, or other documents. This is called merging the database with a text document. This is the process used to generate the personalized mass mailings that you receive in your mailbox.

The first step in creating a mail merge is to create the text document that will be the base form letter for the merge. As you create the letter, the areas that will remain the same for each letter are typed. The changing portions of the letter, also called fields, are filled later after the fixed portion is completed. Fig. 10.10 displays a memo that will be sent to employees. Notice that the addressee area was intentionally left blank.

MEMO

May 20, 1994

From: E. Ramos

To:

This is to inform you that as of June 1st your office telephone number can be accessed by pressing the last four digits of the number.

Fig. 10.10 Form document to be used for memos

The personalized data that is to be used for the mail merge resides in a database. In order for Works to access the database, it must be loaded into memory. A sample database is displayed in list view in Fig. 10.11.

Title	Last	First	Home	Business
Ms.	Bonfort	Sally	232-6658	541-5897
Mr.	Bostell	James	456-8777	541-7789
Mrs.	Coolins	Judith	111-2547	541-2356
Dr.	Crossford	Mark	564-7898	541-7968
Mr.	Falkin	Paul	232-7895	569-7899
Ms.	Hewsell	Jennie	232-4568	444-7896
Mr.	Jennings	Howard	456-7714	328-7877
Mr.	Petersen	Douglas	456-8898	232-4465

Fig. 10.11 Database to be used for memos

The last part required to complete the form letter is the inclusion of the fields into the text document. For this process we move the pointer to the first insertion point in the text document, which is the "To:" portion of the memo. Select the Merge Fields option from the Document pull-down menu (see Fig. 10.12). The possible databases from which you can choose fields are displayed in the dialog box, along with the fields contained in them (see Fig. 10.13).

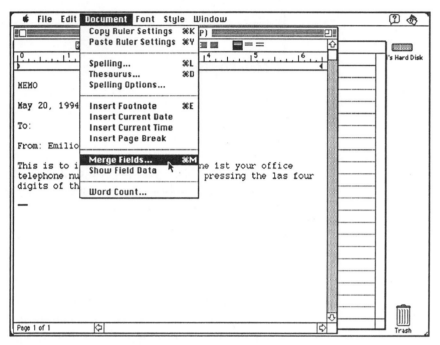

Fig. 10.12 Document pull-down menu showing Merge Fields option

In this case the fields Title, First, and Last are inserted in the proper place in the document by moving the pointer to the insertion place, highlighting the field to be inserted, and then clicking on the Merge button. This process is repeated until all the required fields are in the document. Insert spaces, as necessary, when identifying and placing fields in the document. Initially the data that Works places in the word processor document is the actual field data from a record in the database. Works can also be instructed to display the field names instead of their data. This is done by displaying the Document pull-down menu and selecting the Show Field Data option (refer to Fig. 10.12). The result is a display like that shown in Fig. 10.14.

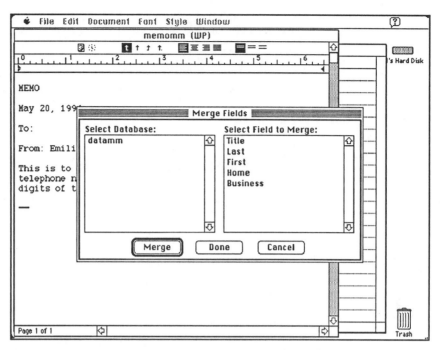

Fig. 10.13 Dialog box displaying all fields available

MEMO

May 20, 1994

From: E. Ramos

To: <<Title>> <<First>> <<Last>>

This is to inform you that as of June 1st your office telephone number can be accessed by pressing the last four digits of the number.

Fig. 10.14 Text document with database fields inserted

Printing the Merged Document

To print the merged document, display the File pull-down menu and select Print. Works will respond with the print dialog box. Select the Print Merged Fields check box if necessary (it should have an X in it to print the merged fields). The memos will be printed and, for each memo, Works will substitute the data stored in the database records for the corresponding field names in the document. Thus, in this example, eight personalized memos will be produced.

Hands-on Integrating Documents with Works

PART I

Including a Spreadsheet in a Text Document

In this section you will integrate a spreadsheet into a text document. The first step is to create the document and the spreadsheet.

1. Use the word processor tool to type the document displayed in Fig. 10.15. Then use the zoom box (on the right end of the title bar) to maximize the window on the desktop.

2. Save the document as TEXTINT, and keep it in memory.

July 12, 1994

Ms. Alice Hitech
2001 Chip Drive
Silicon Valley, CA 20304

Dear Ms. Hitech,

These are the figures that you requested last week. I would be happy to discuss them with you. Please call me at your convenience.

Sincerely,

Howard Thompson

Fig. 10.15 Text document

You will include a spreadsheet as part of the document.

3. Use the spreadsheet tool to create a spreadsheet containing the data in Fig. 10.16 (using formulas and functions as appropriate). After completing the spreadsheet, maximize the window using the zoom box.

4. Save the spreadsheet as DATAINT, and keep it in memory.

	A	B	C	D	E
1		Smally Department Store			
2		First Quarter Sales			
3					
4		Jan	Feb	Mar	Total
5					
6	Clothing	1,400	1,600	1,800	4,800
7	Toys	800	700	800	2,300
8	Housewares	1,200	1,600	1,700	4,500
9	Jewelry	900	1,100	700	2,700
10					
11	Total	4,300	5,000	5,000	14,300

Fig. 10.16 Spreadsheet data

Incorporate the spreadsheet data into the letter.

First select the data in the spreadsheet

5. With the spreadsheet active, move the cell pointer to cell A1 in the spreadsheet.

6. Press and hold the ⌐.

7. Drag the pointer to cell E11.

8. Release the ⌐.

9. Select Copy from the Edit pull-down menu (see Fig. 10.17). The highlighted data is now placed on the clipboard.

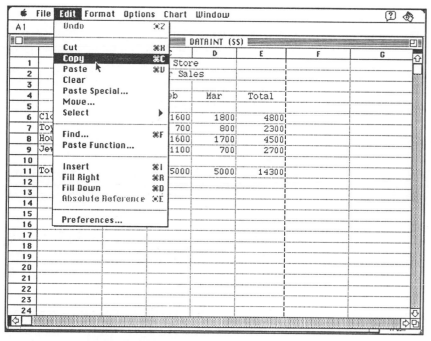

Fig. 10.17 Edit pull-down menu displaying Copy option

Now the data is on the electronic clipboard, which can be accessed by any of the Works applications. Place the contents of the clipboard in the text document.

10. Select the Window pull-down menu.

11. Select the name of the word processing document (TEXTINT) (see Fig. 10.18). Now the word processing document window is in the foreground and is active.

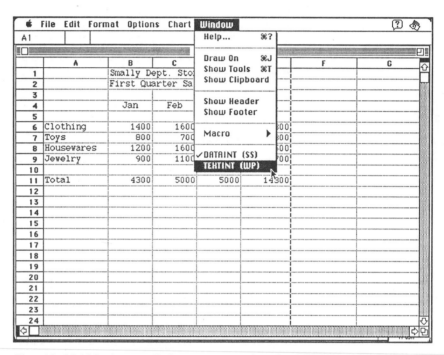

Fig. 10.18 Window pull-down menu showing TEXTINT file name

12. Move the pointer to the line following the paragraph (above the word "Sincerely"), and position it at the left margin.

13. Click the ⌧ to create an insertion point.

14. Select the Paste option from the Edit pull-down menu (refer to Fig. 10.17). The process is now complete, and your document window should look similar to Fig. 10.19.

15. Select Save As from the File pull-down menu to save the integrated file, and name the document TEXTDATA.

Integrating documents in Works involves copying and pasting from one window to another. The process to copy data among the other tools is the same as the one described above.

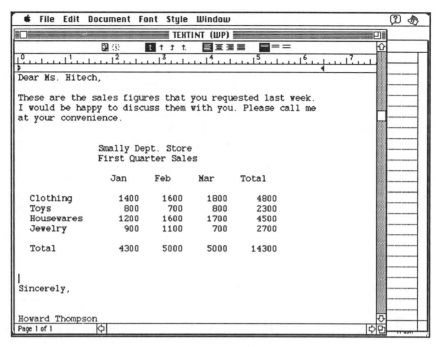

Fig. 10.19 Integrated document

Including a Chart

Charts created with the spreadsheet and the charting tool can be included in a text document to enhance the appearance and effectiveness of the document. Before the chart can be added to a document, it must be created. The process used to create a chart is presented in Chapter 7 of this book. If you need to review chart creation, do the Hands-on section of Chapter 7.

1. Using the sales data in the worksheet just created, create a chart like the one shown in Fig. 10.20. (Use the Window pull-down menu to make the spreadsheet window active.) Name the chart First Quarter Sales.

You will now incorporate this chart into the text document, which currently contains text entered with the word processor and data created with the spreadsheet.

2. With the chart window active (with handle boxes displayed), select the Edit pull-down menu, and select Copy.

3. Select the name of the text document (TEXTDATA) from the Window pull-down menu (refer to Fig. 10.18).

4. Move the pointer to the bottom of the document, and make sure that it is on a line by itself (the line below the name Howard Thompson).

5. Select the Edit pull-down menu.

6. Select Paste.

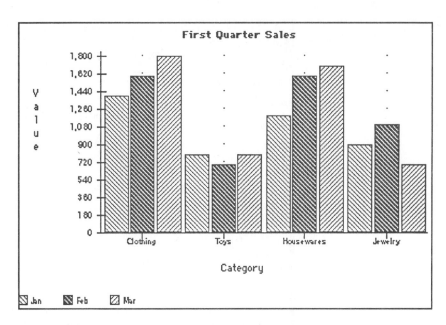

Fig. 10.20 Chart to be included in text document

The chart should now be visible at the bottom of the document.

> 7. Select Draw Off from the Window pull-down menu (see Fig. 10.21).

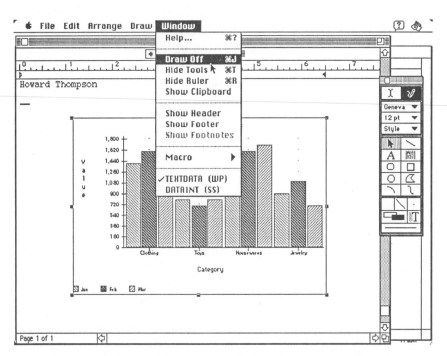

Fig. 10.21 Window pull-down menu showing Draw Off option

Move the lines of text containing "Sincerely" and "Howard Thompson" and the blank lines above and between them below the chart.

> 8. Point to the beginning of the line just above the word "Sincerely."

9. Click the ⬭ to create an insertion point.

10. Drag the pointer to the line below "Howard Thompson."

11. Release the ⬭.

12. Select Cut from the Edit pull-down menu.

13. Press ⦗ **return** ⦘ several times, until the insertion point moves below the chart.

14. Select Paste from the Edit pull-down menu.

The document is now complete.

15. Select Print Preview from the File pull-down menu to preview the completed document.

16. If the chart crosses a page boundary, move it as necessary by using the Draw On option from the Window pull-down menu. (One solution is to drag the chart to the top of the second page; another is to resize it, if necessary, and keep it on the first page.)

17. Select Draw Off from the Window pull-down menu once the chart is positioned.

18. If the chart was moved, arrange the surrounding text as necessary to provide a readable document. (Move the closing lines up or down until they are positioned below the chart, and make other changes as necessary.)

The completed document now includes the text, the spreadsheet data, and the chart.

19. Select Print Preview from the File pull-down menu to review the final document.

20. Select Print from the Print Preview window to print the final document.

21. Select ⦗ OK ⦘ on the print dialog box.

The completely integrated document should print.

Saving and Exiting

The text document now contains text, a spreadsheet, and a chart. At this time the document can be saved for later retrieval.

1. Select Save As from the File pull-down menu, and save the completed document with the name CHARTINT.

The document is now saved on your disk and can be retrieved at a later date for viewing, modifying, or printing.

2. Select the close box on the left end of the title bar.

3. Select the Quit option from the File pull-down menu.

4. Select the close box on the Microsoft Works 3.0 Folder.

You should now be at the Opening System Disk window.

PART II

Creating Form Letters

As stated previously, the database and the word processing tool can be used together to create form letters. This process is called mail merge.

The first step is to create the form letter that will serve as the base for all letters. The form letter will contain text that is the same on all letters to be mailed.

1. To create the form letter, open the Works application program, create a new word processing document, and type the text shown in Fig. 10.22. Then save it, and name it MEMOMERG.

MEMO

May 20, 1994

To:

From: Fred Brown

This is to inform you that as of June 1st   will be your office telephone number. Please make note of this and begin using the new number promptly.

Fig. 10.22 Base document for mail merge

The next step is to create the database that contains the data to be inserted into the text document. The process used to create a database is covered in Chapters 8 and 9 in this book.

2. At this point, create a database from the data shown in Fig. 10.23, save it, and name it PHONES.

You will insert the First, Last, and Business fields into the text document. After all fields are in the memo, you will perform a merge operation that will replace the name of each field in the document with data from the database. This will print a form letter for each record in the database.

Title	Last	First	Home	Business
Ms.	Bonfort	Sally	232-6658	541-5897
Mr.	Bostell	James	456-8777	541-7789
Mrs.	Coolins	Judith	111-2547	541-2356
Dr.	Crossford	Mark	564-7898	541-7968
Mr.	Falkin	Paul	232-7895	569-7899
Ms.	Hewsell	Jennie	232-4568	444-7896
Mr.	Jennings	Howard	456-7714	328-7877
Mr.	Petersen	Douglas	456-8898	232-4465

Fig. 10.23 Data used in mail merge

3. With both the memo and database files in memory, make the text document active by selecting the name MEMOMERG from the Window pull-down menu (see Fig. 10.24).

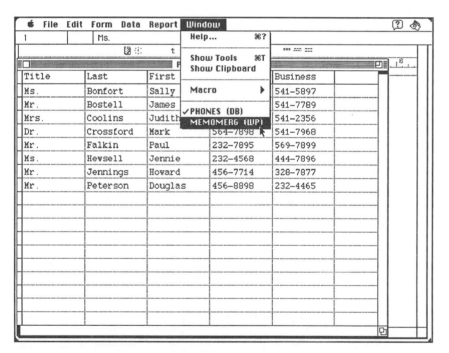

Fig. 10.24 Window pull-down menu showing MEMOMERG file name

4. Move the pointer to the right of the colon after the word "To."

5. Click the ⬭ to create an insertion point.

6. Press ‖space‖ once to insert a blank.

7. Select the Merge Fields option from the Document pull-down menu.

You should see the Merge Fields dialog box displayed (see Fig. 10.25).

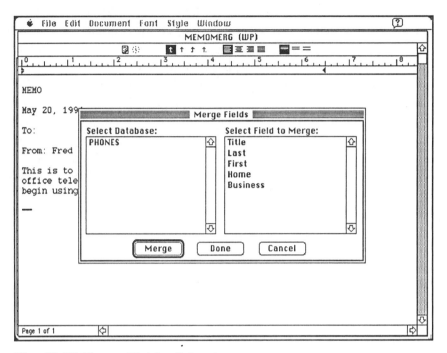

Fig. 10.25 Merge Fields dialog box

8. Select PHONES in the database list box if it is not already high-lighted.

9. Select First in the fields list box.

10. Click on [Merge].

11. Select Last in the fields list box.

12. Click on [Merge].

13. Click on [Done].

14. Move the pointer to the left of the "w" in the word "will" in the first line of the memo paragraph.

15. Click the ⬡ to create an insertion point.

16. Select the Merge Fields option from the Document pull-down menu.

17. Select Business in the fields list box.

18. Click on [Merge].

19. Click on [Done].

You should now see a first name, last name, and phone number added from the database to the memo or the names of the three fields displayed in the memo.

20. If you have an actual first name, last name, and phone number displayed in the memo, select Show Field Names from the Document pull-down menu to display the database name and field names in the appropriate locations in the memo. (If the field names are already displayed, the pull-down menu will have a Show Field Data option displayed, which is used to show the actual data.) The document should now look like Fig. 10.26.

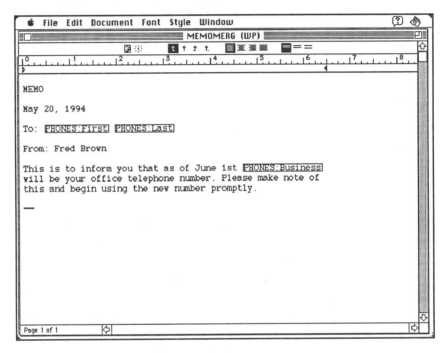

Fig. 10.26 Completed form letter

Printing the Form Letter

The text document is now completed, and it is ready to be merged with the database to produce the letters.

Make sure your printer is on.

1. Select the Print option from the File pull-down menu.

2. Select the Print Merged Fields option in the print dialog box if it is not selected (it should be on).

3. Select OK.

The personalized memos will now print on the printer with appropriate data from each record in the database replacing the field names in the text document.

Saving and Exiting

You will now save the form letter for later reference.

1. Select Save As from the File pull-down menu.

2. Type the name **FORMMEMO**, and click on ⌐Save⌐.

The form letter is now saved, and you can leave Works. Whenever you need the form letter again, just retrieve it and the data file, and print it again.

3. To close the FORMMEMO file, select the close box on the left end of the title bar.

4. To close the PHONES database file, select the close box on the left end of the title bar.

5. To close the Works application, select the Quit option from the File pull-down menu.

6. To close the Microsoft Works 3.0 Folder, select the close box on the left end of the title bar.

You should now be at the Opening System Disk window.

Summary

The application tools included with Microsoft Works can be used independently of each other. However, since they share a common interface, information can be transferred among the different tools by copying and pasting from one application window to another.

In order to integrate two or more applications, they all must reside in memory. To copy data, the Window pull-down menu is activated and the name of the document containing the data to be copied is selected. Using the Edit pull-down menu, the required data is selected and copied to the clipboard. The destination document is then activated. Finally, the pointer is moved to the target location in the document. Then by selecting Paste from the Edit pull-down menu, the data is pasted into the destination document.

Form letters involving mail merging can be created by first using the word processing tool to create a base or form document. Then fields from a database are placed into the form document. By selecting Print from the File pull-down menu and including the merge option, all form letters with appropriate data are printed on a printer.

Questions

1. Which applications in Works can be integrated?

2. Can more than one file be in memory at the same time in Works?

3. How many files are active at one time in Works?

4. Define the term "clipboard."

5. Give three examples of instances when you may want to integrate data from one application area to another.

6. Describe the process used to insert a spreadsheet into a text document.

7. Describe the process used to insert a chart into a text document.

8. What is a form letter?

9. How can you generate mass mailings?

10. List at least four advantages of using integrated application software.

Exercises

Exercise 1

1. Type the memo below using the word processing tool.

   DATE: March 28, 1994

   TO: all employees

   FROM: Department Manager

   SUBJECT: price increases

   These are the numbers for the items that will be discussed in today's meeting. Take time to decide whether the prices are appropriate. If an item has a price too low, then how much would you increase it by?

2. Create a spreadsheet containing the following data.

Item	Cost
101	2.34
102	4.56
103	1.25
104	5.67

3. Insert the spreadsheet created in step 2 into the document.

4. Save the text document and the spreadsheet.

5. Print the text document.

Exercise 2

1. Retrieve the integrated text document and spreadsheet created in Exercise 1.

2. Using the charting tool create a bar chart of the cost data outlined in Exercise 1.

3. Insert the chart at the bottom of the memo.

4. Save the document and the spreadsheet.

5. Print the document.

Problems

Problem 1

Create a database containing five records and including the fields specified in the form letter below. Create the form letter that is displayed. Produce form letters for each of the persons in the mailing list using the mail merge feature.

```
<<First>> <<Last>>
<<Address>>
<<City>>, <<State>>  <<Zip>>

Dear <<First>>,
Please find attached the information promised to you. I hope that
everything included is to your satisfaction. If there is any other
information that I can provide you, please do not hesitate to
contact me.

Sincerely,

Paul Azzingger
```

Problem 2

Integrate the spreadsheet and chart from Exercises 1 and 2 into the following letter. Create a database of 10 names and addresses including all fields shown in the letter. Produce 10 form letters using the mail merge feature.

<<First>> <<Last>>
<<Address>>
<<City>>, <<State>> <<Zip>>

Dear <<First>>,
Please find attached the information promised to you. Please review the data carefully. If there is any other information that I can provide you, please do not hesitate to contact me.

----- the spreadsheet data goes here -----

----- The chart goes here -----

Sincerely,

Paul Azzingger

Appendix A
Tool Palette

The tool palette is accessible from all of the applications. It is found in the Window pull-down menu. Choose the option Show Tools to display the palette when it is not visible. The tool palette is displayed on the desktop (see Fig. A.1). It can be moved anywhere on the desktop by pointing to the title bar and dragging it. The tool palette is closed by selecting the close box on the title bar or by selecting the Hide Tools command on the Window pull-down menu.

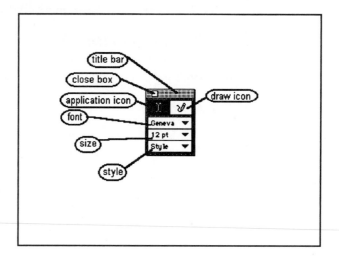

Fig. A.1 Tool palette

The tool palette contains similar information for the word processing, spreadsheet, and database applications. The title bar is across the top; it contains a close box on the left end of it. In the lower part of the palette are three boxes that reference pop-up list boxes to set the font, size, and style of the currently referenced data. The current font and size are displayed in the boxes, and the word "style" is displayed in the third box in the current style. A pop-up feature is referenced by pointing to the appropriate box, then pressing and holding the mouse button. Another setting is selected by dragging the pointer to it and releasing the mouse button. Directly underneath the title bar is an icon button for the application on the left and a pencil icon button for the draw feature on the right. The spreadsheet palette also contains a chart icon button in the middle. The icons are used to transfer control between the application and the draw feature, and are selected by pointing to them and clicking the mouse button. The database palette contains similar information in design view to those of other applications, but differs somewhat in data and list views.

Appendix B
Draw

The draw feature in Works allows you to place a drawing in a word processing, spreadsheet, database, or draw document. The drawing is positioned on a transparent layer above the document, thus allowing it to overlay parts of the document without destroying them. Objects in the drawing can also be overlaid without destroying portions of them.

The draw tool is accessed by selecting Draw On from the Window pull-down menu, or by selecting the Draw tool icon from the tool palette when the tool palette is displayed. To exit Draw, choose Draw Off from the Window pull-down menu, or select the application icon from the top row of the tool palette.

The draw application extends the tool palette to include various options to assist in creating drawings (see Fig. B.1). With the draw feature displayed, the tool palette appears in three sections. The first section contains the general features of the tool palette (refer to Appendix A), the second section contains shapes which can be drawn, and the third section contains formatting features of the drawing. The draw features are generally the same, regardless of which application is involved.

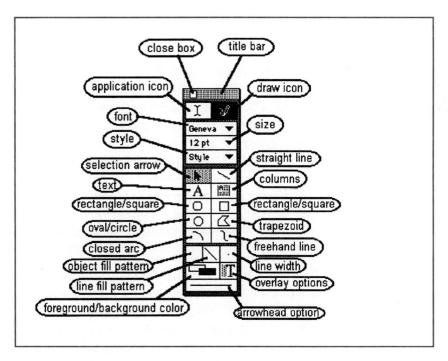

Fig. B.1 Draw feature's tool palette

The second section of the draw palette includes symbols indicating the type of drawing to be done. The left column contains the selection arrow, an A to indicate text entry, a square with rounded corners to indicate rectangles or squares with smooth corners, a circle to indicate ovals or circles, and a curved line to indicate a closed arc. The right column contains a line to indicate straight line, enclosed text to indicate columns, a square to indicate rectangles or squares with pointed corners, a trapezoid to indicate a series of connected lines, and a curved line to indicate a freehand line drawing.

An option from the second section is applied by first pointing to the option and clicking the mouse button to select it. Then create a drawing relating to the option. Text is entered by using the pointer to create an insertion point, then typing the text desired. Lines and shapes (circles, squares, etc.) are created by pointing to where one end or corner will be and dragging the pointer to the other end or diagonal corner, then releasing the mouse button. Trapezoids are created by moving the pointer and clicking the mouse button at the beginning and end of each line segment.

The third section of the draw palette contains several formatting options that can be applied to the drawings. The empty square in the upper left corner of the third section is used to specify a fill pattern for an object. The square to its right, containing the diagonal line, is used to specify a pattern for the line used to draw the object. The square to its right, containing a dot, is used to specify the width of the line used to draw the object. Further down in the third section, the two connected rectangles are used to set foreground and background color. The icon to their right, containing a T, is used to set an overlay option, which includes the option to erase the selected drawing. The horizontal line at the bottom of the third section is used to include an arrow head at either or both ends of a line.

Each of the options in the third section is selected by pointing to it and pressing the mouse button. The color, pattern, and width options display a palette of options. The overlay and arrow options display a list of options to choose from. Drag the pointer to the selection and release the mouse button. The overlay list can be displayed separately and continuously by dragging the list box to a new location before releasing the mouse button.

There are a number of features available on the menu bar that can be used to modify or enhance an object or group of objects in a drawing. The typical edit features are located in the Edit pull-down menu. Other features are found by selecting the Arrange or Draw options from the menu bar.

You can cut and paste an object by selecting it, then selecting the Cut option from the Edit pull-down menu, activating a destination location, and selecting Paste to place the object in the new location. A copy and paste operation can be done using the same procedure and selecting Copy, then Paste. The Clear command can be used to clear a selected object from a drawing. The Select All command will select all objects in the drawing.

On the Arrange pull-down menu, the Group and Ungroup commands can be used to combine selected objects into one object, or to separate objects that have previously been combined. The Bring to Front and Send to Back options can be used to move an object to the foreground or background relative to other objects in the same space. The Grid Settings option can be used to define the distance between grid lines, and the Snap to Grid option, when active, connects an object being drawn to the nearest grid line.

The Smooth option on the Draw pull-down menu causes the connecting points in an object to form smooth rather than pointed edges, in effect creating a curved rather than a straight-line edge. The Rotate option allows you to rotate an object a specified number of degrees, or flip the object horizontally or vertically. The 3-D Effect option adds lines to give an object a three dimensional effect. The Shadow option adds a shadow shading to an object. The Break Up and Join options can cause parts of an object to become separate objects or combine connected objects or parts into a single object. The Lock Objects option will lock a selected object into the drawing and not allow it to be referenced or manipulated. The Add Handles and Remove Handles options can be used to place many handles on an object for reshaping or modifying any part of the object.

In summary, there are many features available in the Draw application of Works. A drawing can be done independently of other applications, or a drawing can be integrated into the other Works applications.

Appendix C
Communications

The word processor, spreadsheet, chart, and database tools in Works can be used by themselves to accomplish a task. However, there is another component available in Works that can be used, if additional hardware is available. This is the communications tool.

The communications tool is used to connect your personal computer with other computers to exchange information.

The hardware required to use the communications tool includes the following:

1. Your personal computer.

2. A modem connected to your computer.

3. A telephone line.

4. A host (receiving) computer with a modem.

5. Communications software (the communications tool in Works).

The Communications Process

Computers process information in digital form, using bits and bytes of data. A bit is the smallest unit of data that the computer can represent. Personal computers use seven or eight bits to represent alphabetic characters and other special characters inside the computer. An eight bit combination is called a byte.

When two computers communicate with each other, the information is exchanged by passing individual bit combinations that represent the characters of data. If the computers are in close proximity, a coaxial cable can be used to connect them. If they are far apart, then a telephone line can provide the connection medium.

When a telephone line is used, the data must be in analog rather than digital format. This requires the use of a modem to convert the data from digital to analog format as it is passed from the sending computer to the telephone line and from analog to digital format as it is passed from the telephone line to the receiving computer.

The Modem

A modem is an electronic device that converts (modulates) the digital communications between computers into audible tones that can be transmitted over telephone lines. The received data is then converted (demodulated) from the audible tones to digital format that can be processed by the receiving computer. The term *modem* is an acronym derived from the words MOdulator and DEModulator.

Most modems for personal computers can dial numbers, redial busy numbers, automatically answer calls, and set the proper communication speed. For the Works communication tool to take advantage of these features and others, your modem must be a Hayes modem or a Hayes-compatible modem. If it is not a Hayes or a compatible, you can use the communications tool, but you will not be able to use the advanced features described above.

Modems can be external or internal. An external modem is placed next to the computer. It is connected to the computer's serial port with a serial cable, and it is connected to the telephone line with a telephone cord. An internal modem is placed inside the computer by using an available expansion slot. It is connected to the telephone line by a telephone cord. Once the modem is connected to the computer and the telephone line, its function is controlled by the communications tool in Works. Your modem will include instructions regarding how to connect it to the computer and to the telephone line. You can install it yourself or have your computer dealer install it for you.

Software Communications Terminology

By considering the factors listed below, you will be able to communicate with electronic bulletin boards or services (BBS). Before an actual connection is made, your modem and software need to have the same settings as the receiving or host computer that you are trying to access. These settings are common to all communication setups; they include the following:

1. Baud rate. This is the rate of transmission of data. One baud equals one binary bit per second. Settings include 300, 1200, 2400, 4800, and 9600. A higher baud rate inherently means a faster rate of transmission and a shorter waiting time for data transmission.

2. Data bits. These are the number of bits that make up a character. Most mini- and mainframe computers use seven bits.

3. Stop bits. These indicate the number of bits used to identify the end of a character. In most cases, one stop bit marks the end of a character.

4. Handshake. This refers to the manner in which one communicating computer knows when the other computer is sending or receiving

data, or when it is doing something that might interfere with the transmission signals. This is part of the communications protocol, which refers to all the conventions that must be observed in order for the computers to communicate with each other.

5. Parity. This is a method of checking for errors in data communications. You should refer to the host machine to find out which type of parity is being used, then select the appropriate setting on your computer.

The Communications Tool

To access the communications tool, select the "Comm" icon from the Works opening dialog box, or select New or Open from the File pull-down menu when in the Works application. A communications window will be displayed, and a communications menu bar will be accessible to you (see Fig. C.1). Before connecting to another computer, you should review the communication settings and change them as necessary. Select Connection from the Settings pull-down menu. The Connection Settings dialog box should then be displayed (see Fig. C.2).

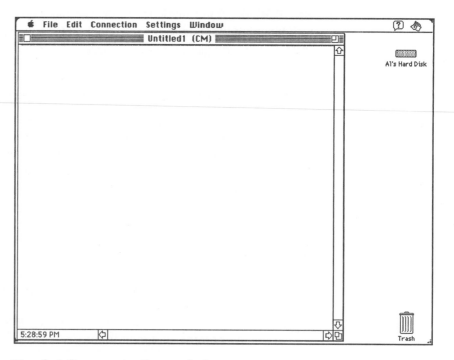

Fig. C.1 Communications window

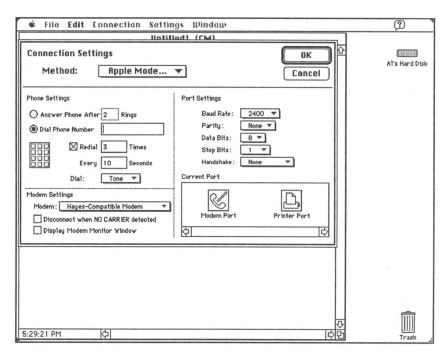

Fig. C.2 Connection Settings dialog box

If you are connecting to a pay-per-hour service, you should have a packet of information that defines the settings needed. If you are not familiar with the host system, get the settings from someone who is familiar with it. If you cannot get the settings, you can perform some trial attempts to find the proper settings.

Some possible settings are 2400 for Baud Rate, None for Parity, 7 for Data Bits, 1 for Stop Bits, and XON/XOFF for the handshake. To change one of the parameters, point to the arrow in the entry box, press and hold the mouse button to see the pop-up list, drag the pointer to the appropriate option, and release the mouse button. The Current Port selection should match the option selected on the back of the computer. The terminal emulation type is found by selecting Terminal from the Settings pull-down menu, and a possible setting is VT102 Tool (see Fig. C.3).

Making the Connection

After all the parameters have been properly set, you can connect to the host system by selecting the Open Connection option from the Connection pull-down menu. To call a computer or information service, first open the communications document for the computer or information service, then select the Open Connection option from the Connection pull-down menu, then enter a phone number if necessary. After connecting, enter your identification number and password if necessary. If you need to log off, choose Close Connection from the Connection pull-down menu.

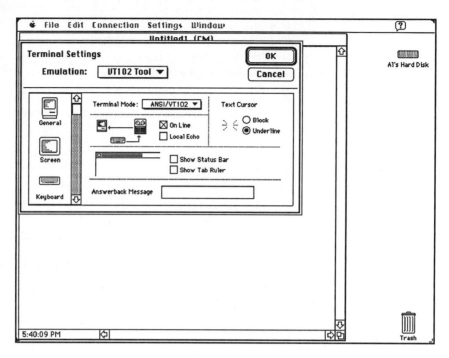

Fig. C.3 Terminal Settings dialog box

Appendix D
Keyboard Control

Word Processing

Key or keys	Moves the insertion point
LEFT ARROW	Left one character
RIGHT ARROW	Right one character
UP ARROW	Up one line
DOWN ARROW	Down one line
HOME	To start of document
END	To end of document
PAGE UP	Up one window
PAGE DOWN	Down one window

Spreadsheet

Key or keys	Moves the active cell
LEFT ARROW	Left one cell
RIGHT ARROW	Right one cell
UP ARROW	Up one cell
DOWN ARROW	Down one cell
HOME	To start of spreadsheet
END	To end of spreadsheet
PAGE UP	Up one window
PAGE DOWN	Down one window

Database

List View or Data View

Key or keys	Moves the active entry
LEFT ARROW	Left one field
RIGHT ARROW	Right one field
UP ARROW	Up one field or record
DOWN ARROW	Down one field or record
COMMAND/=	To the next record
COMMAND/-	To the previous record

Appendix E
Keyboard Shortcuts

Use the following keys to enter commands directly.

Word Processing

File

New	⌂ ⌘ N
Open	⌂ ⌘ O
Close	⌂ ⌘ W
Save	⌂ ⌘ S
Print	⌂ ⌘ P
Quit	⌂ ⌘ Q

Edit

Cut	⌂ ⌘ X
Copy	⌂ ⌘ C
Paste	⌂ ⌘ V
Find	⌂ ⌘ F
Replace	⌂ ⌘ H

Document

Spelling	⌂ ⌘ L
Thesaurus	⌂ ⌘ D
Merge Fields	⌂ ⌘ M

Style

Bold	⌂ ⌘ B
Italic	⌂ ⌘ I
Underline	⌂ ⌘ U

Window

Help	⌂ ⌘ ?
Draw On	⌂ ⌘ J
Show Tools/ Hide Tools	⌂ ⌘ T
Show Ruler/ Hide Ruler	⌂ ⌘ R

Spreadsheet

File

New	⌃ ⌘ N
Open	⌃ ⌘ O
Close	⌃ ⌘ W
Save	⌃ ⌘ S
Print	⌃ ⌘ P
Quit	⌃ ⌘ Q

Edit

Cut	⌃ ⌘ X
Copy	⌃ ⌘ C
Paste	⌃ ⌘ V
Find	⌃ ⌘ F
Insert	⌃ ⌘ I
Fill Right	⌃ ⌘ R
Fill Down	⌃ ⌘ D

Window

Help	⌃ ⌘ ?
Draw On	⌃ ⌘ J
Show Tools/ Hide Tools	⌃ ⌘ T

Database

File

New	⌃ ⌘ N
Open	⌃ ⌘ O
Close	⌃ ⌘ W
Save	⌃ ⌘ S
Print	⌃ ⌘ P
Quit	⌃ ⌘ Q

Edit

Cut	⌃ ⌘ X
Copy	⌃ ⌘ C
Paste	⌃ ⌘ V
Find	⌃ ⌘ F
Select All	⌃ ⌘ A

Data

Next Record	⌃ ⌘ =
Previous Record	⌃ ⌘ -

Form

List View	⌃ ⌘ L

Insert Record	⌃ ⌘ I
Match Records	⌃ ⌘ M
Define Filter	⌃ ⌘ K

Window

Help	⌃ ⌘ ?
Draw On	⌃ ⌘ J
Show Tools/ Hide Tools	⌃ ⌘ T

Communications

File

New	⌃ ⌘ N
Open	⌃ ⌘ O
Close	⌃ ⌘ W
Save	⌃ ⌘ S
Print	⌃ ⌘ P
Quit	⌃ ⌘ Q

Edit

Cut	⌃ ⌘ X
Copy	⌃ ⌘ C
Paste	⌃ ⌘ V
Select All	⌃ ⌘ A

Connection

Open Connection	⌃ ⌘ D
Close Connection	⌃ ⌘ K
Send File	⌃ ⌘ U
Receive File	⌃ ⌘ L

Settings

Connection	⌃ ⌘ 1
Terminal	⌃ ⌘ 2
File Transfer	⌃ ⌘ 3

Window

Help	⌘ ?
Show Tools/ Hide Tools	⌘ T

Draw

File

New	⌘ N
Open	⌘ O
Close	⌘ W
Save	⌘ S
Print	⌘ P
Quit	⌘ Q

Edit

Cut	⌘ X
Copy	⌘ C
Paste	⌘ V
Select All	⌘ A

Window

Help	⌘ ?
Show Tools/ Hide Tools	⌘ T
Show Ruler/ Hide Ruler	⌘ R

Index

Adding
    columns 167, 178
    data 186, 259
    fields 243, 254, 270
    footer 107
    formatted text 114
    page number 107
    records 238, 245, 253, 268
    rows 167
ALU 4
Application software 3, 6, 11, 18, 33, 51, 135
    computer graphics 19
    database 18-20, 33, 227-230, 282-285
    spreadsheet 12, 19, 20, 25, 33, 126, 202, 204-208, 211-221, 322-324, 326-328, 332, 335
    telecommunications 18-20, 33
    word processing 12, 18-20, 33, 50, 55, 322, 328, 338
Arithmetic/logic unit 4
Automating
    database 229-230
    spreadsheet 127, 128
    word processing 51-52

Background 22, 28, 207
Bar chart 198-200, 208, 210, 221
Bar graph *see* Bar chart
Bit 4
Block operations 60-61
Boldfacing 19, 92, 93, 97, 100, 115, 116
Booting 4, 10, 13, 35
Browsing records 252
Business graphics 19, 198
Buttons 30, 54, 95, 110, 112, 288, 294
    mouse 6
Byte 4, 9, 10

Capabilities
    spreadsheet 128
    word processing 128
CD-ROM 10
Cell 126, 130-135, 137, 164-169, 171-174,184, 189-190, 205
    copying contents 173
    deleting 189
    deleting contents 172
    formatting 169, 184
    moving contents 172
    pointer 131, 137, 172-174, 238, 242
    pointer control in list view 242
    reference 131
Centering 92, 97-99, 114
    option 113
Central Processing Unit 3, 4
Changing to list view 266

Chart 20, 198-221, 328, 335-337
    bar 198
    changing type 214
    definition 207, 220
    duplicating 218
    enhancing 205-207
    features 201
    grids 206
    including in a document 335
    labels 206
    line 201
    location 206
    managing 207
    modifying the definition 220
    moving 211
    pie 200
    printing 205, 212
    range 206
    saving 205, 211
    series 208
    size 206, 211
    titles 205
    tool palette 207
    viewing 204
Check box 30, 132, 206, 285, 288, 290, 331
Click 23, 32
Clipboard 26, 61, 78, 79, 174, 180, 243, 244, 333, 334
    using 326
Close box 28, 34
Closing
    files 40, 72, 149
    tool palette 205
Column 126, 131, 204
    adding 178
    deleting 167-168
    width 168, 182
Column Width dialog box 183
Command key 236-237, 242
Communications 4, 20
Comparisons 4
Components 2, 3
Computer graphics 19
Copying
    cell contents 173
    data 179
    files 32, 41
    folders 32
    text 60, 78
CPU 4, 5, 7
Creating
    chart 202
    database 230, 245, 262, 294
    document 38, 52, 54
    fields 295
    folders 31

form letters 338
pie chart 213
report format 289, 292, 308
report with rules 312
series chart 208
spreadsheet 140

Data 2, 4-6, 9-12, 18-19, 282
    label 132
    manipulation 132, 166, 172
    selecting 282
    sorting 283
    summarizing 284
    value 133, 166, 206
Data view 233-237 245-262
    window 232-234
Database 12, 18-20, 33, 227-230, 282-285
    automating 229-230
    changing to list view 266
    creating 229-230, 245, 262, 294
    data view 233-240, 245-262
    design view 238
    display options 174
    entering records 236, 251, 265
    formatting fields 234, 242, 257, 272
    list view 241-245, 262-275
    multiple views 240
    planning 228
    printing 237, 245, 260, 274
    restructuring 239-239
    retrieving 237,
    saving 236, 251, 308
    updating 237, 244
    window 230, 232-234
Define Chart dialog box 203-204, 215
Deleting
    cell contents 172
    cells 189
    columns 167
    documents 44
    fields 243, 257, 272
    files 32
    folders 32
    records 244, 269
    rows 167
    text 50-52, 59, 75
Design view 232
    option 249
    window 232-233
Dialog Box 11, 25, 26, 30
    Column Width 183
    Define Chart 203-204, 215
    Document 94
    Duplicate Report 292-293
    Header 290
    File Save As 35, 56
    Find/Match 285-287

Format Cells 170-172
Format Field 235-236
Merge Fields 330-331
New/Define Filter 287-289
New Field 234-236
Page Setup 94
Print 62
Spelling 58, 67, 68-69
Sort 285-286, 300
Works Opening 33-34, 53
Daisy wheel printer 8
Disk cartridge 10
Disk
    backup 31, 44
    floppy 9-11, 21, 24
    hard 9-11, 21
    icon 24
    preparing 11-12
Display options 174
Displaying formulas 139
Document 25, 31, 33
    creating 34, 38
    editing 58
    enhancing 92
    entering 54
    formatting 90, 93-100, 103-115
    icon 25
    integrating 326
    moving 44, 58, 106
    planning 50, 90, 106
    renaming 42
    retrieving 73-74, 102
    saving 34, 39
    viewing 96-97
Document dialog box 94
Dot matrix printer 8
Double click 23
Drag 23, 32
Duplicate Report dialog box 292-293

Editing
    cell 137
    deleting text 50-52, 59, 75
    document 58-60, 66, 75-77
    inserting text 52, 59
    selecting text 60
    spreadsheet 152
Enhancing
    chart 205-207
    document 92
Empty Trash command 45
Entering
    documents 54, 63
    formulas 134, 144
    labels 143
    list view mode 241
    records 236, 251, 265
    values 143
Exiting Works 34, 40

Field 228, 229, 232-240, 242-244, 247
    adding 243, 254-255, 270
    creating 247-248, 263
    deleting 243, 257, 269, 272

formatting 234-235, 242, 257
    updating 237-238
    moving 243, 256, 273
    naming 242
    width 242, 267, 271
File management 30
File Save As dialog box 35, 56
Files 11, 12, 24-26, 30-32, 41-43, 52
    closing 40
    copying 41
    creating 31, 38
    deleting 32
    moving 44
    renaming 32, 42
    saving 39
Financial applications 127
Find/Match dialog box 285-287
Floppy disk 9-11, 21, 24
Folder 21, 24-26, 28
    copying 32
    creating 31, 43
    deleting 32
    icons 24-27
    managing 30-31
    moving 32
    renaming 32
    Works 3.0 34, 64
Footers 95, 107
    window 95-96, 108
Form letter 20, 329, 330
    creating 338
    printing 341
    saving 342
Form view 36, 167, 237
Format Cells dialog box 170-172
Format Field dialog box 235-236
Formatting 11, 12
    cells 169, 184
    disk 36
    document 50, 90, 93-100, 103-115
    field 234-235, 242, 257
    text 97
Formula 134-135, 165-167, 172, 294
    displaying 139, 147-148
    entering 144
    printing 147-148
Formula view 139
Function keys 5
Functions 128, 132, 135, 164, 167,
    174-176, 294
    SUM 135, 153, 154, 174

Graph see Chart
Graphic tablet 6
Grid lines 174, 205, 206, 291

Hard disk 9-11, 21
Hard disk icon 24, 35
Hardware 2-4, 10, 18, 20, 21
Header dialog box 290
Headers 95-96, 285
    window 96
Hierarchy of operations 134
Horizontal scroll bar 28, 29, 54, 59

Icons 11, 22-27, 30, 32, 33, 96
    document 25
    folder 24-26
    program 24-25
Impact printer 7, 8
Indenting text 92, 94, 100, 103
Input devices 3-6
Inserting text 52, 59, 75
Insertion point 32, 54, 55
    moving 58-59
Integrated application software 20, 322
    using 323

Justification 54, 92, 97, 98, 112, 114,
    option 113

Keyboard 3, 5, 11, 21, 51
Kilobyte 4

Label
    column 168
    data 126-127, 132-133, 137
    define 203-204
    row 167
Laser printer 8
Layout
    features 90-92
Legends 202, 205
Light pen 6
Line graph 198, 201
Line spacing 52, 54, 91, 92, 97, 111
    option 99
List view 231-233, 241, 242, 262,
    266-268, 285
    changing to 266
    option 266
    printing in 245, 274
    window 232-233
Logical operations 2, 4

Macintosh computer 4, 6-10
Macintosh desktop 21, 22
Main memory 3, 4, 10, 11, 31, 33
Managing
    charts 207
    database 245, 262
    files 30
    folders 30
    report formats 291
    spreadsheet 164-166
Manipulating data 166
Margin settings 93, 94, 105, 106, 289
Menu bar 22, 26
Merge Fields dialog box 330-331
Microcomputer 2-6, 9-11, 19
Microsoft Works 12, 20-22
Modem 19, 21
Modifying
    chart definition 220
    report 291
    worksheet 167-169
Monitor 3, 6, 7
Mouse 5, 6, 11, 22-24
    actions 23-24

pointer 22-23
Moving
    cell contents 172
    chart 211
    data 28, 166, 177
    field 243, 256, 273
    files 32
    folders 32
    insertion point 58
    text 60, 79
Multiple
    field entries, matching 287
    level sorts 300
    records, finding 303
    tools 322, 323
    windows 323

Naming fields 242
New/Define Filter dialog box 287-289
New Field 234-236
Nonimpact printer 8
Numbering pages 90, 96, 107, 290
Numbers and tables 126

Opening dialog box 33-34, 53
Opening System Disk window 22
Operating system 3, 10-12, 21
Operations
    hierarchy 134
Output devices 3, 4, 6, 9

Page numbering 90, 96, 107, 290
Page Setup dialog box 94
Photographic camera 9
Pie chart 198, 200, 204, 213, 215-217, 220,
    221
Planning the document 50, 90, 106
Plotter 9
Point 23
Presentation features 90
Press 23
Print dialog box 62
Print Preview 96-97, 109-110
Printers 6-8
Printing 50, 51
    chart 205, 212
    document 61, 81
    in list view 245
    merged document 331, 341
    record 237
    report 245, 291
    spreadsheet 146, 148, 155, 184, 188
Program icon 24, 25

Radio button 30
RAM 4, 9, 11, 21
Range 132, 135, 165, 166, 168, 169,
    172-175, 177, 184, 190, 204-206, 283
Records 228, 229, 231, 234,
    adding 238, 268
    browsing 252
    deleting 238, 244, 269
    entering 236, 265
    modifying 253, 269

moving 245
printing 274, 260
searching 285-287
sorting 285
updating 244
Relational operators 282-283
Renaming
    documents 42
    files 32
    folders 32
Reports 19, 165, 229, 237, 245, 260, 274,
    284, 285, 299-301, 305, 308-313
    formatting 291, 292, 315
    printing 291, 315
    Report Writer 289
Restart command 11, 35
Restructuring the database 238
Retrieving
    database 308
    document 73
    spreadsheet 151, 175
Rows 126, 131, 132, 143, 152, 153, 165,
    168, 176-180, 183, 187
    adding 167
    deleting 167

Saving
    chart 205, 211
    document 34, 39, 55, 322
    database 236, 251, 265, 308, 316
    spreadsheet 136, 144, 155, 205
Searching 57, 285-287, 302
    database 285, 302
Secondary storage devices 3
Selecting
    group of records 287, 304
    data 282, 291
    text 60
Shift-click 23
Shutting down 46
Size box 28, 29, 42, 43, 325
Software 2-6, 11, 18-20, 32, 33, 51, 63,
    128, 135, 141, 245, 246, 262, 295, 322
Sort dialog box 285-286, 300
Sorting 283-285
Spell checking 57
Spelling dialog box 58, 67, 68-69
Spreadsheet 12, 19, 20, 25, 33, 126-144
    automating 127, 128
    creating 124-135
    in a text document 332
    printing 137, 146, 188
    retrieving 151
    saving 135, 139, 144
    window 129-131, 335
Storage devices 3, 9, 10
SUM function 135, 153, 154, 174
Summarizing data 284, 292, 310
System commands 11
System software 3, 4

Telecommunications 18-20, 33
Trash can 22, 24, 26, 32, 37
Text entry box 30

Title bar 23, 28, 30, 34, 40-43
Titles 92, 126, 202, 205
Tool palette 203-204
Touch screen 6
Types of icons 24

Underlining 90, 92, 97, 100, 115, 116
Updating
    field 237
    record 244

Value
    data 133, 166-206
Vertical scroll bar 28, 29, 54, 59
Viewing
    chart 204
    documents 96-97, 109-110
Voice 6, 9

Windows 11, 22-24, 28-30, 322-325
Word Processing 12, 18-20, 33, 38
    automating 51
    in industry 50
    in the home 50, 51
    window 38, 52, 53
Work area 28, 54, 69, 131, 144, 204, 255
Works interface 33
Works Opening dialog box 33-34, 53
Wordwrap 55
Worksheet 33, 126, 128, 164-169, 335